to Dave Vig —

Victory on Two Fronts

Here's to another World Series!

Best,

[signature]

VICTORY ON TWO FRONTS

The Cleveland Indians
and Baseball through
the World War II Era

Scott H. Longert

Ohio University Press   Athens

Ohio University Press, Athens, Ohio 45701
ohioswallow.com

Cover photo: Lou Boudreau applies the tag in Bob Feller's attempted pickoff of Boston's Phil Masi in game one of the 1948 World Series. Umpire Bill Stewart made the infamous "safe" call, and moments later, Masi scored the game's only run. *Cleveland Press Collection-Michael Schwartz Library, Cleveland State University*

Printed in the United States of America
Ohio University Press books are printed on acid-free paper ∞ ™

31 30 29 28 27 26 25 24 23 22 21 5 4 3 2 1

Library of Congress Cataloging-in-Publication Data
Library of Congress Cataloging-in-Publication Data
Names: Longert, Scott, author.
Title: Victory on two fronts : the Cleveland Indians and baseball through the World War Two era / Scott H. Longert.
Description: Athens : Ohio University Press, [2022] | Includes bibliographical references and index.
Identifiers: LCCN 2021032497 (print) | LCCN 2021032498 (ebook) | ISBN 9780821424711 (hardcover) | ISBN 9780821424728 (paperback) | ISBN 9780821447703 (pdf)
Subjects: LCSH: Cleveland Indians (Baseball team)—History—20th century. | World War, 1939–1945—United States. | Baseball players—United States—History—20th century. | Discrimination in sports—United States—History—20th century. | Baseball—United States—History—20th century.
Classification: LCC GV875.C7 L686 2022 (print) | LCC GV875.C7 (ebook) | DDC 796.357/640977132—dc23
LC record available at https://lccn.loc.gov/2021032497
LC ebook record available at https://lccn.loc.gov/2021032498

CONTENTS

ILLUSTRATIONS

Following page 120

Chapter 1

WAR AND BASEBALL

With a stout endorsement from President Franklin Roosevelt, Major League Baseball drew up plans for the 1942 season. It was still January, but many important issues needed to be considered. The most glaring concerned every Major League team's roster. Bob Feller and Hank Greenberg, two of the game's greatest stars and gate attractions, were already in the military. As the months went by, players faced a ramped-up selective service or felt a strong urge to show their patriotism by enlisting. Those who thought ahead enlisted in the navy, where their chances of remaining stateside and playing armed forces baseball were good. The Great Lakes Naval Training Center in Illinois offered a first-class baseball team, as did other bases in Norfolk, Virginia, and Oahu, Hawaii, if one could get transferred there. Many ballplayers opted for this safer opportunity.

Others were bolder, taking their chances and waiting to be called into the army, where overseas duty likely awaited. With hundreds of thousands of names for the draft boards to sift through, a player might be lucky enough to play a full season or more before the draft notice arrived.

The question of revenue weighed heavily on the minds of the team owners. With eligible men leaving for the service in huge numbers, gate receipts were certain to be affected. Civilians who were too old or were rejected for health reasons were joining the defense industry, working

1

hours that conflicted with afternoon and even night ball games. Add the diluted rosters filled up with career minor leaguers and you find anxious owners scrambling to make a profit. Teams with perennial attendance problems, like the Boston Braves, Philadelphia Phillies, and St. Louis Browns, had to be alarmed at their prospects for the 1942 season and beyond.

For the short term, the transportation system in the United States was running smoothly, but much of the rail system would eventually have to be allocated to move soldiers and sailors from base to base. Hotels near army camps and naval bases would soon become makeshift quarters for housing the servicemen. Major League owners had to be keenly aware of pending difficulty in mapping out rail schedules and accommodations for their teams.

In Cleveland, owner Alva Bradley and general manager Roger Peckinpaugh studied their roster and tried to fit the pieces together. Fortunately, the 1941 infield was intact for now, with Hal Trosky at first base, Ray Mack at second, player-manager Lou Boudreau at shortstop, and Ken Keltner at third. Jeff Heath and Roy Weatherly were still around to play the outfield, but several holes needed to be filled. The absence of Feller already had the pitching staff in a questionable state.

Boudreau, having been given his new job in late 1941, had yet to pilot a single game, but he had the strong backing of Bradley and Peckinpaugh. How the twenty-four-year-old was going to whip the players in shape and keep them in line was still to be seen, but he seemed to have support among players and ex-players alike. In early January, the great Napoleon Lajoie spoke highly of Lou. "Larry," enjoying his retirement in Florida, told the *Cleveland Plain Dealer,* "A player-manager is a great asset to a club. I've never seen Boudreau play, but I've heard he is one of the greatest young players to break into the Major Leagues in years." Cleveland pitcher Al Milnar told the local sportswriters "he was willing to work his head off for [Boudreau]."

Still, Boudreau faced the inevitable task of dealing with Roy "Stormy" Weatherly and Jeff Heath and their proclivity for ruining the harmony of any clubhouse. In mid-September of 1941, Weatherly had been abruptly sent home by then-manager Peckinpaugh for lack of hustle and insubordination. Heath was something of a malcontent, whether holding out over salary issues or coming in conflict with umpires, teammates, and opposing players. At an extremely young age for a manager and with only three full Major League seasons as a player, Lou had to find a way to earn and keep his players' respect, no easy task for even an experienced manager.

In mid-January, the Cleveland baseball writers honored Jeff Heath as the Indians' 1941 player of the year. With Heath's nemesis, manager Oscar Vitt, gone, the outfielder had enjoyed a tremendous year at the plate. He had batted .340, fourth in the American League, and compiled 24 home runs and 123 runs batted in. He was first in triples, with 20, and barely missed the 200-hit mark at 199. Except for batting average, all were career highs.

Heath received a fine set of golf clubs from the writers and predicted optimistically that attendance would increase despite the thousands of men headed for Europe and the South Pacific. Alva Bradley smiled at the prediction but told writers he expected a downturn in customers of anywhere from 20 to 30 percent. In 1941, the Indians had drawn nearly 746,000 fans, but Bradley thought the figures for the upcoming season might bottom out at 500,000.

Taking a few days off from his duties as assistant basketball coach at the University of Illinois, manager Boudreau appeared at the banquet. "We are going to hustle and gamble much more than in the past," he told the writers. He then spoke about the role of baseball while the country was at war, saying, "Our biggest job by far is to provide the moral background for the war effort for the army and navy and we in the game of baseball will cooperate to the fullest."

A short time later, Gene Tunney, former heavyweight boxing champ and current lieutenant commander of the Great Lakes Naval Training Center, visited Cleveland on a recruiting trip. Tunney heaped praise on Bob Feller for his dedicated work as a physical fitness instructor at the center. He mentioned he had at least fifty speaking requests on his desk for Feller from cities all around the country. The navy had a priceless asset in Bob, who turned out to be a boon for recruiting. Wherever he traveled, preaching about the great life of a sailor, recruits were sure to follow. Tunney related how Bob had insisted on active duty in the South Pacific, but for now his services were needed at home. There might even be some time to pitch a few stateside ballgames.

On February 19, just four days before the opening of Major League spring training, the Indians were stunned by Hal Trosky's announcement that he was retiring from baseball. In the latter part of the 1941 season, Trosky, still just twenty-eight years old, began suffering from severe migraine headaches, which impaired his play in the field and at bat. His vision would become so blurred that he had difficulty following the flight of the baseball. The headaches persisted through the off-season and were showing no signs of letting up. Trosky told the *Plain Dealer,* "I have considered the matter seriously and know that by retiring I will be serving the best interests of the ballclub, the public and myself."

Two weeks prior Hal had written a letter to Alva Bradley, asking to be placed on the voluntary retirement list at least for the 1942 season. Bradley had said nothing to the reporters about it, hoping that Hal might change his mind and take another shot at playing. The Indians could not afford to lose their powerful lefty, who in eight full seasons had averaged 27 home runs and 113 RBIs. With Feller gone indefinitely and now Trosky, the Indians' chances for contending looked dim.

To replace Trosky, Boudreau announced that Les Fleming would be the starting first baseman. Playing for Nashville in the Southern Association, the twenty-six-year-old had led the league in batting with a robust .414. Previously, the native Texan had bounced around the minor leagues for seven years. He had played two games for the Indians in September of 1941 and was seen as a utility player and backup for Trosky.

The Indians began reporting to the Clearwater, Florida, training camp, checking in at the Fort Harrison Hotel—that is, all but Jeff Heath, who decided to hold out, seeking a hefty 50 percent raise. His action was poorly timed, given that he had a new manager who sorely needed him in camp. Without Feller and Trosky, Heath was Cleveland's marquee player, an All-Star capable of picking up a lot of the slack. While visiting friends in California, Heath said he might travel to Clearwater and sit down with Roger Peckinpaugh to talk about money. Nobody in the Cleveland front office was holding their breath, and Bradley told the reporters they were so far apart on numbers that he saw no reason to negotiate.

On the first day of training, Boudreau gathered his players to affirm his goals for the season. "I am going to lay particular stress on the point of team loyalty," he told them. "We have to function more as a unit this year as ever before." He noted the loss of his two key players, Feller and Trosky, and asked everybody there to step up their game.

Boudreau scheduled workouts for 10:15 in the morning and 2:15 in the afternoon. The early workout featured calisthenics, pepper games, and throwing exercises, while afternoons were set aside for batting

VICTORY ON TWO FRONTS

practice. The Indians invested in a pitching machine to lessen the strain on important arms in camp. Pitchers, including Jim Bagby Jr., Al Milnar, and Al Smith, now could spend their time on more productive things such as throwing in game situations.

The spring training schedule would feature thirty-one games, including fifteen against the New York Giants. This marked the ninth season of barnstorming with the familiar National Leaguers. The two ball clubs planned a stop at Camp Shelby in Hattiesburg, Mississippi, where many Ohio infantrymen were training. It would be the first of times the ballplayers would entertain the troops headed for overseas duty. Both Major Leagues were planning to donate money and spearhead war bond drives, but the best way they could cheer the soldiers up was by showing them a well-played American ballgame.

By early March, Boudreau started to put his team together. One of his two main concerns was catcher. Rollie Hemsley had been sold to Cincinnati, leaving Gene Desautels as the only experienced catcher in camp. The front office signed Otto Denning, a ten-year minor leaguer, and there was a young prospect named Jim Hegan, who seemed to be a year or two away.

The other concern was the outfield. For the time being Weatherly seemed to be past the ugly incidents of the previous season. Heath would likely show up at some point, but whether in a couple of weeks or sometime in April, nobody knew. With a spot open, or maybe two, Boudreau turned his attention to Oris Hockett, a thirty-two-year-old journeyman.

Oris had quite a history behind him, having played minor league ball since 1932. Born in 1909 in Bluffton, Indiana, he moved with his family to Dayton, Ohio, where he played football at Roosevelt High School. After graduation he enrolled at Denison University for one year, then bolted to Mobile, Alabama, where he got a job in the lumber business. He played semipro ball for a time, until several coaches from Alabama Polytechnic Institute, now Auburn University, convinced him to enroll and play football. He studied medicine there for a year, then left abruptly for his parents' home in Dayton. He stayed in town a year and a half, bought a used Model T Ford, and took off for California. He got as far as Omaha, Nebraska, where his money ran out. Hockett sold the car for $15 and auditioned for the Norfolk ball club in the Nebraska State League. Thinking he might want to return to college and play more football, he signed his name as Jim Brown.

Oris was a true wanderer, unable to stay in the same place for any length of time. In 1933, he left Nebraska and traveled to Sioux Falls, South Dakota. He played baseball there for a year, disappeared in 1934, then returned the next season to hit .335. His contract was sold to the Chicago White Sox, but Oris, without explanation, once again packed his bags and set sail for Dayton. He stayed with his family for a time, worked at General Motors, then played for the Dayton ball club of the Mid-Atlantic League. In 1938, the Brooklyn Dodgers bought his contract, and he saw brief playing time at the end of the season. He spent the following year in Milwaukee, then moved on to Nashville in 1940. A year later he batted .359, usually good enough to lead the league but far behind teammate Les Fleming's spectacular .414. The Indians bought Hockett's contract for the 1942 season.

It appeared his wandering days were over, but just before spring training a machine shop offered Oris $150 a week to work as a machinist. A skilled operator, he mulled over the proposition, but the strong pull of Major League Baseball got the best of him. He reported to Clearwater and made a good impression on manager Boudreau, who must have hoped he would stay put.

On March 6, many Cleveland fans noticed a classified ad in the local papers for a family of four looking to rent a two-bedroom furnished home with a fenced-in yard. The ad was placed by Jeff Heath, leading to the belief the holdout might be over. Two days later, Heath signed for $15,000, a bit less than the $18,000 he wanted. Alva Bradley put in a bonus clause stating that if attendance reached a certain number, Heath would get an unspecified amount. With the current situation in the United States, it seemed any bonus money based on attendance was a longshot. Heath told reporters, "I still think I was entitled to more money on the strength of my work last year, but Mr. Bradley thought otherwise and he's the boss." How long Heath would remain contrite was anybody's guess.

That same day the Indians opened the exhibition season in Tampa with a 5–3 win over the Cincinnati Reds. Commissioner Kenesaw Mountain Landis was in the stands along with 2,200 soldiers and sailors who got in without being charged admission. In the ninth inning, a foul ball twisted into the stands, where Landis made a fancy one-handed grab, much to the delight of the servicemen.

As spring training went on, Boudreau continued tinkering with the lineup. Other than the departed Feller, the remaining players appeared safe from any immediate letters from Uncle Sam. Other teams were not so lucky, with Boston losing pitchers Mickey Harris and Earl Johnson, Washington losing Cecil Travis and Buddy Lewis, and the Philadelphia Athletics saying good-bye to Sam Chapman and Al Brancato. In fact, the Indians received some good news when Mel Harder signed his contract for the upcoming season.

Harder had gotten off to a good start in 1941, but somewhere in June–July he injured his pitching elbow. He tried to gut his way through it, but eventually gave up and decided on surgery. The Indians handed Mel his release but welcomed him back to spring training as a free agent to test out the arm. Early results were promising, and Mel signed on with the Indians once more. Now the Indians had a probable rotation of Bagby, Smith, Milnar, and Harder.

As the players gradually rounded into shape for the start of the regular season, Boudreau got high marks from visiting reporters for his handling of the club. Lou told Gayle Talbot of the Associated Press, "It's the greatest thrill I've ever had. I didn't know how some of the fellows would like to take orders from me." But once they arrived and started training, "every worry disappeared." The honeymoon had a way to go, and the real test would come when the season began.

On March 27, the Indians broke camp to begin their tour of the country with the Giants. They would play games in Texas, Louisiana, Arkansas, Oklahoma, Kansas, Mississippi, Missouri, and Indiana, as well as at Camp Shelby in front of 1,500 grateful Ohio soldiers. At almost every stop, homesick servicemen crowded into the small grandstands to see their favorite sport and converse with the players. Within months they would be shipping out overseas, but for now seeing a ballgame gave the boys a sense of the lives they had enjoyed and were bravely leaving behind. For two hours the soldiers would laugh, applaud, and yell at the umpires just like they did back home. The ballplayers had to have felt good knowing that.

While the Indians and Giants made their way toward Cleveland, word came that Bob Feller was now pitching for the Norfolk Naval Base. On April 3, Feller took the mound to face the University of Richmond. Nearly 10,000 sailors, marines, and pilots in training watched Feller toss three scoreless innings and strike out three batters. Asked how Feller looked, the Richmond coach replied, "We don't know. My boys didn't see the ball at all." Feller's days stateside were numbered, but he would have more occasions to play baseball before shipping out.

With the start of the regular season a week away, manager Boudreau made his first questionable decision: he banned his team from playing poker until further notice. Perhaps something had happened on one of the train trips, but Lou did not like the idea of his boys gambling. He believed that if a player lost too big it might affect his play on the field. Some of the guys must have raised an eyebrow at the edict, but nothing was said in public. To pass the hours, they would have to read a lot of newspapers and magazines.

Shortly before opening day, clubs on the East Coast made contingency plans in the event of a surprise German air raid, though the likelihood of that seemed remote. Yankee Stadium had water barrels installed on the roof and an extra supply of fire extinguishers. In case of attack, the front office believed, 15,000–20,000 fans could be safely moved under the concrete stands for protection. The Dodgers and Giants were not afraid to schedule night games, but just in case of an air attack they had engineers modify the light switches to ensure darkness within thirty seconds. The teams were prepared to pipe music and entertainment through the loudspeakers while fans huddled under the stands. At the Polo Grounds, where the Giants played, eight men were hired to guard the roof and watch for any suspicious airplanes flying too low. In Boston, the Braves and Red Sox hired air wardens to patrol the upper deck and watch the skies at each game. In case of a raid, both clubs added printed instructions to every seat for fans to study and note the proper exits. Being roughly five hundred miles from the East Coast, the Indians had little to worry about, but they made plans just to be sure. Alva Bradley worked with the city to have the entire lighting system shut off with only two switches. Making use of the loudspeakers, fans would be instructed to stay in their seats until the "all clear" was given. Extra police and fire personnel were to be on duty at least for the early part of the season.

Many of the owners firmly believed their concrete-and-steel stadiums could withstand any bombardment the feared Luftwaffe had to offer. They expected their players to remain calm on the field during any attack to keep the fans from panicking. This naïve assumption did not involve consulting any of the ballplayers themselves. The best-case scenario for everybody concerned was that no German planes would ever reach the American coast.

On the eve of the regular season, Alva Bradley received a letter from Petty Officer Bob Feller. Still stationed at the Norfolk Naval Base, Feller proposed a game between his guys and a Major League all-star team to be held at Cleveland Municipal Stadium. A July night game was mentioned, with the proceeds going to the armed forces. Bradley hopped on the idea, getting the Cleveland Advertising Club on board and writing for permission from American League president Will Harridge. If carried out properly, Feller's plan might raise a fortune for the soldiers. The venue could accommodate a huge crowd, the Cleveland fans would be eager to see Bob pitch, and bringing in some all-stars would virtually ensure fans came from out of state. A win-win for all involved.

Chapter 2

SUPPORT THE TROOPS

With all the anxieties hanging about like storm clouds, Major League Baseball finally began the regular season. The papers estimated crowds of up to 200,000 people for the eight openers. Jack Mahon, writing for the *International News,* brought things into perspective: "200,000 fans are expected to cheer their favorites on and incidentally to serve notice on Hitler and his stooges that it will take more than their frantic threats and mouthing to halt the game all America loves." Mahon was speaking for the people unable to serve in the military, who would be thumbing their collective noses at Hitler and all of Germany. Supporting baseball in wartime was a means to prove to the Axis powers that Americans would not allow their daily lives to be interrupted. Attending baseball games was indeed fighting back.

On Tuesday, April 14, Cleveland was in Detroit to open the curtain on the season. The Tigers had a fine crowd of 39,267, one of the best opening day totals in their history. The Indians lineup was:

> Weatherly cf
> Hockett rf
> Keltner 3b
> Heath lf
> Fleming 1b
> Boudreau ss

Mack 2b

Desautels c

Bagby p

In the top of the first inning with two down, Ken Keltner blasted the first Indians home run of the year for a 1–0 lead. Jim Bagby was in excellent form, at one point retiring sixteen Tigers in a row. In the top of the seventh, the game was tied at 2–2 when the Indians plated two more runs. An inning later, Les Fleming, the heir apparent to Hal Trosky, powered a solo home run high over the 415-foot sign in right center field. Fleming had three hits for the game, leading the Indians' thirteen-hit attack in a 5–2 win.

The total attendance for the eight openers reached 190,675 fans, for an average of nearly 24,000. In view of the circumstances, that was certainly an impressive figure. No one could know what the upcoming games might bring, but baseball would adapt as needed with the rest of the country, war and air raids be damned.

The Indians dropped their next two with the Tigers to limp home with a 1–2 record. On Friday, Mel Harder got the assignment to pitch against forty-one-year-old Ted Lyons and the Chicago White Sox. The April weather cooperated, with temperatures in the upper sixties and just a few scattered raindrops. The players marched to the center field flag-pole along with a contingent of local marine recruits and smartly raised the Stars and Stripes. With that ceremony accomplished, the game was on and a pitcher's duel took place between the two wily veterans. The White Sox scored a lone tally in the second inning, and Lyons was able to hold the Indians scoreless, winning 1–0. Harder, looking sharp in his first game since his arm surgery, went seven full innings. The 24,569 fans saw a brilliant pitching matchup, but it was the third loss in a row nonetheless.

On Saturday, Jim Bagby took the mound, attempting to stop the three-game losing streak. Though attendance was light, there was a special guest sitting in the owner's box next to Alva Bradley. Bob Feller had gotten a three-day pass to visit his old teammates and work out with them for a couple of days. Early in the game, several dozen young ladies made a dash to where Feller was sitting in hopes of grabbing an autograph from the good-looking navy man. He patiently obliged, then spoke to reporters about his activities at the Norfolk base. "We play ball in our spare time when we have any," he told them, "but mostly they keep us too busy to allow any time to practice." Feller talked enthusiastically about the training he received, firing machine guns and riding in planes with landing forces on simulated missions.

Bagby shut out the White Sox through the first eight innings. At one point he mowed down twenty straight Chicago hitters. The Indians were unable to put anything on the board either, carrying their runless streak to nineteen innings. But in the bottom of the ninth, backup outfielder Buster Mills singled and reached scoring position on a groundout. With two out, Boudreau sent in Fabian Gaffke, another backup, to pinch-hit. The move paid off when Gaffke lined a single to score Mills with the game winner.

With Feller in town, plans for the All-Star–Armed Forces game were revealed in greater detail. The game would be played on July 7 at Municipal Stadium, one day after the Major League All-Star game at the Polo Grounds in New York. The winning side from the Major League classic would hop on a train to Cleveland to face the military team, with Feller as the starting pitcher. Some of the servicemen signed up to play were shortstop Cecil Travis, outfielders Buddy Lewis and Sam Chapman, and ex–Indian catcher Frankie Pytlak. Mickey Cochrane, the former Detroit star catcher and current athletic director at the Great Lakes Naval Training Station, agreed to manage and coach the armed forces.

In addition to the all-star exhibition, Major League Baseball announced each club would donate the entire proceeds of one home game to the Army Emergency Relief Fund and the Navy Relief Society. The U.S. government had not yet had time to set up proper organizations to deal with the families of servicemen killed or wounded in action. Until it had, the two bodies would take the role of providing the wives or parents of the deceased much-needed relief.

Baseball planned to do big things for the army and navy, donating baseball equipment to the boys in Europe and the South Pacific and selling war bonds by the thousands. Play-by-play transcripts of games would be wired to the troops fighting on both fronts. Major League Baseball had no intention of leaving the boys overseas without their favorite pastime.

After winning three straight from St. Louis at home, the Indians went on the road. They took two from the Browns; then it was on to Chicago for two more wins, three in Philadelphia, and another two in

Washington for a team-record thirteen-game winning streak. In the last game against the Senators, Jeff Heath went three for four with a double, triple, home run, and five RBIs, and Jim Bagby, doing his best Bob Feller impression, picked up his fifth straight win.

Earlier in the winning streak, Mel Harder, after pitching well in his first game of the year, continued his timely comeback with a 2–0 four-hitter at St. Louis. Mel was in full command throughout, allowing only a walk over the last five innings. With Cleveland fans marveling at Harder's performance, Jim Doyle, writing for the *Plain Dealer*'s Sport Trail, penned one of his classic rhymes:

> *It used to be hell bo*
> *On that sore arm melbow*
> *To get the ball up to the platter.*
> *But let's give a yell bo,*
> *For him it's all well bo.*
> *(Just ask any St. Louis batter.)*

At the end of April Jeff Heath was hitting .362, Les Fleming had fans forgetting about Hal Trosky, and Roy Weatherly was batting over .300 while making several outstanding plays in center field. Manager Boudreau was managing like Miller Huggins and Joe McCarthy put together, pulling all the right strings on the field. When the Indians left Washington to continue their road trip in Boston, they were the talk of baseball with a Major League–best record of 14–3.

In the dining car on the way to Boston, the players were startled when the glamorous Hollywood actress Marlene Dietrich strolled by. Whether they were still star-struck when they played the Red Sox on Sunday is not clear, but Jeff Heath dropped two fly balls and Ray Mack bobbled a double-play relay to help Boston end the streak with an 8–4 win. At Fenway Park 33,000 eager fans came to see the red-hot Indians cooled off.

The next day, despite fifteen hits, including another homer from Jeff Heath, Cleveland suffered another defeat. Al Milnar lasted only three innings, giving up six runs in the 11–8 loss. The defeats began to pile up, with one more in Boston, then one in New York and another in Detroit, to drop their record to 14–8. On May 10 they were back home to play a double-header with the Tigers. They lost the first 5–1 to extend the losing streak to six games, having scored a grand total of one run over the last three.

The second game looked like it would be a carbon copy of game one. The Tigers scored three runs in their half of the third inning to take an early lead. During the Detroit rally, shortstop Bill Hitchcock rounded third and slid hard into catcher Gene Desautels. The crowd shuddered as Desautels rolled on the ground in obvious pain. Otto Denning, the only other receiver on the squad, came in to catch. X-rays confirmed that Desautels's leg was fractured.

The Tigers added two more runs in the sixth and went into the ninth inning holding a comfortable 5–0 lead. The 23,429 fans, or what was left of them, waited for the inevitable disappointment. Detroit rookie pitcher Hal White, who had been cruising along to this point, issued a walk to Buster Mills. White then hit Lou Boudreau in the foot to put runners at first and second. Jeff Heath rolled a grounder to second baseman Jimmy Bloodworth, who threw the ball away to load the bases. The suddenly engaged fans edged up in their seats as Les Fleming lined a base hit to center, scoring Denning and Boudreau. Tigers manager Del Baker walked slowly to the mound and waved for veteran Johnny Gorsica to come in. Ken Keltner then lined another single to score Heath and pull the Indians within two. Ray Mack laid down a sacrifice bunt, moving the runners to second and third. Otto Denning hit a weak ground ball back to Gorsica. Fleming started for home, put on the brakes, but was run down for an easy out number two, the other runners moving up. Boudreau sent in Roy Weatherly to pinch-hit and Stormy got the fans screaming when he singled to score Keltner and cut the lead to one. With the fans in utter disbelief, Oris Hockett singled past the infielders to score Denning with the tying run. Buster Mills, batting for the second time, struck out, but the Indians' thrilling rally had sent the game to extra innings.

Joe Heving, in relief, set the Tigers down in the top of the tenth. Boudreau led off the bottom half with a triple to deep right field. Heath and Fleming drew intentional walks, setting the stage for Ken Keltner. Once again the crowd stood up, yelling for Keltner to end it right now. The third baseman took a big swing and did just that, slamming a drive to the wall in center field. Boudreau trotted home and the Indians salvaged the split, 6–5. The losing streak was over.

Immediately after the game Boudreau went to his office and called the Indians' top minor league affiliate, the Baltimore Orioles, asking for Jim Hegan to be sent up as soon as possible. The Orioles were in

Montreal, but word got to the young catcher to board the quickest train to Cleveland. His time in the minors was finished.

Jim Hegan was born August 3, 1920, in Lynn, Massachusetts, ten miles north of Boston. During its heyday, there were over two hundred shoe factories in Lynn, sending all types of quality footwear across America and around the world. Jim's father, John, was a Lynn police officer. At English High School Jim starred as a receiver in football, a center in basketball, and a catcher in baseball. Before the start of his senior year, Jim, now standing 6'2" and weighing 195 pounds, played on the Lynn American Legion team, which advanced all the way to the finals of the Legion World Series, held in New Orleans, Louisiana. They were matched against the Zatarains, a local club led by pitcher Howie Pollett, who would become a twenty-game winner for the St. Louis Cardinals. Lynn swept the first three games of the best-of-five series to claim the national championship. Jim, batting cleanup, led the way with seven hits in fourteen at bats and five RBIs. In the final game, he collected four big hits and stole three bases, including a steal of home plate. The winning players each received two free tickets to the 1937 World Series and a trip to Niagara Falls.

Jim's exceptional play had scouts knocking at the Hegans' front door. Bill Bradley, Cleveland's longtime scout and former third baseman, pushed his way to the front of the line. After graduation, Jim signed with the Indians and reported to Class C Springfield, Ohio, of the Middle Atlantic League, where he could expect a salary of just $75 monthly.

In 1940, he advanced to Wilkes-Barre of the Eastern League and the following year to Oklahoma City, in the Texas League. With his career path on track, Jim married his nineteen-year-old high school sweetheart, Clare Kennedy. They had met when she was a sophomore and he was a senior. The couple would have a long and happy marriage.

At the end of the 1941 season, Jim got a chance to catch sixteen games for the Indians. Then-manager Roger Peckinpaugh was impressed with his defensive skills but saw that he needed to improve his hitting. Jim played well enough in spring training the following year to go north with the club, but soon was optioned to Baltimore. When Gene Desautels broke his leg, Jim got his chance to prove he belonged with Cleveland. Until Boudreau found the right time to insert Hegan into the lineup, Otto Denning would do the bulk of the catching.

On Monday, May 11, while the new catcher was boarding his train to Cleveland, the Indians were at League Park, locked in a 5–5 thriller with the Tigers. There were two outs in the bottom of the ninth when Les Fleming came to bat with Buster Mills on second and Jeff Heath on first. Rookie pitcher Charlie Fuchs threw a curveball that Fleming launched high over the right field wall and far across Lexington Avenue. The 8–5 win was the second late-inning comeback in a row and even more exciting than the Sunday win.

All were happy except Heath, who was branded a loafer in the next day's edition of the *Plain Dealer.* Gordon Cobbledick took Heath to task for not running out an infield pop fly and jogging to first on an infield roller that could have been a scratch single. The fans apparently directed some loud comments at Heath, making this a test for Boudreau. Three managers before him had faced similar issues with Heath, and now Lou would have to decide whether to overlook Heath's poor behavior or call him into his office for a stern chat. In the next few days nothing was reported in the newspapers, leading fans and writers to assume the manager preferred not to upset the status quo.

A few days later, the Indians announced plans for a May 25 Army-Navy Relief Fund game at League Park against the White Sox. All proceeds from the game were earmarked for the servicemen's families. Everyone attending, including players, umpires, front office, reporters, and concession workers, would have to pay admission. It was hoped that loyal Clevelanders would turn out in big numbers to support the troops and give a boost to civic pride. In addition, fans were asked to send in donations to allow up to 1,000 soldiers and sailors to attend the game for free. Former League Park ushers, who now included bankers, judges, and doctors, volunteered to work the game to extend personal service to the anticipated large crowd.

The realization that the country was at war and sacrifices had to be made was beginning to sink in with the people living at home. Besides the benefit games, the government, through the War Production Board, announced steep cutbacks on the manufacturing of breakfast beverages. A shortage of cargo ships arriving from South America had driven imports down severely. Supplies of the can't-do-without morning cup of coffee were down as much as 25 percent from prewar levels, tea 50 percent, and cocoa for the kids 30 percent. Many people would have to make do with water or substitutes like Postum or chicory.

There were no promises that the situation was temporary. Products including sugar (now available only through ration books), rubber for tires, and gasoline were needed for the military, and that translated to scarcities in the near future. Car owners were asked to drive no faster than thirty-five miles per hour to conserve fuel. Soon additional coupon books were rolled out to all families, including for food and clothing, allowing them to make only the purchases allotted to them each week. Rationing would be the challenging norm for the foreseeable future.

Alva Bradley had arranged fourteen night games, double the amount played in each of the past three seasons. In consideration of the wartime conditions, Bradley wanted to give working people more opportunities to get out and see ballgames. The Indians played their first night game on Saturday, May 23, after the game the night before had been postponed by rain. An air raid test was carried out during the game, involving the Cleveland fire and police departments. Fifty firemen were on duty, five of them on the stadium roof with sandbags and twenty more walking the grandstand with fire extinguishers in hand, and a thousand-gallon water pumper waited outside in the event of an actual fire. At 10:27 p.m., the lights were turned out and the loudspeakers instructed all fans to remain in their seats and immediately put out all cigarettes, cigars, and pipes. As the stadium fell into darkness for exactly one minute, the crowd stayed completely calm, laughing and joking. The test was deemed a success and the game went on, but unfortunately the Indians lost in ten innings, 2–1. At least city officials could relax a little knowing the stadium had passed muster in case of the far-fetched event of an air attack.

On Monday afternoon, the Indians and White Sox squared off in the Army-Navy Relief Fund game. Even with all the hype about the contest, for some reason only 7,959 fans paid their way into League Park. The admission netted $9,390.86, barely half what had been expected. Other clubs did much better, with the Dodgers–Giants game drawing 40,000 fans and the Red Sox–Athletics nearly 12,000. The numbers in Cleveland were disappointing, but the $9,000 would help more than a few families.

By June 1, the Indians, losers of eleven of their last thirteen games, had plummeted all the way to fourth place, putting them eight and a half games behind the first-place New York Yankees and erasing the memories of the April–May thirteen-game win streak. The pitching, other than Jim Bagby and Mel Harder, had fallen apart, while the hitting had slowed considerably. Rumors began to swirl that Lou Boudreau had asked to step down from his managerial duties and return to player-only status. The *Columbus Dispatch* reported that Indians coach Burt Shotton would be named manager within days. Roger Peckinpaugh insisted that Lou was the manager and there were no plans to replace him. At this point the Indians appeared to be already out of contention and, without Bob Feller, just a middle-of-the-pack club.

A few days later Alva Bradley hosted a luncheon for 140 of Cleveland's business leaders. The owner made a plea to the gentlemen to purchase as many tickets as possible to the July 7 All-Star–Armed Forces exhibition. Mickey Cochrane, in town for the luncheon and to drum up support, told the gathering, "We're not going into that game with any idea of defeat. I know we will be up against a great team, but we'll have a great one ourselves." He added that plans were being made to bring former Red Sox pitcher Mickey Harris to the game. Harris was stationed in the Panama Canal Zone, but Cochrane believed the navy would fly him all the way to Cleveland just to pitch a few innings. The government explained to the business leaders that within twenty-four hours of its receipt of the funds, the money would be distributed to the families of the killed or wounded.

Some members of the public questioned what good it did to keep the players here in the States when the fighting raged in Europe and the South Pacific. In response, the Great Lakes Naval Training Station explained that the armed forces teams had three objectives: to entertain the sailors and soldiers, to boost enlistment, and to raise money for relief, and enlistments had gone up 15 to 40 percent since the exhibition games began.

The newspapers reported that all types of sports throughout the United States were raising money for relief funds. Bob Hope and Babe Ruth played a golf match with all proceeds donated, Aqueduct Racetrack set aside days for all receipts to be given to the fund, and the AAU Track and Field championships did the same. In addition, sports celebrities, including boxing's Joe Louis, football's Ace Parker, and tennis star Don Budge, were on the road raising money. College football's Army-Navy game was expected to bring in $500,000 and would contribute the entire amount. Overall, professional and amateur sports were clearly a big plus for relief funds and would play a major role in all aspects of the home front war effort.

By June 20, ticket sales for the All-Star–Armed Forces game had reached a respectable 20,000. Cleveland's largest businesses had stepped up, with Warner & Swasey buying 12,000 seats, Thompson Products,

2,000, and White Motors, 1,000. The Indians front office remained confident, knowing ticket sales to the public were not expected to peak until early July.

Jim Bagby, Lou Boudreau, and Ken Keltner were named to the American League All-Star team, meaning that if the American League beat the Nationals, the three Indians would likely face Bob Feller the next day. That would surely bring out the Cleveland fans in great numbers. If that was not enough, the Americans had nine Yankees on the roster, led by Joe DiMaggio, in his seventh appearance, Joe Gordon, and Tommy Henrich in the starting lineup, along with Spud Chandler, who would be the starting pitcher. The Nationals had stars like Johnny Mize, Mel Ott, Joe Medwick, and pitcher Carl Hubbell, in his ninth appearance. Certainly that would attract a fair contingent of fans from outside of Ohio.

A week later Feller reported to Great Lakes to begin practice along with Sam Chapman (A's), Fred Hutchinson (Tigers), and Johnny Sturm (Yankees). Already in camp were fellow sailors Johnny Rigney (White Sox), Don Padgett (Browns), and former Indians catcher Frankie Pytlak (Red Sox). Hank Greenberg received an invitation but declined as he was amid training at the Army Corps Officer Candidate School. Even without Hank the armed forces had a talent pool that could compete with either of the Major Leagues' All-Star teams.

Several tanks from the motorized battalion at Camp Custer in Michigan would arrive in Cleveland before the game. The tanks, equipped with .37 mm guns, would drive around the outfield in the pregame ceremonies. The coast guard would be sending 150 men with rifles to join the parade, and a crack marine drill team would also be taking part. The game and the activities were going to be a spectacular example of American pride.

On July 2, the Indians were in Chicago for the home team's relief fund game. A fine crowd of 29,062 was on hand, raising a total of $33,352 for the soldiers and sailors. The Indians won 7–5, on their way to a four-game sweep of the series and moving to ten games above .500. The Indians were 17–12 in June, a good month but not enough to lift them into contention. Les Fleming and Jeff Heath continued to spark the offense, while Jim Bagby picked up his ninth win at Chicago. Bagby had a reasonable shot at twenty wins for the season.

All eyes were starting to turn toward the All-Star–Armed Forces game on July 7. The Erie Railroad announced a special train leaving from Sharon, Pennsylvania, stopping in Youngstown, Ohio, before proceeding north to Cleveland. Within a short time 2,000 reservations were made. The army camp at Port Clinton, Ohio, planned to send two twenty-eight-ton "General Grant" tanks for display on game day.

On July 5, the armed forces team arrived in Cleveland for two days of practice at Municipal Stadium. Mickey Cochrane told reporters that after Bob Feller had pitched an inning or two, Johnny Rigney would do most of the pitching since he had gone through all of spring training and part of the early regular season. Mickey Harris would also pitch. Tigers outfielder Pat Mullin, a last-minute addition to the squad, would hopefully add some punch to the lineup.

The traditional All-Star game took place on Monday, July 6, in front of 33,694 fans at the Polo Grounds. Lou Boudreau, leading off the game for the American League, slammed a Mort Cooper fastball 420 feet into the left field seats. Tommy Henrich slashed a double. Ted Williams and Joe DiMaggio failed to hit safely, but Rudy York smashed another long home run for a 3–0 advantage. The score stayed the same until the bottom of the eighth inning, when NL pinch hitter Mickey Owen homered to close the gap to 3–1. The Tigers' Al Benton retired the Nationals in the eighth and ninth without any further damage and the Americans gained the victory, allowing them to battle the armed forces team. A marvelous total of $95,000 was raised for the relief funds, with the same amount or better expected Tuesday night.

By the morning of the seventh about 45,000 tickets had been sold, with estimates of 60,000–70,000 fans by game time. Each ticket had an extra dollar added to the price to go toward purchasing government war bonds. Emil Bossard's grounds crew worked overtime hanging red, white, and blue bunting all around the upper deck, alternating with large photos of General Douglas MacArthur. On the stadium roof flags were placed representing all the Allies fighting against Germany and Japan.

The evening schedule started with batting practice at 6:30. At 7:30 the Columbus, Ohio, Fort Hayes military band, eighty-five strong, had a selection of patriotic songs ready to go. At 8:20 the tanks from Camp Custer and Port Clinton started their engines and stirred up the crowd, and at 8:55 the marine drill team led a march to center field to raise the flag.

Moments before game time, a fired-up Mickey Cochrane told sportswriters, "We came here prepared to win and we've got the power and defense and we'll give 'em more than they are figuring!" With that slightly overconfident statement, the opposing American League All-Stars took the field. Even as the game was underway, fans kept piling into the stadium, swelling the total to over 62,000 paid admissions. For those who stayed home or were too far away to attend, the game was broadcast nationally and to Hawaii and the Mediterranean Sea. Leading off the broadcast play-by-play was local favorite Jack Graney, calling all the action for the first three innings, then yielding the microphone to Bob Elson and Waite Hoyt. For the past ten years, Cleveland fans had had the great pleasure of hearing Graney's exciting radio calls. For this evening, listeners from all over the United States and many servicemen on duty could hear him.

At precisely 9:00 p.m., the American League All-Stars took the field, with Jim Bagby on the mound. The armed service starting lineup was as follows:

> Pat Mullin cf Army (Private)
> Benny McCoy 2b Navy (Coxswain)
> Don Padgett lf Navy (Coxswain)
> Cecil Travis ss Army (Private)
> Joe Grace rf Navy (Storekeeper Third Class)
> Johnny Sturm 1b Army (Corporal)
> Ernie Andres 3b Navy (Specialist First Class)
> Vince Smith c Navy (Seaman Second Class)
> Bob Feller p Navy (Chief Boatswain's Mate)

All told, the military roster had thirteen navy men and eight army men. They were stationed in nine different states and one (Harris) at the Panama Canal. By far the greatest number on the roster, nine, were from the Great Lakes station. All the players had Major League experience except for third baseman Ernie Andres, who had recently played for the Class AA Louisville Cardinals.

The starting lineup for the American League All-Stars looked like this:

> Lou Boudreau ss (Indians)
> Tommy Henrich rf (Yankees)
> Ted Williams lf (Red Sox)
> Joe DiMaggio cf (Yankees)
> Rudy York 1b (Tigers)
> Bobby Doerr 2b (Red Sox)

Ken Keltner 3b (Indians)
Buddy Rosar c (Yankees)
Jim Bagby p (Indians)

Jim Bagby had a rocky first inning, walking two batters and allowing a single, but managed to escape without yielding any runs. A moment later the armed forces men jogged to their positions while a rousing ovation shook the huge stadium. Bob Feller walked slowly to the mound wearing a white uniform with a large black *N* on the left front of his jersey. The roar continued throughout Feller's warmup tosses to catcher Vince Smith.

The first hitter to face the longtime Cleveland ace was his old teammate and likely future boss, Lou Boudreau. Once again the fans rose to their feet and cheered when Boudreau lifted a high fly to center fielder Pat Mullin. Tommy Henrich hit a roller to the side of the mound that Feller could not reach, Ted Williams drew a base on balls, then Joe DiMaggio lined a single to center, scoring Henrich for the first run of the game, Williams taking third. Next up was Rudy York, who sent a deep fly ball to right field that Joe Grace ran down. Williams tagged up and trotted home with the second run.

Feller escaped further trouble, but in the second inning Ken Keltner drove one of his fastballs a mile to deep center field for a triple. Buddy Rosar singled to score Keltner, forcing Mickey Cochrane to call time and walk to the mound. Feller's day was finished, but not before another mighty ovation from the fans.

Johnny Rigney shut down the All-Stars over five scoreless innings to keep the game close at 3–0. For the armed forces, Mickey Harris gave up two more runs over the last two innings on a double by Phil Rizzuto and triples by Williams and sub George McQuinn. The final score was 5–0, yet there was no cause for disappointment. The fans knew the armed forces team had received little time to practice on top of their military duties. They played exhibition games when possible, while the All-Stars had gone through spring training and had been playing daily games against Major League competition. The result, nonetheless, was a highly entertaining event and a massive donation of approximately $130,000 to the relief funds. Bob Feller's April letter to Alva Bradley culminated in one of the greatest benefit baseball games of the twentieth century.

Chapter 3

FINDING HELP

In early August of 1942, the Indians' season peaked when their record climbed to a lofty 60–47, thirteen games over .500. Despite playing good baseball, they found themselves a distant second to the streaking Yankees, who were leading by eleven and a half games and had the pennant just about clinched. Les Fleming was hitting .302, but most of the other Indians were struggling at the plate. Jim Hegan was playing great defense, but his batting average was hovering around the .200 mark. Jim Bagby and Mel Harder continued to pitch exceedingly well, but the rest of the staff could not be counted on for much support. One highlight occurred on August 11 against the Detroit Tigers. Al Milnar and Tommy Bridges were locked in a 0–0 pitcher's duel. Neither pitcher would yield; there was still no score after fourteen innings when curfew halted the game. Milnar pitched the game of his life, allowing only two hits despite not getting a single strikeout. The first hit against him came with two outs in the ninth inning.

As the Indians went further into August, their record tumbled down toward .500. The sportswriters and fans mostly gave manager Boudreau a pass for his first season, figuring he would learn from any mistakes and use his experience for better results in 1943.

The impact of the war seriously hindered the latter stages of the Major League season. More players were being called to the military, one of the biggest being the Yankees' Tommy Henrich. Minor leaguers, many of whom were single guys without dependents, were being drafted at a steady rate, and the minor league owners worried about possibly having to fold their teams for lack of bodies.

During this period, an editorial in the communist newspaper the *Daily Worker* floated a novel idea: the time had come for Black ballplayers to be given tryouts for the Major Leagues. The dilution of talent in the big leagues, said the writer, could be stemmed by bringing in the best players from the Negro Leagues. Though the piece made a lot of sense, it was not likely to catch on with the baseball owners, most of whom were comfortable with unofficially keeping the game White.

Sportswriters, too, felt that the idea was impractical due to the social conditions of the day. Gordon Cobbledick, in the *Cleveland Plain Dealer*, wrote that Black players would face all kinds of obstacles, the least of which was being banned from staying in the same hotels as their White teammates. Cobbledick predicted that in the southern cities of the minor leagues fans might riot or stay away from the ballparks. A dissenting opinion came from Ed Bang of the *Cleveland News*, who wrote that if Black ballplayers could fight in a war and protect their country, they should be getting the chance to play in the Majors. Franklin Lewis of the *Cleveland Press* thought Blacks should get a chance but believed most players in the Negro League were suited for Class AA baseball, not the American or National League.

Soon rumors flew that several stars of the Negro Leagues were getting tryouts with the Pittsburgh Pirates. The names tossed about were catcher Roy Campanella, second baseman Sam Hughes, and pitcher Dave Barnhill. Alva Bradley received a letter sent by Cleveland Buckeye third baseman Parnell Woods on behalf of himself and two other Buckeyes requesting tryouts: outfielder Sam Jethroe and pitcher Eugene Bremer.

Having to make an uncomfortable decision, Bradley replied that he would send one of his scouts to watch the three, and if the reports were favorable a tryout would follow. He was evasive on who would scout them and on what criteria. It is not clear whether Bradley was at all serious or trying to blow smoke to push the issue further away. A scout could be instructed to say the players were not good enough or were a few years away. John Fuster, writing for the *Call and Post*, Cleveland's Black newspaper, wrote a column arguing that all three of the Buckeyes had been selected for the East-West All-Star game, which put them among the

VICTORY ON TWO FRONTS

elite of Black ballplayers. Woods, a college graduate and schoolteacher, was hitting .376, Jethroe, a real speedster, was hitting .436, while Bremer had an impressive won-loss record of 11–2.

A week later Bradley remained noncommittal, saying that his chief scout, Bill Bradley, had charge of the assignment and the two had not spoken recently. Bradley was in Tennessee and might not return to Cleveland for a time. Coincidentally, the East-West All-Stars were playing a second game at Cleveland Stadium on August 18. Bremer, Woods, and Jethroe would surely be in the West lineup, making it easy for the Cleveland front office to have one of their scouts attend. The East pounded the West 9–2. Possibly due to nerves, Jethroe and Woods went hitless, while Bremer was chased in the third inning, when the East scored five runs. The poor showing of the three Buckeyes made it easy for Alva Bradley to issue a statement that none of the Cleveland players were Major League material. Whether he had any real intention of giving the prospects a fair look will never be known. However, he did send a letter to Parnell Woods advising him that if the Indians decided to look at Negro Leagues ballplayers next spring, the three would get first consideration. Bradley was polite, if nothing more. Sam Jethroe absolutely had Major League ability, as his three seasons (1950–52) with the Boston Braves prove. He led the National League in stolen bases twice and scored 100 runs in his first year. But the issue of breaking the color barrier faded until after the war ended.

In the meantime, the Indians bought the contract of first baseman Eddie Robinson from the Baltimore Orioles. Bradley and Peckinpaugh had maintained a shrewd working agreement with the International League team, allowing the Indians to buy any two Orioles for a total price of $10,000. In return, Cleveland, after spring training, sent their best prospects to Baltimore to bolster their roster. They paid $5,000 for Robinson, leaving them another $5,000 if they wanted to choose another player. Without the agreement, Robinson's purchase price would surely have been much higher, probably in the $20,000 range.

Eddie Robinson was born on December 15, 1920, in Paris, Texas. Sitting on the eastern border of Oklahoma and Texas, Paris was known as a regional railway hub. Eddie grew up an only child, spending his after-school hours playing whatever sport happened to be in season. The Depression years were hard on the Robinsons, forcing young Eddie to pick cotton and take on any odd jobs he could find. In his highly readable autobiography, *Lucky Me: My Sixty-Five Years in Baseball*, Eddie said his high school did not have a baseball team. Instead, he ran track along with football in the fall and basketball in the winter. In the summers he played baseball on a local amateur team.

After his 1938 graduation, Eddie played more amateur ball, then signed with Knoxville of the Southern League. The next spring Knoxville loaned him to Valdosta, a Class D club in the Georgia-Florida League. In his first season, he hit only .249, with 7 home runs. The next year at Valdosta, Eddie found himself, raising his average to .323 while collecting 184 hits. His improved play caught the attention of the Baltimore Orioles, who bought his contract and assigned him to Elmira of the Eastern League. He continued to hit well there, prompting the Orioles to bring him back for the 1942 season. Eddie's manager at Baltimore was Tommy Thomas, a former Major League pitcher with eleven years of experience in the big time. He worked with Eddie on his hitting, and the results showed: 27 home runs, 104 RBIs, and a batting average of .306. The Indians were watching and took advantage of their deal with Baltimore to receive a potential starting first baseman at a bargain price.

A short time later the Indians announced they would be calling up more prospects from Baltimore, including third baseman Bob Lemon, outfielder Hank Edwards, and pitcher Steve Gromek. They would have to wait until the end of the International League schedule but were sure to get some playing time under Boudreau. The player-manager had recently accepted a generous three-year contract from Bradley to manage through the 1945 season. This was the only time in Bradley's tenure he had given a manager three years. With this security, Boudreau could work alongside Roger Peckinpaugh, trying to build a winner without looking over his shoulder. Most of the Indians commented that they were pleased with the deal and liked playing for Lou. Maybe they could do something in 1943 to give the fans a reason to fully support them.

Even with the good news about Lou, the Indians continued to plummet in the standings, falling toward fourth place while the Yankees held a comfortable lead over Boston. On August 23, the Yankees scheduled a relief fund doubleheader against the Washington Senators. To truly escalate the gate receipts, Walter Johnson agreed to attend and throw a few pitches to Babe Ruth between games. Billy Evans, the former umpire and current general manager of the Detroit Tigers, would call balls and strikes to judge who got the better of it. Over 69,000 fans jammed into Yankee Stadium to see the two Hall of Famers square off.

Johnson threw seventeen pitches, two of which went sailing deep into the right field stands. The Babe hit his second home run on the last pitch, enabling him to drop the bat and trot slowly around the bases. The New York fans gave him a tremendous ovation, one that Babe surely loved. The final receipts totaled a whopping $80,000 for the relief fund, the highest total for a regular season game. By the end of the 1942 relief fund drive, baseball had raised an impressive $517, 964. But there was more to come. Commissioner Landis informed the news outlets that both leagues had agreed to donate a huge portion of the World Series receipts to the Army-Navy fund. Estimates in the $400,000–$600,000 range were given, with part of the proceeds set aside for the Red Cross and the United Service Organizations (USO).

Around the same time, Washington owner Clark Griffith and National League president Ford Frick announced the creation of the Ball and Bat Fund. The idea was to raise money for two types of kits to be sent to Europe and the South Pacific. Kit A would contain twelve baseballs and three bats, while kit B would hold a complete catcher's outfit. The two men believed $140,000 would cover the costs of preparing and shipping the kits. Griffith had done a similar act of charity during World War I, when he filled a cargo ship with baseball equipment to be sent overseas to France. On the journey a German U-boat sunk the ship, but Griffith, undaunted, sent a second ship that reached its destination.

In early September, the Indians were ready to call up Eddie Robinson and their three prospects from the Orioles. In addition, they planned to bring up the two best pitchers from their Wilkes-Barre farm club, Paul Calvert and Allie Reynolds. Reynolds had an outstanding 18–7 record and an impressive 204 strikeouts. With Mel Harder and Al Smith well into their thirties and Al Milnar fading, Cleveland would need some youth on the pitching staff. The 1943 spring training season was shaping up to be a terrific opportunity for Gromek, Calvert, and Reynolds to grab a spot or two in the rotation. Billy Evans, the Indians' general manager in the late 1930s, called Reynolds the best pitching prospect he had seen in ten years. The compliment raised hopes for Cleveland fans about to see a revamped pitching staff in the years ahead.

Albert Pierce Reynolds was born in the small town of Bethany, Oklahoma, on February 10, 1917. Allie's grandmother on his father's side happened to be a full-blooded Creek Indian. Being Native American and a Major League ballplayer meant you were destined to be nicknamed "Chief" or, in his case, "Superchief," like players of the past such as Charles Albert Bender of the Athletics and John Meyers of the Giants. More recently, Bob Johnson of the A's was not known as "Chief," but as "Indian Bob." Surely the players would have preferred their given names, but that was baseball and society at the time.

Allie's father, David, was a minister for the local Church of the Nazarene, which had appropriated land in central Oklahoma for its members. Bethany at the time of Allie's birth had a population of less than five hundred people, almost all of whom were connected to the church. The town's blue laws banned alcohol, cigarettes, gambling, and sports on Sundays. The last became a problem for Allie, the oldest of three brothers and a budding athlete.

As a teenager he attended Capitol High School, starring on the football field and running track. He did not play any organized baseball, partly due to the blue laws and partly to his development as a phenom on the gridiron and a premier sprinter. His track prowess landed him a scholarship to Oklahoma A&M in Stillwater, which later became Oklahoma State University.

Though he was on a track scholarship (worth $20 a month), Allie tried out for the football team and soon developed as a starting halfback and sometimes fullback. He had reached his full adult weight of 195 pounds and proved adept at smashing through the line and turning on the jets when he broke into the secondary. In a game against Kansas State, Allie took a handoff on his own one-yard line, broke through the line, and dashed ninety-nine yards for a touchdown. The Aggies played a tough schedule against the likes of Oklahoma, Texas Tech, and Arkansas, and the losses piled up, but Allie held his own, scoring hard-earned touchdowns.

Allie did not attempt to play baseball, but while he was practicing with the track team fate intervened. Hank Iba, the legendary college basketball coach, also oversaw the baseball squad at the time. During practice he spotted Allie heaving his javelin to distant fields. Iba walked over to the track star and asked him if he would throw some batting practice. Several of his pitchers were on the bench with sore arms.

With nothing to lose, Allie reared back and fired several fastballs. Seeing immediately that the javelin thrower possessed a better heater than any of the A&M pitchers, Iba persuaded Allie to pitch for the varsity. Because of his limited baseball experience, Allie still had much to learn about the fine art of pitching. A friend from boyhood had taught him to throw a curveball, but Allie knew nothing about holding runners on base or how to use the strike zone. The transition to complete pitcher did not happen overnight, but with practice Allie became one of the better college pitchers in the country.

At the end of his senior year, he was drafted by the National Football League's New York Giants. Unsure about his future, he spoke with Coach Iba about whether to pursue a career in pro baseball or football. Iba knew that Major League Baseball at that time paid considerably better than the NFL. The coach got in touch with his baseball contacts, which resulted in scouts from various teams coming to Stillwater. The Indians made the best offer and signed Allie to a deal that included a $1,000 signing bonus, a huge amount of money for a minister's son. Ironically, before the Indians came by, a scout from the Yankees, for whom he would later star, watched Allie pitch a bad game and decided he was not of Major League caliber.

In the summer of 1939, he reported to Springfield, Cleveland's Class C affiliate in the Mid-Atlantic League. On the ball club were future teammates Jim Hegan, Bob Lemon, and pitcher Red Embree. Most of them were earning $75 monthly, but Allie, due to some clever negotiating by Coach Iba, received $200 a month. Despite the emerging talent, Springfield finished in seventh place, but Allie managed a winning record of 11–8. It was a successful first season, but he would comment later that the hard muscles he had developed in playing football hindered his transition to professional baseball. He believed it took a year or so until he felt in shape to pitch in top form.

The next two years found him in Cedar Rapids, where he put up good numbers but was far from a league leader. Promoted to Wilkes-Barre in 1942, he flourished with 18 wins and a hefty 204 strikeouts. At age twenty-five and a married man, Allie got his first chance to stick with a Major League ball club.

Over the rest of the schedule Boudreau did his best to get the new ballplayers some game experience. On September 9, the Indians faced the Athletics. A Municipal Stadium crowd of barely over 4,000 saw a thirteen-inning battle with the A's prevailing, 5–4. Hank Edwards played the entire game in center field, knocking in two runs with a double and a single. Bob Lemon entered the game as a pinch runner, while Eddie Robinson got his first at bat, popping up to the infield.

Two days later the Red Sox hammered the Indians 15–2. With the score 12–0 in the seventh, Lou emptied the bench, placing Bob Lemon at third, Edwards in center field, and Robinson at first. Steve Gromek came on to do the pitching. The three fielders combined to go 0 for 6, while Gromek in two and two-thirds innings allowed three runs and walked three but did record four strikeouts. With this one-sided loss, the Indians were on their way to dropping six straight home games to slip five games below .500.

Allie Reynolds had to wait until September 17 for an opportunity to pitch. The Indians were still at home, playing Washington in front of a thousand hardcore fans at League Park. In the top of the second, with Cleveland trailing 4–1, Reynolds got the call from Boudreau. In four solid relief innings he walked four batters but gave up only a single run as the Indians came back to tie and send the game to extra innings. Cleveland scored in the bottom of the eleventh to win the game 6–5 and send their friends and families in the stands home with something positive to think about. Allie was not the pitcher of record, but he had acquitted himself well in his first Major League appearance.

The Indians completed the 1942 campaign in fourth place with a lackluster 75–79 record, a distant twenty-eight games behind the first-place Yankees. From August 1 to the end of the season they managed to win only eighteen games and drop thirty-two. One of the bright spots was pitcher Jim Bagby, with a record of 17–9, an ERA of 2.96, and four shutouts. Mel Harder finished with a record of 13–14, but after his elbow surgery in the fall of 1941 those numbers were encouraging.

On the hitting side, Les Fleming led the ball club in batting average, home runs, and RBIs. Not quite the spitting image of Hal Trosky, but more than adequate. Disappointingly, Jeff Heath did not repeat his 1941 stellar season, seeing his average drop sixty-two points to .278 and his home runs and RBIs fall as well. Fans booed him throughout the season, expecting him to play at an All-Star level.

Attendance fell below 500,000, close to Alva Bradley's winter prediction. The owner cautioned fans that 1943 would be even tougher, with more players drafted into the service and probably limits placed on travel. Bradley believed the game would continue, however. "Unless a definite order comes from Washington to stop baseball, I think we will, and I think we should[,] go on next year. I thought last year that baseball provided the people with an outlet for emotions stirred up by the war and I thought it was a useful service." Bradley added that he would look for ballplayers who had families rather than single men who were classified 1-A.

Before the Cleveland owner could sketch any plans, news came that Les Fleming had decided to take a job at a Texas defense plant. Despite his success in 1942, Les advised Bradley he would not be playing baseball until after the war ended. The Indians reached out to Hal Trosky at his Iowa farm, but the retired first baseman said no thanks. Eddie Robinson would have been the next choice, but he had already signed up with the navy. Another candidate would have to be found among a rapidly diminishing supply.

Though he was a nonswimmer, Jim Hegan enlisted in the coast guard and would probably be lost to the Indians for the duration of the war. The club believed Hegan would be their catcher for many years ahead, but his enlistment had them scrambling for a backstop with Major League experience. Most of the ball clubs had similar worries. Boston's Ted Williams was training to be a navy pilot along with his teammate shortstop Johnny Pesky. The Yankees were already without Tommy Henrich and would now be without Joe DiMaggio. The 1943 season had yet to begin, and it was apparent rosters would have to be filled with journeymen and career minor leaguers.

In this turbulent off-season, many ballplayers chose to work in the defense industries, which would exempt them from being called into the service. This seemed to be the best course of action for those who wanted to remain stateside. The caveat was if they left their jobs to play baseball, the protection would end. Among the Indians, Mel Harder, Oris Hockett, Hank Edwards, Ray Mack, and Jim Bagby had taken defense jobs. Still to be seen was how the War Manpower Commission might interpret their eventual resignations. One of the commission rules stated, "A statement of availability shall be granted to workers desiring to change jobs if they can prove that their transfer would be in the best interests of the war effort." It could be argued that playing baseball helped the general morale of the people and therefore qualified as helping the war effort. Believing the commission might interpret the rule that way, Bradley urged his players to take the defense jobs. This was not a certainty, however, and ballplayers had to take their chances.

At the end of November, Joseph B. Eastman, chairman of the War Transportation Board, wrote to Judge Landis and league presidents Will Harridge and Ford Frick. Fuel and railroads were needed for transporting troops and equipment, and Eastman asked that Major League Baseball review its travel schedule and significantly reduce the mileage.

Eastman, who had vast experience in the transportation industry, had three suggestions.

First, he asked if the teams could consider training at a location near their home base. Since none of them were in a warm climate, this would mean using an indoor facility like a gymnasium or fieldhouse. He also asked if they could shorten their exhibition schedules to cut down on travel.

Second, he urged the leagues to avoid long trips during the regular season. This would mean, for example, that if a game was rained out, a team should not make a special trip to make it up, such as traveling straight to St. Louis after finishing a road trip in New York. Instead, the game should be made up the next afternoon if the teams had a day off in the schedule, or as part of a doubleheader when the teams met again.

Finally, he asked that teams use secondary trains as much as possible, even if they did not have a sleeper car. Players could snooze in their seats rather than the comfortable lower berths they were used to.

Eastman's suggestions were not unreasonable given the situation, but owners still seemed to prefer training in Florida and California. Some arm-twisting from Landis might be needed.

Less than a week later, the winter meetings took place at the North Side Hotel in Chicago, where Judge Landis kept a suite. The commissioner's health was beginning to become a concern, serious enough that the owners did not want him to leave his residence. The seventy-six-year-old judge had been weakened by a recent bout of pneumonia, but he still kept long hours in the office and a close eye on the game itself. His plate was crowded with wartime issues and how to keep baseball a going concern.

While Landis and the owners met, Bob Feller made an unannounced visit to the hotel. Along with him was his fiancée, Virginia Winther from Waukegan, Illinois. Given several days of leave before he departed for the South Pacific, Feller was taking the opportunity to visit family and friends. He appeared eager to enter the fighting and ready to board the battleship USS *Alabama* to lead a gun crew. After he said his farewells, he was off to do his duty for the duration of the war.

The owners considered the travel limitations, expansion of rosters, and whether the season should begin a week later than usual. If it did, and they planned to keep the 154-game schedule, an additional number of doubleheaders would be necessary. Clark Griffith, the Washington

VICTORY ON TWO FRONTS

owner, asked for permission to schedule more night games, which everybody agreed to. Griffith was allowed a total of twenty-one games, while the other clubs had the option to play as many as fourteen.

The meeting concluded with little consensus on anything else, including the travel question. Many of the owners still wanted to take their teams south. The season would probably start a week later in April, and the rosters would remain at twenty-five men per team. More benefit games would take place, but plans were sketchy at best. The July All-Star game was awarded to Connie Mack and the Philadelphia Athletics, with the proceeds from ticket sales (Shibe Park could hold about 33,000) to be given to the Ball and Bat Fund for the servicemen.

As the owners sat back and waited, Judge Landis conferred with Joseph Eastman. Consulting a map of the United States, they drew up what became known as the Eastman-Landis line, which determined where the teams would train. Clubs would have to stay north of the Ohio and Potomac Rivers and east of the Mississippi. The western boundary did not apply to the Cardinals and Browns, just across the Mississippi in St. Louis. No matter what locations the teams selected, they would not resemble Florida or California.

With the new boundaries decided, the clubs began to scout locations in the Midwest and East. The Indians inspected several colleges and the city of Indianapolis before deciding on the fieldhouse at Purdue University in Lafayette, Indiana. General manager Roger Peckinpaugh liked the dimensions of the track-and-field facility, which measured 360 by 160 feet. The floor had an earth covering that allowed for ground balls and some careful sliding practice. Peck announced that the plan was for morning sessions inside the fieldhouse then afternoons outside, weather and snowstorms permitting. There would be some conflicts with the Purdue indoor track team, but Peck believed they would be worked out with the college's athletic director.

Gradually the other Major League teams revealed their spring training sites. Indiana got six ball clubs, including both the White Sox and Cubs in French Lick, the Tigers in Evansville, the Reds in Bloomington, the Pirates in Muncie, along with the Indians in Lafayette. The Yankees would train in Asbury Park, New Jersey, and the Dodgers curiously chose a resort in Bear Mountain, New York. There was some method to their madness, since they were five miles from the West Point Military Academy, which had an indoor baseball facility.

In years past, spring training had involved three to four hours of hard work every day, then lots of time for golf, swimming, fishing, and movies. The players liked to go out for a steak dinner, then take a leisurely walk back to the hotel for a few hands of poker. The new reality promised snow squalls and freezing temperatures. The carefree days in a warm climate would be on hold for several long years to come.

Chapter 4

A NEW SPRING TRAINING

The months of January and February 1943 saw a flurry of activity for Major League Baseball. Much to the dismay of the owners, stories appeared in the national newspapers wondering if baseball might be shut down for the year. Many looked to the War Manpower Commission to designate ballplayers as essential or nonessential workers. Paul McNutt, the former governor of Indiana, chaired the commission, which studied the labor needs of the armed forces, industry, and agriculture. McNutt had the power to rule on baseball and compel players who were not in the military to work year-round in the various plants and shipyards.

Whether McNutt planned to exercise that power was unknown to the public. Judge Landis stated that he would not go to Washington to ask for any special favors regarding the game. The owners took the same stance. New York columnist Bob Considine, in a syndicated story, accused the owners of being frightened to contact McNutt and confront the commission. William Duncan of the commission's office called Landis, Frick, and Harridge "the Timid Trio" for not attempting to get any clarification. Duncan said, "It simply amazes me to think that the leaders of the game in such a crisis assume the attitude we had better say nothing to the president or Mr. McNutt or they might say no."

In February, Judge Landis issued his famous statement on the matter: "Baseball this year as long as there are nine men for each side." Ty

Cobb, still a keen follower of the game, told writers, "Baseball has a definite place in the daily life of Americans wherever they happen to be on this Earth." Although gas rationing would make it more difficult for people to drive or take taxis to the games, Cobb said he believed baseball could thrive in war conditions, with fans taking the subway and street-cars or even walking to ballparks. Connie Mack, one of the few owners who had the nerve to speak out about the topic, said he wanted baseball to continue if possible or until the government said otherwise.

Cleveland's Roger Peckinpaugh, noting the number of players now in the armed forces, doubted baseball had the means to put a representative product on the field. The latest figures disclosed 244 players in the military, with the number growing monthly. Additionally, 24 Major Leaguers were still in war jobs, and their status remained unclear. The question writers and fans were tossing about was how sixteen Major League clubs could fill out their rosters and still be competitive. The answer would probably not come for several months.

Though much of the talk about baseball's future centered on the Major Leagues, the brunt of the hardships fell on the minors. Their better players were being called up to the parent clubs, while few if any replacements were available. Rosters were further depleted by the large number of young guys being drafted into the army. Leagues faced the prospect of shutting operations down temporarily, and a number of them did, including the Texas League, the Three-I-League, the California League, and the Mid-Atlantic League. Larger organizations like the Pacific Coast League, the International League, and the Southern League had the financial strength to sustain themselves for the difficult stretch ahead. But these were trying days for everyone.

In mid-March, with little fanfare, the Major League clubs assembled for spring training. The owners kept a low profile, hoping and praying the War Manpower Commission would somehow fail to notice the spring training activity and concentrate on other pressing issues. When the Indians arrived in Lafayette, Indiana, they quickly noticed a shortage of cabs to take them to the Fowler Hotel, their training headquarters for the next few weeks. With all the difficulty surrounding the teams' locations, including harsh weather conditions and an abbreviated exhibition schedule, it was important for all players to report on time. Not so for the perennial holdout, Jeff Heath. Once again, the troublesome left fielder did not care for his salary offer and stayed in Seattle. After his disappointing season, the Indians wanted to drop his salary to $10,500, while Heath demanded $13,500. Despite having little or no leverage to use against Bradley and Peckinpaugh, he still tried to play hardball. For their part, though they would miss him in left field, the two were willing to move on without him.

Heath added a new facet to this year's holdout, asking to be traded to any other ball club. He told the local writers he strongly disliked Municipal Stadium because of its massive outfield dimensions. Heath was certain his many four-hundred-foot fly outs would have been home runs and triples at League Park and most American League stadiums. Bradley seemed to have reached his limit with the enigmatic player, telling the newspapers Heath should resign from baseball and be done with it. Mercifully, in December of 1942 the Indians had traded with the Yankees for veteran outfielder Roy Cullenbine and catcher Buddy Rosar in exchange for Roy Weatherly and reserve Oscar Grimes. With Oris Hockett, rookie Hank Edwards, and Cullenbine, the Indians could field a team without Heath and his antagonistic attitude.

The Indians had high expectations for Edwards, a resident of Norwalk, Ohio. Friends called him a natural, someone who played baseball on a much higher plane than his peers. After starring in high school, he moved on to summer ball with the local Keller News. Along with his brother Paul, they played all comers, including a late-season exhibition game against the Toledo Mud Hens. The Cleveland scouts did not have to travel far to sign Edwards, and the team assigned him to Mansfield of the Class D Ohio State League. In 1939, he tore up the circuit, winning the batting title with an average of .395. A few promotions later he was a member of the varsity, in line for a starting spot in the outfield.

The Indians mapped out a sixteen-game exhibition schedule, less than half of what they had played in 1942. With the reduced travel, they would play the Pirates at Muncie and Indianapolis and the Reds in Indianapolis, Springfield, Ohio, Dayton, and two final games in Cincinnati. Considering the probability of rain and cold weather, the schedule would surely wind up being curtailed. The pitchers needed the most work of all, but with the limited schedule there was little chance of their getting much.

For ten days, Cleveland practiced in the fieldhouse, occasionally venturing outdoors to brave the cold. Two batting cages inside helped them get their swings no matter what the weather. The fieldhouse was large, but they had to share the space with several hundred navy recruits going through training and the Purdue track team preparing for an up-coming meet. Somehow all three groups were able to get their work done without too much interference or somebody getting leveled by a shot put.

In the second week of camp, temperatures reached the mid-fifties, giving the Indians a chance to work outside for several uninterrupted days. On March 26, the thermometer climbed to sixty-three degrees, allowing three hours of outdoor batting practice. The Purdue Relays forced the Indians to remain outside for several days, but fortunately the weather stayed reasonable. On the last day of the month, temperatures in Lafayette soared to seventy-four degrees, almost Florida-like. When time to break camp arrived, the club had had seven days of outdoor work, a real bonus for them and the other teams in Indiana.

Just as things were coming together, Oris Hockett suddenly left camp without any explanation and returned home to Dayton. The outfielder and part-time machinist still had job offers at $150 weekly, causing the front office to believe they had seen the last of the footloose ballplayer. Hockett was AWOL for nearly a week, giving no clues to what his inten-tions might be. With two starting outfielders unavailable, the Indians, hard-pressed for replacements, sent several coaches and pitchers into action.

As suddenly as he had left, Hockett returned to camp, claiming his father was ill with pneumonia. In different circumstances, Boudreau might have lowered the boom on him, but he allowed Hockett to suit up without any serious consequences. Hockett owed thanks to Jeff Heath, whose absence made him all the more valuable.

On Friday, April 2, Cleveland traveled to Muncie for two games against the Pirates. They lost the first game 4–3 in ten innings, though Jim Bagby debuted with a strong outing. The next day's game could not be played due to the temperature dropping well under forty degrees. On Sunday the Indians packed their bags for a week's stay in Indianapolis and games against the Pirates and Reds.

On Tuesday they were beaten by the Pirates 5–3. The game featured an unusual incident. A few days earlier Boudreau had told his team the new sign to steal would be when he pulled out his handkerchief and pretended to blow his nose. Trailing by one run in the middle innings, the Indians had Oris Hockett on second and rookie Eddie Turchin on first. Boudreau, sitting on the bench, suddenly jerked his head forward and sneezed. Without thinking he grabbed his handkerchief and loudly blew his nose. On the next pitch both runners took off, and Hockett was thrown out at third by five feet. After a moment of confusion, the players realized what had happened and cracked up. Later, with a sheepish grin, Lou told the sportswriters it was a big mistake, but at least his runners were paying attention.

Five of the nine remaining games with the Reds had to be canceled because of constant rain and cold. Only Jim Bagby was able to pitch six innings; the rest of the staff pitched no more than three or four. This did not bode well for the beginning of the season. The lack of good weather proved to be a significant problem for the Indians, who would not be in the best of shape to start the season.

Good news came when Jeff Heath finally signed his contract and was able to play in the last exhibition game. Showing little rust, Heath banged out three singles, prompting Boudreau to pencil him in for the opening day lineup. The Indians' home schedule had forty-five games at Municipal Stadium, with fourteen under the lights, and thirty-two at League Park. Gradually, Alva Bradley was increasing the number of games at the stadium while cutting back on contests at League Park, though at no time did he indicate a departure from the old grounds.

Before opening day, Emil Bossard and his grounds crew worked overtime to completely resod the stadium. The previous summer had seen army tanks and soldiers marching over the field, and in the fall football games tore up what was left of the grass. Major work had to be done, and Bossard and his crew were up to the task. Bossard, regarded as one of the best groundskeepers in baseball, worked tirelessly around the clock to keep the huge stadium in top condition.

On Wednesday, April 21, with temperatures at a chilly forty degrees, the Indians opened the season at home against the Tigers. At the pregame ceremonies, Boudreau received a large square cake in the shape of Municipal Stadium. Steve O'Neill, the longtime Cleveland player, coach, and manager and currently the Tigers manager, got one in the appearance of a shamrock. On hand for the ceremonies were former champion boxers Johnny Kilbane and Barney Ross.

Though Kilbane was a native Clevelander, Ross received the bigger ovation from the crowd, which knew that Ross was a war hero. Not only one of the great boxers of recent memory, he had enlisted in the marines and, rather than spend the war shaking hands stateside, insisted on being sent to the front lines. Though already in his thirties, he was ordered to the South Pacific. At Guadalcanal, amid heavy fighting, Ross was in a foxhole with three other marines. Two of them were killed and the third was wounded, but Ross, despite being wounded himself, picked up their weapons and held off several squads of Japanese soldiers. When the shooting stopped, he carried the one other marine alive back to safety. For his incredible bravery he was awarded the Silver Star and a citation from President Roosevelt.

Jack Graney was behind the microphone, ready for the start of another Cleveland baseball season. Always creative, Graney continued as one of the game's best play-by-play men. He did the home games live and re-created away games with colorful observations in the studio. One of his new routines occurred when the ticker tape described a foul pop-up near the stands. He would yell for his engineer to "Watch out," then bang a baseball on his wooden desk to make it seem as if the ball had just missed them.

For the Tigers, the team's former star Harry Heilmann was at the mike, sending a live broadcast to Detroit. Improvements in technology had made it possible to smoothly relay long-distance broadcasts back home, and soon Graney, like many other broadcasters, would travel with his team to bring the live action home.

At 3:30 the Indians ran onto the field with four new faces in the lineup. After an impressive spring training, rookie Hank Edwards got the start in center field. Otto Denning had won the first base job by default, and newly acquired Buddy Rosar did the catching. Playing his first game for Cleveland was Roy Cullenbine, starting in right field. Cullenbine, in his fifth Major League season, was an upgrade from Roy Weatherly and a solid, if not spectacular, outfielder. On the bench sat Oris Hockett, last year's starter, who was being given a moment to think about abandoning the ball club two weeks prior.

The pitching matchup featured two veterans: Jim Bagby against thirty-six-year-old Tommy Bridges. For eight innings the game was scoreless. After Bagby retired the Tigers in the top of the ninth, Roy Cullenbine drew a leadoff walk. Otto Denning fanned, but Buddy Rosar crushed his third hit of the day, a ringing double down the third-base line. Ray Mack was intentionally walked to load the bases. Up came Jim Bagby with a chance to win his own ballgame. On the first pitch from

Bridges, Bagby lined the ball to deep right field. Rip Radcliffe made a running catch, but Cullenbine tagged up at third and easily scored to win the game 1–0. Despite the cold temperature and small crowd, the Indians had their first win in the books.

Bagby was in midseason form, allowing only three scattered hits and a single walk. He also had two base hits to go along with Rosar's three. The only other Indian to hit safely was Jeff Heath with a single. Tommy Bridges pitched just as well until he tired in the ninth. Apparently the hurlers did not need as much spring training as most experts thought.

The next day the teams met again, this time at League Park. A tiny crowd of 2,500 watched another pitcher's duel between Mel Harder and Virgil Trucks. The score stood at 1–0 after seven innings, but Detroit scored two more runs off Harder in the eighth and went on to a 4–0 win.

In the Cleveland locker room, the hitters were complaining about the baseball and its inability to go anywhere after contact. They knew the pitching was good, but could something else be going on? It wasn't only the Indians and Tigers; of the twelve Major League games over the first four days of the season, eight were shutouts. Cleveland sportswriters checked into the baseball and discovered some changes had been made since last season. Due to the needs of the armed forces, the core of the baseball was being made with reprocessed rubber and a new type of cement between the layers of wool. The result was a ball much like the ones used early in the century, when low-scoring games were the norm.

The complaints reached Judge Landis, who checked with the manufacturers of the inferior ball. Spalding promised a new, improved version in two weeks. But for the time being the pitchers would have a measurable advantage over the hitters in both leagues.

The dead baseball wasn't the only problem baseball had at the beginning of the season. Attendance lagged far below the figures from 1942. Opening day crowds totaled 192,000 that year, as opposed to 82,000 for the current campaign. Rain, cold temperatures, and muddy playing fields led to an inferior quality of play. The owners saw empty seats all around their ballparks and fretted about draft call-ups.

On May 5, the National League teams received their supplies of new, livelier baseballs. The American League had to wait three more days. The Indians were in St. Louis when they arrived. Bill DeWitt, the Browns general manager, bounced samples of the old and new from a height of nine feet. The new baseball bounced forty-two inches as compared to the inferior version's twenty-eight—not quite double, as had been reported, but still a significant difference.

As of May 9, the effect of the new baseball was apparent. The Indians, in the first game of a Sunday doubleheader, racked up sixteen hits in a 6–5 thirteen-inning win. Jeff Heath exploded for a single, triple, and home run along with four RBIs. Cleveland lost the second game, but Heath bashed three more hits to give him six for the day. With the team heading home to Cleveland and a ball to their liking, things were looking up. They had a 10–6 record; the weather was about to turn around; and attendance was beginning to trend upwards. What could go wrong?

Mel Harder had pitched Saturday in St. Louis, going the distance in a 3–2 loss. But in the top of the eighth inning he slid hard into second base and his spikes caught the bag, giving his ankle a severe jolt. After a few moments of flexing the leg, he walked to the Indians' bench, then came back out and pitched the bottom half of the inning, allowing what would prove to be the winning run. On Sunday he was able to walk around the hotel, limping slightly when he put weight on the ankle.

When the Indians arrived home, they immediately sent Mel to see Dr. Edward Castle, the team physician. X-rays revealed a broken ankle that would take at least two months to heal. The injury threw the pitching staff into disarray, since Harder and Bagby had been the only two reliable performers to that point. Manager Boudreau would have to look at guys like veterans Vern Kennedy and Chubby Dean to fill the gap, or possibly Allie Reynolds, wasting away on the bench. In 1943, quality pitchers were at a premium, so trading for a veteran starter was probably not going to happen.

The lack of exhibition games in March and April came back to haunt the Indians. With only eight games played, Boudreau had not been able to get a good read on his pitchers, other than Bagby, Harder, Smith, and Al Milnar. The other candidates had appeared sparingly, unable to show much of what they could do. Boudreau had the unenviable task of reshaping his starting rotation with pitchers who were still in extended spring training.

On Thursday afternoon, while the Indians were hosting the Washington Senators, fans listening to the game on WHK were puzzled when Jack Graney's longtime partner, Pinky Hunter, took over at the mike in the fourth inning. At the end of the previous inning Graney had received a note that his son, army lieutenant John G. Graney, had been seriously injured in a plane crash at Fort Bragg, North Carolina. Graney rushed home to pick up his wife, then drove to the WHK building, planning to charter a private plane to fly them to North Carolina. At the office, Graney learned his son had died from severe head injuries. The younger Graney had qualified for officer candidate school and graduated as a field artillery instructor. He was on the airplane observing ground maneuvers when the pilot somehow crashed into a tree in midflight. Jack and his wife flew to North Carolina to claim the body and bring their son home for a Monday funeral.

Graney had seen his share of tragedies. In August of 1920, while he was playing for the Indians, he had seen his close friend and roommate Ray Chapman hit by a pitch that fractured his skull. Graney helped carry Chapman to the clubhouse and stayed with him until an ambulance arrived. Chapman died early the next morning, leaving Jack in a terrible state. Now disaster had struck again with the death of his only son. It would be several weeks of grieving before he resumed his broadcast duties.

While Graney was at home mourning, the Indians took three straight at home against the Yankees. On Saturday, May 22, Jim Bagby won his fifth of six decisions, beating New York 9–2. The next afternoon Cleveland swept a doubleheader behind Al Smith and Chubby Dean, 3–1 and 5–2, to move into first place with a record of 16–11. The real test would come on the first eastern road trip of the season, when the Indians played fifteen games against Boston, New York, Washington, and Philadelphia. They were out to prove that their good start was not a fluke. A successful road trip would keep them close to or at the top, but a losing one meant they still had work to do.

The road tour began with a rare morning-afternoon doubleheader. The Red Sox were trying to determine if they could draw working men who worked afternoon or evening shifts to Fenway Park. But apparently they preferred sleeping in, as attendance at the morning game was less than 2,000. The afternoon crowd was not much larger. But the Red Sox, despite the near-empty ballpark, won both games, 2–0 and 4–3.

The Indians salvaged the last game in Boston, only to drop all three in New York. In the Sunday doubleheader, with 53,000 watching, Allie Reynolds pitched four innings in extended relief, giving up one run with five strikeouts. The one run, on a homer in the bottom of the ninth by former Indian Roy Weatherly, was the margin of victory in a 3–2 loss.

After losing three out of four games in Washington, the Indians continued the discouraging road expedition with four games in Philadelphia. In the first game, on Thursday, June 3, a fly ball to left center field led to a tremendous collision between Jeff Heath and Hank Edwards. The promising rookie was down for several minutes before rising to his feet and walking slowly to the Cleveland bench. He was thought to have a concussion and was told to stay on the bench for the next several games. The trip concluded with Cleveland stumbling back home with a dismal 4–11 record.

Back in Cleveland, Edwards, still feeling the effects of the collision, went straight to Dr. Castle's office for a complete exam. As with Harder a month earlier, the X-rays came back with bad news, in this case a broken collarbone that would mean four to five weeks out of the lineup.

Facing a shortage of outfielders, the Indians immediately called up twenty-year-old Pat Seerey from Wilkes-Barre. Seerey was born in Wilburton, Oklahoma, a town of around 2,000 residents known for coal mining and a group of caves that were ideal hideouts for bygone outlaws such as Jesse James, the Younger brothers, and female desperado Belle Starr. The family moved later to Arkansas, where Seerey starred in football and baseball at Catholic High School. In the summers he played American Legion ball for the Little Rock Doughboys, smashing home runs farther than most boys his age. Facing mostly college pitchers, he led the Doughboys to the Arkansas state finals, batting .464 in sixteen games, with four triples and three home runs. One of his homers was a four-hundred-foot blast, astounding his teammates and spectators in the grandstand.

His feats of strength were noticed by Cleveland scouts, who signed him to a contract and sent him to Appleton of the Wisconsin State League. A year later he moved up to Cedar Rapids in the Three-I League, where he blasted 33 home runs. Five feet, ten inches tall, over two hundred pounds, and showing tremendous upper-body strength, Pat hit many tape-measure shots, but struck out at a dizzying rate. Cleveland hoped to use him only as a fourth outfielder until Edwards returned.

Needing more punch, the Indians sent Otto Denning and rookie infielder Eddie Turchin to Buffalo for first baseman Mickey Rocco. A career minor leaguer, the twenty-seven-year-old Rocco had a little pop in his bat, something the Indians had lacked at first base since Les Fleming's departure. Part of Rocco's appeal was in his 3-A draft status, with a wife and child to support and little chance to be called into service.

At home with Rocco installed at first base, the Indians opened a five-game series against the St. Louis Browns. Much to the dismay of the Cleveland fans, the Indians inexplicably lost the first four. They hit bottom on Saturday, June 12, with an ugly eleven-inning 7–6 loss. A frustrated Boudreau used nineteen players in the game, including five different pitchers, who tallied a mind-blowing seventeen walks. In the tenth inning, Boudreau, short on players, moved himself to catcher, sending in pitcher Jim Bagby to play shortstop for the final two innings.

While the Indians were in a complete freefall, Hal Trosky visited the Chicago White Sox and took several workouts with the team. With his migraines cleared up, he had changed his mind about playing baseball and was trying to find out if he was anywhere near playing shape. Trosky advised interested reporters he might talk to Boudreau about applying for reinstatement.

While Indians fans were buzzing about a Trosky comeback, the story had an interesting twist. Before Hal had officially announced his retirement, general manager Peckinpaugh sent him a 1942 contract with his salary slashed 50 percent. Peck was quoted at the time as saying, "Wait till Trosky sees these figures. He'll have a real headache!" It was a thoughtless comment making light of the migraines, and of course Trosky found out about it. Before his Chicago visit, he contacted six teams in the American League, who were generally interested in the slugging first baseman, but the Indians refused to give up their rights to him.

Trosky and Boudreau met in Chicago over breakfast. They had a friendly chat, but Trosky made it clear that things between him, Peckinpaugh, and Bradley needed to be straightened out before a return to Cleveland was possible. The meeting ended with Hal leaving for Norway, Iowa.

Still lacking a power-hitting first baseman, the Indians traveled to Detroit to begin a three-game series. They were shocked to discover thousands of federal troops with rifles lined up on the city streets. Several days earlier, a massive race riot had occurred in the city, and the turmoil was not yet under control. A total of 1,300 people were in police custody, of which a disproportionate 85 percent were Black. Stores in White and Black neighborhoods were looted and burned, while numerous saloons in both areas were trashed and emptied of their liquor supplies.

Detroit was the fourth-largest city in the United States, with a population of roughly 2 million. The auto industry had long attracted people looking for work, but since the beginning of World War II most of the automakers had converted their plants to war production. With the promise of steady employment, a large southern migration of Blacks and Whites came to Detroit, hoping for fair pay and reasonable housing. The southern Blacks arrived to find available only the lowest-paying, most dangerous factory jobs and hardly any housing. The Whites got many of the better-paying jobs, including supervisory ones, and found consider-ably better options for housing. In this situation, with overcrowding and unequal treatment, tensions between the races reached the boiling point.

On Sunday, June 20, thousands of Blacks and Whites visited Belle Island, a popular place to swim, relax, and picnic. Without any warning, fights broke out between youths of the two races, and before the police could get control, the skirmishes spilled into downtown, growing into riot proportions. President Roosevelt sent in federal troops to quell the violence, but by Tuesday all was not quiet, forcing the Indians-Tigers game to be canceled.

The next day the teams played a doubleheader with hundreds of soldiers on duty carrying fixed bayonets. The teams split, with Detroit winning the first 3–1 and the second going eleven innings. With the score tied 6–6, Jeff Heath socked a two-run homer, keying a three-run rally and a 9–6 win. To wrap up the series, the clubs had scheduled a Thursday twi-light game but were notified by the city of an absolute ten o'clock curfew.

Oris Hockett led off the game with a home run, but the Tigers scored four times off Jim Bagby in the bottom of the second inning and cruised to a 7–4 win. The game was over in less than two hours, giving the Indians ample time to shower, dress, and get cabs to the boat dock off Lake Erie. They were surely relieved to get out of Detroit and put some miles between them and the tragic violence that had occurred around the city. Unfortunately, this would not be the last time a Major League Baseball game had to be postponed under such circumstances.

Wednesday, June 30, had been set as the day for ticket sales around the Major Leagues to be donated to the Army-Navy Relief Fund. The Indians played the Yankees at Municipal Stadium before a crowd of nearly 23,000 people. The fans enjoyed a real nail-biter. With the score knotted at 1–1 going into the top of the eleventh inning, New York's Nick Etten, who had already homered off Jim Bagby, doubled to score two more runs. The Indians could not answer in the bottom half of the inning and lost to the Yanks 3–1. The receipts added up to $25,000 for the relief fund, while the seven other games raised $175,000 for an over-all number of $200,000, a welcome amount for the soldiers' families.

In 1943, baseball had greatly upped the ante in raising money for the relief funds and purchasing war bonds. Earlier in the month a group of New York bankers and industrial leaders had worked out a plan to buy large sums in war bonds. They partnered with the New York chapter of the Baseball Writers of America Association to sponsor players from the Yankees, Giants, and Dodgers. In an auction setting, the well-to-do New Yorkers bid for their favorite players. Outfielder Dixie Walker of the Dodgers went for $11,250 in war bonds, while his teammate, shortstop Arky Vaughan, brought in $11,000. Joe Gordon of the Yankees went for $3,500, and Carl Hubbell of the Giants for $3,000. The idea was to monitor a yet to be determined number of games and buying more bonds based on the player's performance. If one of the hitters had a single, his sponsor bought $2,500 in bonds, while a home run was worth $10,000. For pitchers, a win netted $35,000 and a shutout $50,000. Just sponsoring players brought in $123,850 alone. The league was not done yet; with the 1943 All-Star game just weeks away, another large sum was guaranteed to be added to the war effort.

Meanwhile, the Indians kept up their disappointing homestand. They had trouble putting wins together, eventually sliding all the way down to fifth place and a record below .500. There were a few highlights at home, however, including a classic beatdown of the Yankees on July 2. Played at League Park, the game was scoreless going into the bottom of the fourth inning, when Cleveland exploded for twelve runs. Before the side was retired, Ray Mack had singled twice with the bases loaded, Jeff Heath had two singles, and Ken Keltner had a double and single. The twelve runs in one inning were one shy of the Indians record of thirteen, set in 1923 against the Red Sox. Oddly enough, the final score stayed at 12–0, a three-hit shutout victory for Allie Reynolds. The rookie pitcher had claimed his place in the rotation, impressing Boudreau and Peckinpaugh with his mature attitude and lively fastball. With Mel Harder still out, Reynolds and veteran Al Smith had stepped up to fill the gap in the rotation. The thirty-five-year-old Smith pitched so well that he was chosen for the All-Star game along with Jim Bagby, Lou Boudreau, Ken Keltner, Jeff Heath, and catcher Buddy Rosar. The Indians matched the total number of Yankees selected, taking a total of twelve spots between them on the American League roster.

The All-Star game took place at Shibe Park on July 13 in front of 31,000 enthusiastic spectators. In the bottom of the second inning, Bobby Doerr of the Red Sox slammed a three-run homer to deep left field off Mort Cooper, and the American League stars went on to a 5–3 victory, which netted $64,000 for the baseball equipment fund. Ken Keltner was the only one of Cleveland's six representatives to start, going one for four with a double and a run scored. Jeff Heath entered the game to pinch-hit, but the other players did not see any action. That was unfortunate for Al Smith, making the team for the first time in ten seasons. His Indians teammates all had multiple opportunities in their careers, but for Smith this would be his one and only chance.

With the All-Star break concluded, the Indians went back on the road and promptly lost three in a row to St. Louis. For a moment it seemed the boys might be throwing in the towel and tanking the rest of the schedule. But whether Boudreau said something in the clubhouse or several of the veterans got together and spoke, a fire was lit. The Indians swept a doubleheader to conclude the series with the Browns, and over the next four days their pitchers bore down, allowing a single run in thirty-six innings. On July 21, Al Smith threw a shutout, and the next day Bagby gave up the one run, followed by consecutive shutouts from a recovered Mel Harder and a rapidly developing Allie Reynolds. Reynolds's win brought the team back to .500 for the first time in three weeks.

When the Indians returned home, there seemed to be grumbling from the players about the large outfield at Municipal Stadium. Usually it was Jeff Heath doing the bellyaching, but now several others were airing their criticism. They had some justification, since the center field fence was some 470 feet from home plate and the power alleys 435. Alva Bradley listened for a few days, then spoke of applying to the American League office to move in the fences. How serious he was is a matter of conjecture, but a local fence company told the papers they would be willing to do the job for nothing. Bradley asked the company to come forward, but after several days of silence the talk died out and no fences were installed. The cow pasture would remain for the immediate future.

On Sunday, August 8, the Indians played a home doubleheader against the Browns. The first game was tied 5–5 after nine innings. In the top of the twelfth, St. Louis had runners on first and second with one out. The next batter hit an infield grounder, and the throw went to Ken

Keltner for the force out at third. Keltner stepped on the bag, but before he could fire to first for the double play, Browns outfielder Mike Chartak slid hard into him, spiking his ankle severely. Trainer Lefty Weisman raced onto the field to take a look. Keltner had a bloody four-inch gash at the ankle, showing clear through to the bone. Weisman quickly bandaged the injured leg and called for a stretcher. By the time they reached the clubhouse, an ambulance was waiting to take Keltner to Lakeside Hospital. He was admitted for an overnight stay and would be lost to the Indians for at least a month.

Cleveland scored in the fourteenth inning to win 6–5, then took game two behind Jeff Heath's first-inning inside-the-park three-run homer. Heath's blast, hit 450 feet off the right center field wall, illustrated the point that it took a mammoth shot to hit a ball out of the park, except down the 322-foot foul lines.

All through August the Indians remained hot, at one point winning eight games in a row. Manager Boudreau found his batting eye at home, during one stretch rapping out fourteen hits in twenty-one at bats. For the entire month they had a record of twenty-one wins and eleven losses. The early season cold, rainouts, and travel restrictions led to their having to play a five-day, eight-game homestand against the Red Sox, including three doubleheaders. Both teams had to go deep into their pitching staffs throughout the exhausting series. The Indians, with superior pitching, got the better of the Red Sox, five games to three.

With the Indians' second-half rally, home attendance took an upward turn. Among the fans at one game was William Edmunds, the local director for the War Manpower Commission, who told reporters, "I've been rather critical of baseball continuing during this time of war, but the other day for the first time in years I went out to see the Indians play. What I saw completely changed my mind." Edmunds observed the fans yelling encouragement to the players and generally having a great time. He concluded that baseball was truly an excellent vehicle for people to get their minds off the war and relax for a couple of hours. Attendance for all teams was down about 12 percent from 1942, but the game's value in terms of relaxation more than outweighed the numbers.

As far as money for the war effort, the game kept on giving. On one chosen day, the receipts from all eight games played, over $322,000, were donated to the Red Cross. For the October World Series, the $100,000 paid by Gillette Razors for radio advertising rights would be going to several war funds. All told, about $400,000 in series ticket sales would be donated, keeping baseball as one of the most generous funders of the troops overseas.

Moving into September, the Yankees, with a record of 77–46, were running away with the race. With little chance of overtaking them, the third-place Indians had their sights on passing the second-place Washington Senators and getting a good share of the World Series receipts. On September 10 the team was in Detroit for another doubleheader. Jeff Heath, one of the game's hottest hitters, came to bat in the first inning with the bases loaded. Probably salivating at the chance to knock in a few more runs, he looked to the bench and got the take sign from Boudreau. Fuming, Heath obeyed and subsequently fanned. On the way to the dugout he vented his rage at the man in charge. Boudreau promptly benched Heath for the remainder of the game and all of game two. He told the sportswriters, "I guess I have got to quit being a good fellow. I just wish I had started being tough earlier in the season."

Heath did not leave the bench for the next several days, and just when he was ready to escape the doghouse, he developed a bad flu. His condition worsened, prompting a visit to Lakeside Hospital, where he was diagnosed with acute bronchitis. He would not return that year. It had been a difficult season for Heath. In addition to hearing boos from the Cleveland fans, he had a thrown ball hit him squarely in the eye while sliding into second during a July 18 doubleheader at St. Louis. The throw from outfielder Chet Laabs opened a gash above his eyebrow that needed four stiches. Two days earlier at batting practice, an errant throw hit Heath in the back of the neck, sending him to the clubhouse for two hours of ice packs. But he had made the All-Star team, and hit extremely well for most of the second half, including one stretch in which he hit four home runs in four games. In 118 games, Heath hit .274, and would end up leading all Indians batters with 18 home runs and 79 RBIs. If he had played a full season, 20-plus home runs and 90 to 95 RBIs were reasonable projections. Until that final outburst, he had mostly managed to keep his temper in check while helping the Indians to a winning season.

The fans who loved heckling the outfielder were not aware that after many of the home games Heath would come out of the dugout, dragging a player or two with him, and take batting practice for at least a half hour. Whether it was after a good game or a bad one, he wanted to work on his hitting. When fans accused him of loafing after pop flies, they did not realize Heath had judged the ball uncatchable and stopped short to play the ball on the bounce. While giving the other outfielders a pass, they would rag on Heath without giving him the benefit of doubt.

With the season nearly complete, the Indians were in Boston for a weekday game. With no warning, Jim Bagby startled the writers covering the team by airing his grievances with manager Boudreau. He disclosed that Boudreau had fined him $100 at the end of July for not doing his pregame running and being out of shape. For this and other reasons, he wanted out of Cleveland. "I haven't changed my mind," he told the writers. "I still want to be traded, but I'm still pitching to win, no matter what club I'm with." He was tired of being the goat, he said, and he was willing to take a pay cut to get away from Boudreau. For his part, Lou acknowledged that they did not see things eye to eye. The two had recently met to try and clear the air, but failed to reach any kind of truce. Bagby, a two-time All-Star and seventeen-game winner the past two years, was clearly the ace of the staff. He had strong Cleveland connections, including his father, Jim, who helped lead the 1920 Indians to the pennant and their first World Series championship. For him to demand a trade was a strong statement, and losing him would surely be a setback to the starting rotation.

The 1943 season ended with the Indians in third place behind the Yankees and Senators with a record of 82–71. Each player earned a World Series share of about $500. There were many positives, including fine seasons from Bagby and Al Smith. Mel Harder made a strong comeback from his elbow surgery, while Allie Reynolds established himself as a future star, leading the American League with 151 strikeouts and posting an ERA of 2.99. The hitting did not come up to expectations, as not a single regular batted over .300 and the entire starting infield collecting only 19 home runs. Keltner missing forty-two games had something to do with the lack of production, but none of the others were able to hit as many as 10.

Attendance for the year slipped to 438,000, down almost 21,000 from 1942. Still, this figure represented only a 5 percent decline, while Major League attendance overall dropped 13 percent. Even the powerhouse Yankees were down by 303,000 fans. With the number of marginal players on most teams' rosters, including the Indians, many clubs' payrolls had been reduced accordingly to help offset the drop in attendance. How that would play out in 1944 was anyone's guess.

Chapter 5

TO PLAY OR NOT TO PLAY

The first few months of the 1943 off-season went quietly for the Cleveland Indians. In November, local sportswriters named Al Smith Indians Man of the Year. Smith had come a long way in his career since starting in 1929 with Independence, Kansas, of the Western Association.

The Indians cut ties with Hal Trosky, selling his contract to the Chicago White Sox for an undisclosed price. The front office wanted to give Mickey Rocco another chance to establish himself at first base, and it seemed best to allow Hal to try and resurrect his career elsewhere. But they had no other options if Mickey failed.

The winter baseball meetings were held in New York without generating any front-page headlines. The Washington Senators obtained permission to play night games beginning May 5 through the end of the season. Day games were required only on Sundays and holidays. The Browns and Cardinals would play twenty-one night games each, while the rest of the clubs would stay at fourteen. The Washington area contained a great number of government workers whose positions kept them from attending day games. Playing more night games would help raise attendance and thus revenue. The St. Louis clubs, especially the Browns, found they had better turnouts at night. As expected, teams would train once again in the Midwest and East with a limited number of exhibition games.

The only incident of note at the meetings came when Paul Robeson, the distinguished Black actor and singer, requested and received time to address the owners. Robeson appealed to them to allow Black ballplayers to fill the ranks of the minor leagues. He noted that the teams were struggling to complete their rosters, so why not use the talented Black players? If this action was approved and some of the players showed Major League ability, then the owners could do what they thought best. Robeson was supported by editors of several large Black newspapers, including the *Pittsburgh Courier,* the *Baltimore Afro-American,* and the *Chicago Defender.* The owners listened but gave no indication of what they were thinking. By spring training time, the Negro League players came to realize they were not going to be afforded the chance to compete at a higher level.

The meetings came and went with Jeff Heath and Jim Bagby still members of the Indians. Trades were bantered around, but Roger Peckinpaugh heard nothing he liked. He believed a team could win despite a few unhappy campers, and chose not to give away players for the sake of peace in the clubhouse. Manager Boudreau had little choice but to go forward with his two problem children.

In the latter part of December, sad news came of the passing of Chuck Bradley, the older brother of the Indians owner. In 1927, Chuck had been instrumental in working with his younger brother to complete their purchase of the Cleveland franchise. The more outspoken of the two, Chuck had been heavily involved in the front office during the early years of the Bradley ownership. Lately he had put most of his energy into other projects such as operating railroads and taking charge of a downtown department store. The city honored Chuck by lowering the Terminal Tower flag to half-mast for several days.

Upon his death, his shares in the team were almost certainly purchased or at least controlled by Alva. Over time, several of the original shareholders with the Bradleys had died, leaving their wives or sons in possession of the stock. Though owning the majority of the club, few of the families chose to remain active, allowing Alva to call most of the shots without challenge. There was a question of what would happen, though, if an outside party made an offer to purchase the club. Would Bradley, holding less than 50 percent, have enough shareholder support to keep running the team, or would he be forced to sell? At least for the short term, however, he appeared to be safe.

In January, Peckinpaugh stated that the Indians had decided to return to Lafayette, Indiana, for spring training. This was even though the navy would have use of the fieldhouse for the morning and early afternoons, leaving only a few hours for baseball practice. Training camp would start March 13 and exhibitions two weeks later. The Indians planned to bring thirty-one players to camp, enough to stage intrasquad games until the regular exhibitions.

Alva Bradley worried all winter about the kind of team he could field for the 1944 season. The uncertainty of whether his players would be allowed to transition from war jobs to baseball still existed, and several more were facing draft calls. At an ill-timed moment, Bradley spoke candidly to the *Plain Dealer*. He said with some frustration, "It's too good a game to be turned into a farce and that's what will happen if we insist on operating whether or not we've got big league ball players to operate with." Bradley believed that if one club ceased operations the others would fall like dominoes. "I won't consider quitting until there's no other course open to me," he said. "But common sense tells me that time may come whether I like it or not."

The comments soon went national, causing a ruckus among the other league owners. Many believed Bradley was alerting his peers that he planned to shut the team down. Eddie Brannick, secretary of the New York Giants, said, "Baseball will go on with or without the Indians. And I frankly don't think that Bradley would surrender his membership and be the only club to drop out." Warren Giles, general manager of the Cincinnati Reds, said, "We are planning to operate and not with any low form of comedy. If that is all Cleveland can offer [comedy] or expect to offer, it should quit!" Realizing his error, Bradley issued a clarification. "The idea that I'd close up my franchise if the rest of the league kept operating is the most ridiculous thing I've heard in a long time." The Indians were still open for business.

In early February, Judge Landis announced that a committee of American and National League owners was being formed to deal with the future issue of players returning from the war and what to do with them. Currently the armed forces claimed over 400 Major Leaguers and 1,200 from the minors. Until the war ended, there was no way to determine the time frame for their return to baseball. If it happened in mid-season, how would rosters be affected? Should the Major League players have guaranteed jobs while their current replacements were immediately released? The most interesting question concerned the minor leagues. With so many clubs not operating, where would the returning minor league players go?

If Landis had his say, no doubt free agency would be put in place. Those and other questions had to be tossed about by the committee, which included Alva Bradley, Clark Griffith, Red Sox general manager Eddie Collins, Warren Giles, and Branch Rickey. In the meantime, the war went on, with heavy fighting in Europe and the South Pacific.

With the start of spring training a month away, the Indians took stock of their roster. They had thirteen players classified 4-F, which meant there was little or no chance of their being called up. Among the players in that category were Mickey Rocco; relief pitcher Joe Heving, who was thirty-nine-years old, over the draft age; and pitchers Al Smith and Steve Gromek. Mike Naymick, another of the relief pitchers, stood 6'8" tall, which was well above the military's height limit. It is not hard to imagine what might have happened to him charging out of a foxhole toward the enemy.

Lou Boudreau had been classified 4-F since the beginning of the war due to his chronically sore ankles. In a strange twist, his draft board in Illinois reclassified him 1-A (ready for service) and would be calling him for another medical exam. Ken Keltner had a 2-B classification (safe from service) because of his war job but planned to stop working and take his chances with the Indians. He was the first Major League player in 1944 to willingly give up his exemption. In most cases, draft boards waited until a replacement was found at the war job before reclassifying, but Keltner was philosophical about the probable change to 1-A status. He told the papers, "If the army wants me that's okay, but I'm still a ball player by trade and I'm going to play until I'm called." Ballplayers did not want to be unpatriotic, but at this stage of the war they were reluctant to enlist or follow Keltner's lead.

By the second week of March, Cleveland had eighteen players available for spring training. It goes without saying that Jim Bagby and Jeff Heath were not among them. However, there were a few surprises among the missing, including Mel Harder, Al Smith, and Allie Reynolds. The reasons for their absence were not given, but the three were among the best pitchers on the club. They would be needed in camp in just a week's time.

Buddy Rosar, who had a war job with the Buffalo Arms Company, indicated that rather than quitting he would try to obtain a transfer to a

Cleveland company. That would enable him to avoid the draft, and he would likely get permission to play weekends and night games at home. Ray Mack, the Indians' second baseman since 1939, had a war job at Thompson Products in Cleveland. He said that he did not intend to play ball unless the company gave him the okay for home games. Cleveland fans wondered what might happen in the unlikely event that, with Mack working in a factory, both Keltner and Boudreau were drafted. Alva Bradley may have been thinking of such a situation when he made his comments about teams folding.

To make matters worse, Jim Bagby let Peckinpaugh know he was temporarily retiring and joining the merchant marine. Apparently he was serious about his trade demand, and preferred to enter some form of service rather than play for the Indians. Heath was off on his annual holdout and would be out, if history was any guide, until the start of the regular season.

Just days before the trek to Indiana, Boudreau had only eleven players ready to leave for camp, and that number included himself and Keltner, who were both still on shaky ground. The manager fumed about the holdouts and about the players who were slow to make arrangements to report. In the current situation, he said, this was not the time to be absent from camp. As the small group was leaving on March 13 for Lafayette, Boudreau peered out the train window, hoping some of his missing players might board at the last minute.

On the first day of camp, the squad arrived at the Purdue fieldhouse. Vern Kennedy, one of the Indians spot starters, made his way to the pole vault area. Kennedy, who had been a decathlon champ in college, grabbed a pole, took a running start, and vaulted over the nine-foot bar. The players whooped and hollered, but Boudreau ran over and grabbed the pole from Kennedy before he could go again.

The roster status improved over the next few days with pitcher Steve Gromek reporting and Roy Cullenbine and Mel Harder signing their contracts. This marked the seventeenth season for Mel, who was nearing the exclusive 200-victory mark. His 197 wins placed him number one among all Indians pitchers since 1901. The only pitcher who had a chance to outdo him was Feller, and his status remained in limbo. If Harder stayed healthy, he would reach 200 sometime in May.

The most fascinating pitcher in camp was George Hooks, a twenty-four-year-old from Georgia. The Indians had signed Hooks in 1940 and sent him to Flint in the Michigan State League. He pitched well there and advanced to Cedar Rapids the following season, where he struggled with a sore arm. While recovering, he received his draft notice. In 1942, his unit was assigned to the North Africa campaign to aid the British in keeping the Suez Canal open. Hooks's chief job was to deliver supplies from the main base to the front lines. On one of his runs, German planes bombed the convoy and Hooks was gravely wounded. He spent seven months in an army hospital before receiving his medical discharge in July of 1943. While resting and recuperating on his father's farm, he began throwing a baseball around, and found his strength returning along with his fastball and curve. In the winter, he wrote to Roger Peckinpaugh asking for a tryout at Lafayette. Peck had never seen him play and knew little about him but invited him to report to camp with the rest of the team. Peck's humane gesture gave a young war veteran a chance to be a ballplayer again, even if it turned out to be a brief stay. Hooks did not make the club but was sent to Baltimore, where he pitched with limited success for several seasons. In a time of war, this was an inspirational moment for everybody involved, especially for Hooks, who had nearly lost his life while serving.

It was not until Wednesday, March 22, that the Indians were able to play their first intrasquad game outdoors. Lacking enough bodies for two complete teams, Boudreau found a couple of sixteen-year-old boys who volunteered to take the field with the pros. By now Allie Reynolds and Al Smith had reported to bolster the pitching staff, but Jeff Heath was working in Seattle with no progress on a contract.

The Indians, like many of the other clubs, were on the hunt for players to fill their twenty-five-man active rosters. Each year the war continued the talent pool lessened. The Yankees were among the hardest hit, with Joe Gordon, Bill Dickey, Charlie Keller, and Spud Chandler joining DiMaggio and Henrich in the military.

With all the unknown quantities in spring training, American League president Will Harridge declined to make any predictions on the favorites for the pennant race. He would only say to reporters, "The very uncertainties which face baseball as it opens its third wartime season, could produce one of the most interesting and exciting campaigns the sport has ever known." Interesting for sure, but exciting? The fans would have to wait and see.

Meanwhile, spring training weather in Lafayette failed to cooperate, forcing one cancellation after another. On April 2, the Indians managed to play their first exhibition game, against the Cincinnati Reds. They lost the game, but the bigger problem concerned Harder, Reynolds, and Smith, who had yet to make their first appearances on the mound. Only two weeks remained for them to work their pitching arms into semi-shape for the start of the season.

The Indians had played only eight exhibition games by the time they traveled to Chicago for the opener. On April 17, while the White Sox were away selling war bonds, Boudreau secured the grounds at Comiskey Park for a day of practice. Sox manager Jimmy Dykes, not exactly the friendly sort, instructed the groundskeepers to cover the infield and keep it that way. An angry Boudreau peeled away a corner of the tarp to reveal a dry infield that could have been used. While Boudreau made a mental note to return the favor later, all the Indians could do was run in the outfield and go through some calisthenics.

On Wednesday, April 19, the Indians and White Sox got the regular season under way. Cleveland's lineup had six new starters, while the White Sox had an entirely new infield featuring Hal Trosky at first base. Here's how it looked for the Indians:

> Boudreau ss
> Rocco 1b
> Cullenbine cf
> O'Dea lf
> Keltner 3b
> Seerey rf
> Peters 2b
> McDonnell c
> Smith p

Mickey Rocco was with the team in 1943, but arrived well after the season had started. Outfielder Paul O'Dea had been in the Indians' minor league system going back to 1938. At the Fort Meyers training camp two years later, the lefty was standing outside the batting cage waiting for his turn to hit when an errant foul tip careened through a space in the netting, smacking him squarely in the right eye. He lost almost complete sight in the eye, but did not give up, learning how to turn his head slightly to the right while batting in order to see the whole field. It helped that he preferred to go to the opposite field rather than pull the ball. In 1943, O'Dea, a native Clevelander, played Class A amateur ball with Bartuneks Clothing. He hit well enough that the Indians brought him to training camp, hoping he might offset the loss of Hank Edwards to the military.

Jeff Heath signed his contract in Cleveland on the seventeenth and hurried to Chicago to join the club. But since he was not quite ready to go, the outfield had to be reshuffled, and Pat Seerey got the start in right. Utility player Russ Peters took over Ray Mack's second base job, at least until an upgrade could be found. Jim McDonnell, a twenty-year-old good defensive but light-hitting catcher, won the starting job after a passable spring. Buddy Rosar's transfer was still up in the air, and until he returned manager Boudreau would have little experience to choose from at catcher.

After last year's All-Star season, and in the absence of Jim Bagby, Al Smith assumed the role of number one starter. In 1944, having one or two quality starters was as much as most teams could hope for. The difficulty of having to train in a cool climate showed in the first game, as the Indians, now wearing red numbers on their backs, lost to Chicago by a score of 3–1. Smith pitched well enough, but tired after five innings. The offense was led by Jim McDonnell, who had two hits, while his teammates provided little help. The game showed the difficulty of trying to prepare for the season in a midwestern town rather than in a warm climate.

Virginia Feller, Bob's new wife, was in the stands, leading the few cheers for the Indians. She spoke to reporters about his adventures in the South Pacific, directing his gun crew at the battles of the Marshall, Caroline, and Gilbert Islands. It had now been two and a quarter years since Feller entered the navy, and his time away from the ball club was keenly felt by the players, the fans in Cleveland, and around the American League. Like all the soldiers and sailors, Feller would keep on risking his life as long as necessary to bring the war to an end. Surely he missed being a ballplayer, but the job at hand far outweighed the challenge of facing American League hitters.

Two days later the Indians were back in Cleveland to play the home opener against Detroit. The thermometer climbed to a tolerable fifty-five degrees to go along with some light raindrops. A small crowd of 13,000 fans witnessed Allie Reynolds facing off against the Tigers' Frank Overmire. The Indians were trailing 3–2 in the bottom of the sixth inning when Pat Seerey clobbered a three-run homer off the facing of the upper deck in left field. Reynolds zigged and zagged through seven and two-thirds innings before being relieved by forty-three-year-old Joe Heving. The man they called "Grandpa" picked up his first save of the year as the Indians won, 7–4. Ken Keltner had three hits, while Jeff Heath, after missing spring training, contributed two singles.

Missing from the home opener was Jack Graney and his popular play-by-play. National programming, including the vital war news, soap operas, comedy shows, and musical entertainment, pushed the Indians off the radio schedule. In the interim, Graney received front office work for the Indians in addition to doing a daily 6:45 p.m. baseball recap show on WCLE.

Rain on Saturday forced a doubleheader on Sunday. In front of only 6,000 fans, Cleveland dropped both games, 6–2 and 4–3. With only three regulars in the lineup, Rudy York, Pinky Higgins, and Roger "Doc" Cramer, the Tigers managed to win two out of three in the series.

Two road losses in St. Louis gave notice to Cleveland fans not to expect too much from this year's edition. Mel Harder's drive for 200 wins was one bright spot, however. On Friday, the Indians stopped in Detroit, where Harder opposed the Tigers' Dizzy Trout. Russ Peters got on base twice and Mickey Rocco knocked him in both times to give Harder a cushion. The polished old pro scattered ten hits over nine innings, outpitching Trout for a 2–1 win and the 198th victory of his career.

While the club was on the road, Buddy Rosar received word that his transfer to the Weatherhead Company in Cleveland had been approved and that he would be permitted to play home games. Ray Mack applied to his draft board for an okay to do the same, but was refused. Second base would continue to be a problem, but at least the catching situation would have some clarity for the rest of the season.

While Rosar was absent, thirty-six-year-old coach George Susce caught several games for Boudreau. Since joining the Indians in 1941, Susce had appeared in a total of six games. It was a stopgap measure, but Susce handled the job admirably. Rosar's return was a welcome addition, especially for the coach himself, who preferred a seat on the bench to game action.

In the first week of May, Boudreau left for Harvey, Illinois, to meet with his draft board. Boudreau's medical history included a broken ankle in 1934 and another one in 1940, resulting in chronic arthritis. Before every contest he had his ankles heavily taped and usually soaked them in ice afterwards. The attending physician recommended that his status be returned to 4-F, believing the ankles would not hold up in the rigorous life of an infantry soldier in constant marching through the thick jungles of the South Pacific islands or the dense forests of Europe. The draft board agreed and granted Lou his 4-F and a permanent place in baseball.

Decisions like this were open to criticism that ballplayers received special treatment the "average Joe" did not. How could Boudreau play 140 to 150 baseball games a year, slide into bases, get knocked over by runners while turning double plays, but be unfit for the military? If you could play baseball, you should be able to fight overseas. And the army had many positions that did not involve ten miles of daily marching.

The most publicized case of alleged ballplayer favoritism was high-profile Boston slugger Ted Williams. He was originally classified 3-A as the sole supporter of his mother. In early 1942, Williams's draft board changed his status to 1-A. Ted, acting on the advice of others, hired an attorney to appeal the decision. When the draft board reversed its ruling and allowed him to go ahead and play in 1942, people across the country accused him of using his ballplayer status to avoid military service.

The Cleveland sportswriters wanted to know why Williams was given 3-A status and Bob Feller was 1-A, even though his mother, father, and sister were dependents. The elder Feller was suffering from a brain tumor that would ultimately cost him his life. But Feller went ahead and enlisted even before he was called. Since Bob was already in the navy, the argument was moot but shed light on some questionable classification decisions.

A short time later, Ken Keltner reported to Milwaukee for his draft board exam. He passed the physical and was told to expect a call to service within three weeks to three months. With some luck he might be able to stay at third base until mid-August or even later, but his loss would be a real blow to the Indians, who had no plans for his replacement.

On May 10, the Indians opened their first eastern road trip of the season against the Boston Red Sox. Mel Harder had beaten the White Sox a week earlier and was now trying for win number 200. In the top of the first, the Indians scored a run, then followed up in the fifth with three more. Meanwhile Harder was sailing along, not allowing a Red Sox runner to reach third base. In the top of the seventh, the Indians added to their lead when Pat Seerey belted a solo home run, his third of the year. In the eighth, Mel surrendered four straight singles for two runs and gave way to new reliever Ed Klieman. Ken Keltner fumbled an easy grounder, and Russ Peters followed with a wild throw on a double play grounder. With the lead cut to a single run, Klieman, the ex–Baltimore Oriole, saved the day by retiring the next two batters and blanking Boston in the bottom of the ninth for a 5–4 victory. The Indians now had a 9–9 record, the first time they had reached .500 since they started 1–1, and Harder had his milestone.

Harder was delighted to join the 200-win club along with greats such as Chief Bender, Red Ruffing, Carl Hubbell, and one-time Indian Stan Coveleski, who got his 200th after leaving the club. "I've been looking forward to that one for a long time," Harder told reporters. "You've got to give Ed Klieman a lot of credit, I certainly thank him." Always humble in victory or defeat, Harder had given Cleveland fans a mountain of thrills during his long career. When the Indians arrived home, the front office would stage a fitting celebration to honor one of their all-time greats.

While the boys congratulated Harder on the win, Jeff Heath sat in front of his locker with a sore leg. In the first inning he had pulled a muscle running out a ground ball. Oris Hockett replaced him, but he had been idle for the better part of a month, nursing a lame right shoulder, and could barely throw to the infield. But the Indians had no other adequate replacement, forcing Hockett to play while Heath recovered.

Harder's next start was a no-decision in a Cleveland loss, but on May 20 he pitched a three-hit shutout at Philadelphia, not walking a single batter, as the Indians won 5–0. Pat Seerey gave him all the runs needed by walloping a two-run homer off Shibe Park's left field roof. Seerey was still an all-or-nothing hitter, either a long home run or a strikeout. Even when Pat was swinging and missing badly, there was always the chance he would get ahold of a high fast one and knock it to the next county. Even with the K's, his blasts were worth the price of admission. Franklin Lewis, writing for the *Cleveland Press* and *Baseball Digest,* nicknamed him "The People's Choice." Pat was a ballplayer the fans could identify with. He carried around a lot of extra pounds on his 5'10" frame, smoked cigars and cigarettes, and did not take baseball too seriously. Whenever a fly ball was hit to him, Cleveland fans flinched watching him career back and forth before making the catch.

The next day in Philadelphia, twenty-four-year-old Steve Gromek made his 1944 debut as a starting pitcher. He had earned the start by pitching well in long relief earlier in the road trip. He held the A's scoreless until the bottom of the seventh, when they tied the game at two apiece, then scored one more in the eighth for a 3–2 win. But Gromek had pitched well enough to stay in the rotation for now.

Steve Gromek was born in Hamtramck, Michigan, in the Detroit area, on January 15, 1920. His parents were Polish immigrants who came to the city when unskilled jobs at the Dodge Brothers Motor Company were plentiful. In the early part of the twentieth century, most of the residents in Hamtramck came from Poland, swelling the population to 48,000 in 1920.

At St. Ladislaus high school a lack of funding meant there was no football or baseball team, but Gromek excelled on the basketball team, being one of the best players in the area. His father wanted him to peddle newspapers after school, but Steve chose to play sandlot baseball. He graduated to American Legion ball, and in 1938 he was scouted and signed by Cleveland's Bill Bradley, who seemed to be everywhere finding ballplayers for the Indians.

A slick-fielding shortstop in those days, Gromek was assigned to Class D Mansfield in the Ohio State League. One of his teammates there was future Indian Hank Edwards. In August of 1939, Gromek tore a muscle in his left shoulder while swinging at a pitch. Taking no chances, the Indians brought him to Cleveland for an exam with trainer Lefty Weisman. After taking some time off to rest, he still had difficulty reaching down for ground balls, and switched to the outfield when he was promoted to Class C Flint, Michigan. The change in scenery did him well, both on and off the field. He found a favorite restaurant, the Hollywood Diner, which specialized in savory home-cooked Polish food. And his laser-like throws from the outfield warranted a tryout on the pitcher's mound.

Gromek, with a three-quarter rising fastball, found himself climbing the ladder to Baltimore, where he won 16 games in 1943 along with 188 strikeouts. Jim Bagby's enlistment helped Gromek win a place on the Cleveland roster and an eventual spot in the starting rotation, joining Al Smith, Mel Harder, Allie Reynolds, and, for the moment, Vern Kennedy. As the sole supporter of his disabled father, his mother, and a younger sister, Steve had a 4-F classification.

Thursday, May 25, was designated Mel Harder Day at League Park. That afternoon 18,706 fans packed the ballpark, an enormous number for the old ball grounds. Among the celebrities there to honor Mel was

Hollywood actor-cowboy-singer Gene Autry, who waved to the grand-stand and said a few words to the crowd. As the fans cheered, former Cleveland Spider, Cleveland Nap, and Hall of Famer Cy Young ambled to the microphone to pay his tribute. After Cy was thanked and given a $250 war bond, the Indians presented Harder with his own $1,000 bond for his long service. The Ohio Rubber Company, where Mel worked his war job, handed over more war bonds in the amount of $201 to match his lifetime win total. Harder went out and held the Washington Senators to one run over eight innings, but faded in the top of the ninth, when the Senators rallied for three runs and a 4–2 victory.

The Indians had trouble stringing wins together, finishing May with a season record of 19–22. During one game, Boudreau turned his ankle at shortstop, but had to keep playing because Jimmy Grant, the Indians util-ityman, was sitting out with a sore shoulder. Lou thought about putting Steve Gromek at short, but decided to finish the game on one good leg.

In early June, with 27,343 fans looking on, the Indians were play-ing a doubleheader against the Yankees at Municipal Stadium. Team harmony took a hit when Boudreau suspended Vern Kennedy for in-subordination. In the first game, the manager signaled for Kennedy to get warmed up in the bullpen. It was not an unreasonable request, but for some reason Kennedy refused to move, earning the suspension and a fine. On May 31, he had been yanked from the mound after a start of only four and a third innings. At the time, the Indians were leading Boston 5–2, but Kennedy had already issued seven walks. They won the game 7–4, but the early removal may have led to some resentment on Kennedy's part. Whatever the reason, he seems to have wanted a showdown with Boudreau, and lost badly.

Gordon Cobbledick believed Lou had the ears of most of his players and the suspension of Kennedy would probably not change the team dynamics. However, the veteran reporter noted that the young manager tended to ignore his players off the field, spending the bulk of his time with his older coaches. Cobbledick thought a small amount of fraterni-zation with his team, particularly the older players, might not do any harm. Nevertheless, Boudreau had the strong support of Alva Bradley, which trumped most grievances players, and newspapermen, might have had.

On June 6, 1944, people in the United States and around the world received the magnificent news that the Allies had landed on Normandy

Beach and other areas in northern France. The attack, coordinated by General Dwight D. Eisenhower, involved 156,000 American, British, and Canadian troops, 5,000 ships, and 11,000 aircraft. Within a week, German forces were pushed back and hard-fought territory secured. With thousands of additional troops landing, the liberation of Paris and the entire country of France was sure to follow. Sustained advances through France, and later to the German border, brought the end of the war in Europe that much closer.

On Friday, June 16, an intoxicated fan at Municipal Stadium began harassing umpire Bill Summers. Finally Summers called time and waved to the front-row railing, inviting the fan to meet him there. The fan obliged, carrying an empty beer bottle with him. When they were face to face, Summers quickly grabbed the bottle and smashed it against the railing. He then turned to Boudreau, who was standing close by, and ordered the fan tossed from the park. Lou led the fan away, trying to calm him down as they walked. When the fan assured Lou he would be quiet and behave himself for the rest of the game, Lou let him return to his seat, and he gave Summers no more trouble. Lou's actions as a peacemaker got considerable attention in the papers. If there was anything to learn from the incident, it may have been that umpire-baiting, quiet during most of the war, was coming back into fashion.

Later in June the Indians were in Detroit to open a three-game series. Just minutes before the Tigers took the field, Buddy Rosar and Ray Mack came racing into the clubhouse. They had completed their weekly job assignments and their employers had given them permission to travel. The players quickly booked the short flight over Lake Erie and reported to Boudreau, who put them into the lineup, where they helped Allie Reynolds pick up his seventh win of the year, 3–1. Rosar's and Mack's presence in the clubhouse and on the field gave their teammates a lift. The Indians were not about to stage a miracle run for the pennant, but with the two veterans playing more games, they had an opportunity to move up in the standings.

On July 2, the American League announced the selections for the All-Star game. Four Indians made the team, including Keltner and Boudreau for the fifth consecutive year, Roy Cullenbine in his second appearance, and Oris Hockett in his first. Both Cullenbine and Hockett were wise choices, having anchored the Cleveland outfield while Jeff Heath was sidelined with knee problems, forcing Paul O'Dea to play regularly.

The rosters for both squads were missing most of the usual marquee names, but the American League did feature Boudreau and Boston's Bobby Doerr, while the National League included a young Stan Musial of St. Louis and Mel Ott of the Giants. The starting pitchers were Hank Borowy of the Yankees and Bucky Walters of the Reds. A good crowd was anticipated for the game, to be held on July 11 in Pittsburgh, with gate receipts to be donated to the Ball and Bat Fund.

One week before the All-Star game, the Indians played a July 4 holiday doubleheader at Yankee Stadium. There were 40,000 fans in the seats ready to watch the dismantling of the visiting club. In the first game, Allie Reynolds held the New Yorkers to one run through seven and a third innings, but with runners on first and second in the eighth Boudreau called time and motioned for Joe Heving to come in. The next Yankee hitter, Mike Milosevich, rapped a hard ground ball to the third base side of the mound. Boudreau moved quickly into the hole and dived headlong after the ball. Fully stretched out on the ground, he snared the ball with his bare hand and flipped it toward second. Ray Mack grabbed the toss, stepped on second, then rifled a relay to first to get Milosevich. An incredible double play to end the inning!

The Yankee fans stood with their mouths open and eyes wide, not believing what they had just seen. Spontaneously the applause began until almost every fan in the park gave Boudreau a tremendous ovation. Heving zipped through the ninth inning and the Indians had the first-game victory, 3–1. They went on to sweep the doubleheader, the first time they had accomplished this at Yankee Stadium since 1939.

The following Sunday the Indians were in Boston to complete the road trip with another doubleheader. Ed Klicman got the start and was in control throughout the game. Behind two RBIs each from Pat Seerey and Ray Mack, the Indians had a comfortable 8–1 lead heading into the bottom of the ninth inning. The first batter for the Red Sox singled, but Klieman got the next two out. The potential final out laced a double to drive in a run and make the score 8–2. Boudreau signaled for time and called in his closer, Joe Heving. When Lou reached the mound, Klieman, who was livid, let the manager know what he thought. The Red Sox fans let go with a large chorus of boos directed at the Indians' manager. Klieman stormed off the mound and took a seat in the dugout while Heving got the last man out to preserve the win, 8–2.

After the game Boudreau announced to the press that Klieman had been given a $100 fine for his behavior on the mound. Lou would not comment on what was said but explained his decision by noting that it was a "terribly hot day and [he] was not taking any chances." Soon the second-guessing began in earnest. Russ Needham, the sports editor of the *Columbus Dispatch,* wrote that pulling a pitcher with a six-run lead and two outs in the ninth was a serious mistake. He went on to reference the Jim Bagby situation, ripping Boudreau for not trying harder to patch things up with his dissatisfied pitcher. Bagby had won 34 games in 1942–43, he wrote, and letting talent like that simply walk away did not make sense. Fortunately, it was time for the All-Star break and everybody to calm down just a tad.

After the Nationals won the All-Star game 7–1, the Indians were at home to take on the St. Louis Browns, who were sitting in the unfamiliar position of first place. On Friday, July 14, Steve Gromek pitched against Bob Muncrief. After seven well-pitched innings, the score was tied at 2–2. Both pitchers continued to throw out zeros, not allowing another run through thirteen innings. Gromek, still going strong with ten strikeouts, retired the Browns in the top of the fourteenth. In the bottom half, Ray Mack walked and was sacrificed to second, and Gromek rapped a single to score Mack and win the game 3–2. It was only his second win as a starter, but the fans at League Park got to witness a tremendous performance.

That same day, the Indians received the news that Jim Bagby was resigning his position with the merchant marines and requesting permission to rejoin the Indians. Bagby was now classified 1-A but wanted to play baseball again, even with the Indians. An agreement was reached, and the former sailor hustled his way to Cleveland. The Indians' record stood at 39–42, but they were just six and a half games out of first place. Due to the war and the dilution of talent, parity was giving four or five teams a chance to contend for the pennant.

The next day, with Cullenbine and Seerey providing home runs, the Indians pounded the Browns 13–2. With the team just two games below .500 and five and a half out of first, the Indians' fans suddenly got pennant fever. At the Sunday doubleheader there were 32,553 fans at Municipal Stadium, the biggest crowd of the home season. The Indians battled, but lost both games in twelve innings, 8–7 and 2–1. A chance to move within three and a half games of the lead turned into a seven-and-a-half-game deficit. The disappointed fans shuffled out of the stadium fearing that for another year their team was likely going nowhere.

Jim Bagby made his first start on Friday, July 21, and despite being away from baseball and having had no real practice, he pitched a complete game 4–1 victory over Philadelphia. If the Indians had put aside their hard feelings and tried to sign Bagby over the winter, they might have found themselves in a much better position.

In a scheduling quirk, the Philadelphia series ended on Saturday with the Senators in town for the usual Sunday doubleheader. In the sixth inning of game one, Jeff Heath made his first appearance since early June. There were two runners in scoring position when Heath lined a base hit to score both. But on the way to first base he pulled up lame, reinjuring his bothersome knee. It was that kind of season for Cleveland, a quick burst of great play followed by bad luck. They would finish July with a record of 19–13, their only winning month of the year, and a season record of 50–49. But they would soon fall below .500 and further down the standings.

On August 6 at the stadium, the Indians hosted the annual Amateur Day, where the best Cleveland sandlot players got a chance to showcase their talent and raise money for their teams. The two top Class A amateur teams would play four and a half innings each against the Great Lakes Naval Training Station Negro team. This group of all-stars had been consistently steamrolling teams all around the Midwest, and today was no exception, as they clobbered the sandlot boys 14–0. Pitcher John Wright, formerly of the Homestead Grays, dazzled the local teams, and a slick-fielding shortstop named Larry Doby went 3 for 4 with a double and a stolen base. A crowd of close to 17,000 watched the elite Negro team manhandle the local amateurs, while $15,000 was raised for medical care and equipment. The money was sufficient to cover all costs for the 1945 Class A baseball season.

A few weeks later the Allies liberated Paris, putting the once-mighty German army on the run and bringing the war closer to an end. General Eisenhower entered the fallen city to see the sights and acknowledge the cheers of the wildly celebrating French citizens. With much more of Europe in safe hands, a group of Major League players and managers agreed to travel with the USO and visit as many army camps as possible. Among the volunteers to leave in October were Dixie Walker, Rip Sewell, Nick Etten, Johnny Lindell, and managers Luke Sewell and Leo

Durocher. Former ballplayers Lefty Gomez, Carl Hubbell, and Harry Heilmann were added to the group to help with the baseball clinics and demonstrations. After years of seemingly endless fighting, the front-line troops were receiving well-deserved breaks and first-class entertainment.

In September, a pennant race was taking shape in the American League. As of September 9 the Yankees were back in first place, with Detroit trailing by a mere half game and St. Louis hanging tough, only a full game back. The Browns, who in forty-two seasons had not managed to win a single pennant, were the sentimental favorites, matching wins with New York and Detroit, who had been there many times before.

With exasperating problems mounting daily, the Indians did not figure in the race. An examination of Jeff Heath's bad left knee revealed torn cartilage that would need surgery at the end of the season. Allie Reynolds's right arm swelled up, becoming grossly discolored all the way to his fingers. A doctor's visit revealed a blood clot, which abruptly ended his year.

With the team destined to finish in fifth place, the only excitement left for the Indians was Lou Boudreau challenging for the batting title. He went on a hot streak after the All-Star break, dueling Bob Johnson and Bobby Doerr for the lead. On September 25, Doerr was called into service, finishing the year at .325. Four days later, Lou went 3 for 5 against New York, raising his average to .330. When the season ended, Boudreau was at .327. Doerr's .325 average left him in second, with Bob Johnson third at .321. Boudreau's batting crown was the first for a Cleveland player since Lou Fonseca led the league in 1929.

In addition to the batting title, Boudreau had 45 doubles, ahead of teammate Ken Keltner's 41. To complete his exceptional year, Lou banged out 191 hits, second to the Yankees' George Stirnweiss.

On the fielding side, Boudreau had an excellent season, handling 874 chances with only 19 errors and a percentage of .978. He led the American League by participating in 134 double plays. The timing was perfect for Alva Bradley to tell the press he was awarding Lou another three-year contract at $25,000 per year. Earlier Bradley had hinted as much, telling reporters, "I think he has done a splendid job. He's a great boy."

It seemed Bradley had found his ideal manager, having gone through men like Roger Peckinpaugh, Walter Johnson, Steve O'Neill, Oscar Vitt, and Peckinpaugh again before landing on Boudreau. Bradley had done other worthy things in his tenure as well, but winning a pennant, the one thing that defined an owner's success, had eluded him. With the three-year deal, Bradley was certain he had the guy who could help him take his place in Cleveland baseball history alongside Jim Dunn. On the current roster were young pitchers Steve Gromek and Allie Reynolds to build around. Boudreau and Keltner still had good years left to play, and with the Allied progress on both fronts, soldiers and sailors like Bob Feller, Jim Hegan, Eddie Robinson, and Hank Edwards might soon be on their way home. Factor in minor league talent including Bob Lemon and Dale Mitchell, and the immediate future seemed loaded with promise.

Chapter 6

THE END OF AN ERA

On November 17, 1944, a joint commission of American and National League executives met to discuss the future of Judge Landis. His contract as commissioner was set to expire in 1946, but the league personnel wanted to draw up a new, lengthy deal. After some debate, a vote was taken. The decision was unanimous: a seven-year contract at $65,000 annually. The only problem with the agreement was that Landis was lying seriously ill in a Chicago hospital. The seventy-seven-year-old judge had been admitted on October 2 with symptoms of a severe cold. He would suffer a heart attack and die on November 25, eight days after the executives had assembled. Landis had served twenty-four years as baseball's one and only commissioner, cleaning up the game after the 1919 Black Sox scandal and ruling aggressively over players and owners throughout his tenure.

Ford Frick, the National League president, spoke for many when he said, "His passing is a terrific loss to baseball. He contributed more to the game of baseball than any other man." Alva Bradley commented, "I feel it not only as an owner in the league, it is also a personal loss."

Despite the judge's advanced age, the Major Leagues had made no provisions in the event of his death. The league presidents and owners would have to form committees and hold many meetings to determine how they would choose a successor. Other than Clark Griffith and Connie Mack, few if any men remained who had had anything to do with the judge's hiring twenty-four years ago. Would they go with a baseball man like Will Harridge or Frick, or somebody from the federal government? It would probably be months before a new commissioner was selected.

Days before the winter meetings, Lou Boudreau came to Cleveland to visit with Bradley and Peckinpaugh. The three men discussed immediate plans to trade away the unmanageable players Heath and Bagby for the sake of club harmony, but interest was cool among the other American League ball clubs. Of the offers received, most included only fringe players and minor leaguers. The only trade the team managed was sending Oris Hockett to Chicago for outfielder Eddie Carnett. Trading Hockett after an All-Star season might not have seemed to make much sense, but Carnett was only twenty-eight while Hockett was thirty-five.

At the winter meetings in New York, the clubs agreed to establish a ten-man committee, with five executives from each league, for the purpose of finding a successor to Judge Landis. The group would meet in early January to decide how many years the term would be and what salary range to recommend. A month later they would reconvene to bring up names for the job.

In other matters, both St. Louis clubs were given the okay to expand their attendance-driven night game schedules from thirty-five to forty. Once again, Washington had permission to play as many as they could fit in. Everybody else would stay put at the established limit of fourteen games. In anticipation of an influx of men returning from the war, a plan was introduced to increase rosters from twenty-five to thirty players for the entire season.

The owners had concerns about the rising popularity of the National Football League, which now covered all the baseball cities with the exception of Cincinnati and St. Louis. Believing fans were switching sports once the pro football schedule started, they agreed to bar any NFL games in their stadiums before the end of the regular season.

Another issue concerned the uncertainty about the current ballplayers' draft status. The owners had been informed that players between the ages of twenty-six and thirty-eight would not be called into service. However, James Byrnes, the war mobilization director, indicated he would still look at men in that age group as well as all the 4-F's. If Byrnes followed through, another shortage of players would surely occur, of major proportions.

In January, President Roosevelt spoke about the status of baseball for the 1945 season. He recommended that the game continue if it did not harm war production or prevent healthy young men from doing their duty. The president maintained that there were enough 4-F's to have a competitive year in both leagues. Although not an official proclamation, Roosevelt's words seemed to put the idea to rest of reexamining 4-F's for service in the military.

With the likelihood of ample talent to get through the season, the owners turned their attention to the selection process for a new commissioner. On January 5, the committee met for two hours behind closed doors. The main purpose of the meeting was to develop a new agreement, different from the one offered to Landis. The opportunity was there to shift some power back to the owners, in contrast to the absolute authority Landis had held.

A month later the committee met for a second time but did not release any names or come to a vote on Landis's successor. Instead they opted for a new four-man committee to expedite the selection process. Alva Bradley was named to the new group along with Don Barnes from the Browns, Sam Breadon from the Cardinals, and Phil Wrigley from the Cubs. The men were responsible for narrowing the field to three or four candidates to put before the rest of the owners. In addition, they revealed that the top salary of the new boss would be $50,000.

The next meeting was to take place on February 27. Phil Wrigley told the press, "We will make no recommendation for a selection of a successor to Landis. Our group merely does 'bird dog' work until the time all 16 presidents get together." Wrigley added that each member had reviewed all the applications submitted. But February 27 came and went with no committee meeting taking place. The four members did find time on March 5 for another private conference, in which several candidates' names were leaked. Eric Johnston, the president of the United States Chamber of Commerce, was one, along with FBI chief J. Edgar Hoover and former postmaster general James Farley. At least the selection process was advancing toward the decision stage.

On the same day the committee met, Roger Peckinpaugh revealed that March 12 would be the start date for spring training. For the third year in succession, the team would make use of the Purdue fieldhouse in Lafayette, Indiana. Peck, unsure how many players could meet that date, planned for several Cleveland sandlotters to make the trip to fill out the infield and shag fly balls for the first week or two.

The Indians offered a conditional contract to Jeff Heath, stating he would be paid only if he was able to play. Heath had undergone knee surgery at the end of the season, giving the Indians no timetable when he might be ready to join the starting lineup. Asked for comment, Heath said he wanted out: "It's no dice. I'd play baseball allright, in Detroit!" It was not in his nature to stay quiet and attempt to reach a compromise.

Another long holdout seemed inevitable, but this time the Indians held all the cards. If Heath reported to training camp and needed a month or two to rehab his knee, they were not obligated to pay him. If he worked extra hard and was ready for opening day, they could simply change the terms and give him a standard contract. The Indians were not going to allow him to sit on the bench and collect any kind of salary. It was a good payback for all the years of grief Heath had given Messrs. Bradley, Peckinpaugh, and Boudreau.

At the start of training, the league announced the cancellation of the 1945 All-Star game due to travel restrictions. A travel reduction of 25 percent was to be determined by each team's front office. The league urged that when games were scheduled between clubs relatively close to each other such as Cleveland and Detroit or Brooklyn and the Giants, the visiting team should bring only a minimum of ballplayers. This action saved space on the railroads and hotels. There was discussion of having umpires remain in a city for an undetermined length of time rather than move from city to city with each series. The 1945 season promised to be the most stressful of all the war years to date.

On March 12, the Indians reported to spring training with a scaled-down version of the April roster. Manager Boudreau was not there yet, waiting on his release as a crane operator in Illinois. Ed Klieman arrived several days later with one of the more novel excuses. Unable to find any trains running the 176 miles from Cincinnati to Lafayette, he rode several slow buses on a marathon ride to get him to camp. Gradually enough players trickled in, including Allie Reynolds and Pat Seerey, to make intrasquad games possible.

The Cleveland front office announced that the home opener would be played on April 17 against the White Sox. The team would play forty-two games at the stadium and thirty-five at League Park. Once again fourteen night games were on the schedule, plus eleven Sunday doubleheaders, with additional two-game sets on the July 4 holiday and on Labor Day. The July 4 games would be against the Yankees, ensuring a nice lively crowd for the afternoon. Alva Bradley stated that attendance for the 1944 season had risen by 42,000 from the previous year despite the Indians finishing with a losing record. He had an optimistic view of the 1945 season as far as attendance, but was mum on his team's chances.

Bradley also made it known that he and Mayor Tom Burke had reached an agreement on a new five-year lease at Municipal Stadium, pending the approval of city council. The lease stipulated that the Cleveland Baseball Company schedule a minimum of twenty-eight games each year and pay rent of $500 per game. For night games the city would collect $850 for usage of lights and the normal $500 rent for a total of $1,350 at each of the fourteen games planned. The city would receive 3 percent of admissions for the first 400,000 fans and 5 percent for any totals above that figure.

One of the most interesting aspects of the agreement was that the ball club would continue to pay the city $60 per every thousand spectators at a potential World Series game. Bradley had once again exhibited his negotiating skills in limiting what could have been a large windfall for the city. If somehow the Indians were to win the American League pennant in the next five years, Bradley would only have to pay the city 6 percent per thousand and retain a much larger share. For example, if three World Series games were played in Cleveland and they drew a total of 150,000 fans, the city would earn a grand total of $9,000. A pennant was not on the radar for now, but if the Indians beat the odds the city would surely regret the deal.

The Indians retained the right to collect 60 percent of all concessions and souvenirs, with the city getting the remaining 40. Mayor Burke had argued for a fifty-fifty split, but Bradley would not move. All maintenance costs of the baseball and football field were to be paid by the Cleveland Baseball Company on a yearly basis. The amount agreed upon totaled $17,000, with the city agreeing to reimburse the club $2,000 each year for upkeep. Mayor Burke and the city consented to supply all the custodial work at no charge. The Indians would keep all the revenue from radio rights, advertising, and rental of League Park to the Negro American League Cleveland Buckeyes and any college or high school football games.

The mayor's office released figures showing that over the period 1939–44 attendance totaled 3,210,968 and revenue $3,353,367. The most successful year for tenant and landlord was 1940, the only year the Indians were in the pennant race for the entire season, when attendance at forty games soared to 823,884 and revenue to $838,331. The city's numbers showed a range of rent income from $14,228 in 1942 to $33,916 in 1940. For the city to profit, the Indians would need to finish in the first division on a consistent basis. The better the team played, the more fans in the seats and the more revenue for both parties.

The Indians' six-year revenue from concessions was $75,688, with a high of $14,701 in 1940. From the figures as a whole, it is difficult to determine whether Bradley made money for his shareholders other than in 1940. As was the custom with Major League owners, profit and loss figures were kept private. But the fact he'd owned a ball club for eighteen years and never officially put it up for sale suggests that the Indians were bringing in a profit, albeit a small one.

On March 16, Boudreau reported to camp, free from his war job obligation. Five days later, Paul McNutt, director of the War Manpower Commission, issued a welcome ruling that any ballplayer resigning from a war job and joining his team would not be subject to the draft. This was good news to all but Ken Keltner, who had recently received his notice to report to the military. He would be stationed in Hawaii but lost to the Indians for at least the entire season.

The weather in Lafayette turned unseasonably warm, reaching a record of eighty sweaty degrees. For the first time in three years, outdoor practices and intrasquad games were the norm until Major League exhibitions began in April. As per the rules, the travel restrictions applied immediately, preventing all the clubs from going outside of their camps until the end of March. The only games the Indians could schedule other than among themselves were late-month contests against Purdue University.

During the early part of camp, however, they received an invitation to play on Saturday, March 30, against the Camp Chanute army team in Illinois. The plan was to use the University of Illinois field, play the Saturday game, then take on the college team on Sunday. Will Harridge and the American League office had to approve the 190-mile round trip, which they did. It probably helped that the army agreed to send buses and the several thousand soldiers at Camp Chanute were eager to see the Indians in action.

On arriving in Champaign, the Indians found rainy weather and a diamond too wet to play. The games against the army team and the University of Illinois would be played on Sunday. In the meantime, Boudreau took a group of his players, including Pat Seerey, Allie Reynolds, Ed Klieman, Paul O'Dea, and Jim Bagby, to the basketball facility, where he had been a legend a few years back. Boudreau's boys, as the shirts, defeated the skins 10–8. The winning basket was made by Lou, reliving his glory days as a member of the Fighting Illini. A second game, refereed by several sportswriters, ended in a 20–20 tie.

On Sunday the weather cooperated, and the Indians won both games, 5–0 and 9–1. The soldiers in the stands were nowhere to be found. Sunday was payday, and the enlisted men scattered to the wind to spend their money elsewhere. Afterwards the Cleveland players boarded their buses for the ride back to Lafayette and a Monday game against a local semipro team.

When the team returned home, news came that Jeff Heath had agreed to sign his conditional contract and report to camp. A few days earlier a frustrated Peckinpaugh had told reporters, "We paid a thousand dollars for his knee operation and $300 for his hospital stay because we wanted him to know that we would give him every break." Heath had probably heard that and decided it was time to end his yearly holdout. He was already nineteen days late, but assured the team he could be ready for the start of the season.

April 3 brought the exciting news that Bob Feller had returned to the States. He had completed his tour of duty of the South Pacific and was being shipped home to coach the Great Lakes Naval Training Station baseball team and finish out his enlistment. His assignment did not include playing ball, but only managing the squad. Nothing was reported about a discharge date, but it seemed possible that Feller might be in an Indians uniform before the end of the summer.

In the day-to-day life of the Cleveland Indians, it seemed good tidings were always followed by something bad. While fans were happily guessing about Feller's return, the newspapers reported that Jeff Heath had changed his mind and refused to sign the conditional contract. He was demanding a trade while complaining again about his home runs and triples being long outs at Municipal Stadium. Roger Peckinpaugh thought he had an agreement eight days ago, and now he was back to square one. Peck told the papers, "He can sit out in Seattle forever unless I can make a trade which will be of benefit to the team."

Heath's sudden change of heart, though perhaps not surprising, put the Indians in a difficult situation. They were thin at the outfield positions. The players in camp included Pat Seerey, Ed Carnett, Paul O'Dea, and thirty-seven-year-old Myril Hoag, who had played part-time last year. Right fielder Roy Cullenbine was working out at third base in hopes of replacing the departed Ken Keltner. If Cullenbine could not make the switch, a third baseman would have to be found somewhere.

While the Indians worried about an opening day lineup, the owners would be at the Hotel Cleveland on April 24 to vote for a new commissioner. Twelve out of sixteen votes would be necessary to choose Judge Landis's replacement. Back in March, the four-man committee had narrowed the list of candidates. J. Edgar Hoover had not made the final cut. Rumors had National League president Ford Frick as the frontrunner among the three remaining candidates. The owners had dragged their feet through the process, and with the war in Europe nearing an end it was important to make a decision now. A new commissioner would be needed to help baseball deal with all the returning veterans and ensure a smooth transition. The sixteen owners had enough on their hands without trying to handle a major restructuring of rosters for the major and minor leagues.

On Thursday, April 12, the talk of selecting a commissioner came to a sudden halt when news bulletins announced the shocking death of President Franklin Roosevelt at Warm Springs, Georgia. The president had suffered a cerebral hemorrhage while posing for a portrait and died moments later. Roosevelt, who was in his unprecedented fourth term as president, had guided the country through the Great Depression and a world war. At the time of his death, Allied soldiers were sixty miles outside of Berlin ready to pound the German army into submission. Roosevelt would not live to see that historic day, much to the sadness of most Americans and free populations around the world.

Baseball too keenly felt the president's loss. Clark Griffith, the Senators owner and one of the grand old men of the game, remarked, "Only last month Mr. Roosevelt said in his own words that he was the number-one night baseball fan. We've lost a warm, personal friend and a great champ of baseball." Griffith had recently delivered Roosevelt's annual pass with and received assurances from the president he would throw out the first ball on opening day. That duty now fell to Harry Truman, the former vice president. Baseball announced that all Saturday exhibition games would be canceled to honor the late president.

On Sunday, April 15, the Indians arrived in Cleveland to prepare for Tuesday's home opener against Chicago. Manager Boudreau had quite a chore in putting together a coherent starting lineup. With Ken Keltner gone and Ray Mack apparently not leaving his war job, the infield had two large holes to fill with unproven talent. Roy Cullenbine had been trying his best, but his play at third was nowhere near the level of Keltner's. Catcher Buddy Rosar was an unexpected holdout, leaving the club without an experienced catcher. The outfield minus Jeff Heath must have had Boudreau shaking his head about who he could pencil in at the three positions. At least the pitching rotation had Jim Bagby, who claimed he was happy to be back, and the duo of Allie Reynolds and Steve Gromek. Mel Harder kept his war job, missing all of spring training and casting doubt on whether he wanted to pitch another season. That left Al Smith, returning after a disappointing 1944 season, as the only other candidate.

At least the Cleveland players' attitudes seemed to be positive. Several of them spoke about how Boudreau had evolved as a manager and found ways to keep most of them happy. One player who spoke anonymously said, "Lou really has changed—and for the better. All of us, and I mean every word, will really battle for him. I couldn't have said this last season." One thing Lou did was bring back Oscar Melillo, the one coach everybody liked during the Oscar Vitt era. Though the players may have been lacking in skill, the improved outlook in the clubhouse would help them in the long run.

On the eve of the home opener, the navy announced that Bob Feller would be free to pitch while continuing to manage the Great Lakes team. The stated reason was the lack of pitchers available, but every baseball fan, and especially the navy, knew that Feller was months away from his discharge. Finding a reason to get his arm back in shape for his American League return was certainly the right thing to do.

The ceremonial opening of the season was scheduled for Monday the sixteenth, with the Senators hosting the New York Yankees. The weather failed to cooperate, with rain and mist covering the field, forcing a cancellation until Friday. Despite overcast skies the two teams were able to play ball on the twentieth. Will Harridge, Walter Johnson, and Clark Griffith marched solemnly to the flagpole, and as the Stars and Stripes slowly rose, the 24,494 fans stood silent for a moment in memory of President Roosevelt. President Truman was not able to attend, so Sam Rayburn, the Speaker of the House, threw out the first ball. Notably absent was the late Judge Landis. It was the first time in twenty-four years he had not been in a field box, leaning forward, eyes glued on the action.

The Indians had opened their season on Tuesday under clear skies with the temperature at sixty degrees. The 20,558 spectators who watched the Cleveland players take the field in their new flaming red bills and buttons on their caps would have needed their scorecards to know who many of the players were:

Rocco 1b
Hoag cf
Carnett rf
Boudreau ss
Seerey lf
Cullenbine 3b
Cihocki 2b
Ruszkowski c
Reynolds p

Al Cihocki had played briefly in the Cleveland organization before enlisting in the coast guard. After he received a medical discharge, the Indians, out of desperation, brought him to training camp. Nineteen-year-old Hank Ruszkowski, who had caught several games for Cleveland the previous season, won the catcher's job with little competition. Eddie Carnett had played one season as a starter before the trade with Oris Hockett. This lineup had more holes than Swiss cheese, but the Indians were in dire need of experienced help.

Allie Reynolds held the White Sox scoreless for five innings before giving up two in the sixth. The Indians answered with two in the bottom of the inning to tie the score at 2–2, but the White Sox reached Reynolds for two more in the seventh and another in the eighth to spoil the opener, 5–2. The most noteworthy play of the game happened in the sixth inning, when Boudreau took a short lead off third base, only to be tagged out by third baseman Tony Cuccinello via the seldom-used hidden-ball trick. Whether Lou fined himself for falling asleep on the bases is not known, but he must have had his head bowed when he walked to the dugout.

Wednesday brought the usual early season rainout, probably a good thing for the Indians. Reynolds developed an infected finger, while Roy Cullenbine injured his wrist. Boudreau also had a sore wrist and had to miss Thursday's game, replaced by little-known Elmer Weingartner. Cullenbine did start the game at third base but had to leave in the seventh inning, replaced by another minor leaguer, Ed Wheeler. Lou's presence would have made little difference, due to dreadful pitching from Jim Bagby, Hal Kleine, and Pete Center, who combined to allow seventeen hits and walk an ungodly ten batters. The White Sox scored eight runs in the first four innings and won easily, 14–6. Indians fans had to grimace at the late-inning infield of Rocco, Cihocki, Weingartner, and Wheeler. For anybody who was not aware of the acute manpower shortage in Cleveland and around baseball, this game was an eye-opener.

Boudreau and Cullenbine were back the next day, and the Indians notched their first win, beating Detroit, 4–1. Steve Gromek recorded the victory, striking out seven. After the Tigers took the next two games on Saturday and Sunday, Boudreau scheduled an intense off-day workout at League Park. After a 1–4 start, he did not want things to get completely out of hand.

While the Indians struggled, sixteen representatives from all the Major League teams checked into the Hotel Cleveland. On April 24 at 11:00 a.m., they heard the four-man committee present three names for the position of commissioner: War Manpower Commission director Paul McNutt, former governor of Ohio John Bricker, and Senator Albert "Happy" Chandler of Kentucky. Arguments were heard, followed by a unanimous vote for the forty-six-year-old Chandler. He received a seven-year contract at $50,000 per year.

Senator Chandler was born in 1898 in the farming town of Corydon, Kentucky. The product of a poor family, he sold newspapers and did odd jobs to help pay the bills. A huge fan of Ty Cobb, he participated in sports during high school, then attended Transylvania College, where he played football, basketball, and baseball. He was talented enough to play semipro baseball briefly for Lexington, Kentucky, part of the old Blue Grass League. He studied law at Harvard for a year before receiving his degree from the University of Kentucky and seeking a career in politics. In 1931, he became lieutenant governor of Kentucky. Elected governor in 1935, he balanced the budget, built several hospitals, and raised teachers' salaries. He reached his political peak in 1939 as a member of the United States Senate. According to many biographies, Chandler was a jovial man, always with a smile on his face—hence the nickname "Happy."

The new commissioner hit the ground running, promising to take office within sixty days and reinstate the All-Star game provided the war ended before July. Keenly aware of Judge Landis's legacy, he told fellow senators, "I promise you that I will keep baseball clean." Chandler had a difficult act to follow, but with his upbeat demeanor he might just be the person to fill baseball's top job.

At the end of April, the Great Lakes station defeated Northwestern University 12–2. Bob Feller, approaching forty months in the navy, pitched three innings, striking out seven Wildcats. He would still need a lot more turns on the mound, but demonstrated the lively fastball of years past. Navy man Ken Keltner also played, scoring three runs.

Facing few alternatives, Roger Peckinpaugh strengthened the infield by reluctantly trading Roy Cullenbine to the Tigers in exchange for third baseman Don Ross and second baseman Dutch Meyer. It was a fair trade for both teams, as Cullenbine was a solid outfielder and Ross and Meyer were a huge upgrade for the infield. Ross, an average hitter, had played five years in the Majors, while Meyer had two years of limited experience with Detroit. A week before the trade he had been discharged from the army air force after serving for thirty-one months. He would have to play his way into shape as the season progressed, but even out of condition he was the best second baseman the Indians could come up with.

April finished with several frustrating rainouts and seven losses in nine games. The only two wins were by Steve Gromek. Cleveland sorely needed Jeff Heath in the outfield, but he continued his stubborn hold-out. For now they had to muddle along with Seerey, Carnett, and Hoag in the outfield, backed up by Paul O'Dea.

In early May, the Indians were on the road at St. Louis. Allie Reynolds, with his finger healed, pitched probably the best game of his young career. With Commissioner Chandler in the stands, Reynolds allowed a run in the fourth, then held the Browns as the game went to extra innings tied 1–1. In the top of the thirteenth, Ed Carnett singled to drive in Mickey Rocco, then Reynolds retired the Browns in the bottom half of the inning to win his first game of the year in style, 2–1. He had eight strikeouts and gave up only four hits. If the Indians had any dreams of a winning season, they would need the young arms of Gromek and Reynolds to carry much of the load.

Chandler visited several ballparks while juggling his duties as commissioner and senator. One of his first announcements was that he would move his office closer to his home outside of Cincinnati. He then scheduled a meeting with the War Department to discuss draft issues concerning his ballplayers. There was still the question of changing the status of athletes classified as 4-F to 1-A. If one could play a sport, the thought went, they certainly could serve in the armed forces. Taking a contrary point of view, Illinois congressman Melvin Price had recently filed a complaint with the War Department about drafting criteria applied to athletes alone. The congressman believed athletes were being discriminated against, attention being given to their special talents of strength, coordination, and endurance without regard for any possible physical impairments. He stated, "No man should be inducted if he is legitimately 4F." Price wanted a freeze put on drafting athletes until his investigation was completed. Several days later the War Department announced that any athlete classified as 4-F would remain so and those who had already been upgraded to 1-A were subject to review. It was not divulged how many athletes might come under review, but based on Congressman Price's complaints, the numbers were significant.

On May 7, newspaper headlines announced that Germany had surrendered to the Allies. Hostilities ceased at precisely 2:41 a.m., when General Eisenhower received his German counterparts at his headquarters in France, a nondescript small red schoolhouse. The three Allied powers, the United States, Great Britain, and Russia, all agreed to announce the surrender officially on May 8 at 9:00 a.m. eastern time. President Truman, Prime Minister Winston Churchill, and Premier Joseph Stalin would all speak on worldwide radio to share the most historic news of the century. Businesses all through the United States, Canada, and Great Britain planned to close for the day to allow widespread celebrating of VE (Victory in Europe) Day. Almost five years of heavy fighting with horrific casualties were over, leaving millions of people with their lives torn completely apart. VE Day signified the start of a new world that could hopefully rebuild and live in continued peace.

Though Germany had surrendered, the Japanese government had shown no willingness to admit defeat. In April, the United States Army, Navy, and Marine Corps began a massive attack on Okinawa. Once Okinawa was secured, the final assault of the war would commence, one that the American commanders feared would result in losses in the hundreds of thousands. Americans proudly celebrated VE Day but knew in their hearts that more terrible fighting remained in the South Pacific.

After U.S. forces drove the Japanese out of the Mariana Islands, sailors discovered the enemy had recently laid out a proper baseball field. Within days, 6,000 navy men gathered to watch a game between servicemen including pitchers Johnny Vander Meer, Johnny Rigney, and Virgil Trucks. The infield featured Mickey Vernon, Johnny Mize, Pee Wee Reese, and Billy Herman, and Barney McCosky played in the outfield. For several hours the conflict was forgotten in favor of the national game.

Soon talk came to the forefront about returning baseball and football players home to restart their professional careers. More emphasis was put on football, as the beginning of the season still had four months to go, while baseball was in full swing. Apparently the government wanted the National Football League to begin play as smoothly as possible. Baseball had already been disrupted.

American and National League owners let out a collective sigh of relief, knowing that the mad scramble to field a competitive team would gradually be coming to an end. For the Indians' part, they were waiting not only for Bob Feller to be discharged, but for other key members of the team and their minor league clubs. The 1945 season was looking like a disappointment for Cleveland, but there was a lot to be optimistic about in the seasons ahead.

On May 15, Commissioner Chandler was in Cleveland again to be the main speaker at the luncheon for the Cleveland Newspaper Guild the next day. Alva Bradley threw a dinner party for him at the Stadium Tower offices with Boudreau, guests from the front office, and several stockholders. Chandler had a fine time at the dinner, telling humorous stories about his days as a semipro ballplayer in Lexington. He had been planning to see the Indians play the Washington Senators after dinner, but it was rained out and rescheduled as part of a doubleheader the next day.

Chandler's speech to the Newspaper Guild at the Hollenden Hotel emphasized his firm conviction that baseball and horse racing were fine sports but should never mix. He maintained his resolve that gamblers should stay at the tracks and away from baseball parks. A former spectator at many racing events, Chandler told his audience, "As commissioner of baseball I will remain away from the tracks and I have advised all connected with pro baseball do likewise." Why he seemed to have gambling as a top priority is unclear, but possibly Chandler feared the death of Landis might embolden bettors to migrate back into the game and was sending a message to gamblers that the new boss was aware of them and would keep watch.

Asked why he had selected Cincinnati as the new location for the Major League offices, the commissioner reminded the audience that his responsibilities included the minor leagues, which had numerous teams in the upper and lower southern states. Cincinnati provided a central location for both the major and minor leagues. In addition, he maintained a home in Versailles, Kentucky, a two-hour drive from the office.

The doubleheader that day was washed away as well, making eleven rainouts in a single month. A string of late-season doubleheaders had to be scheduled, which would not go well with tired players down the last stretch.

On Saturday, May 19, the skies were finally clear, allowing the Indians to play a doubleheader against Philadelphia. They swept it, as Allie Reynolds tossed a 4–0 shutout in the first game while Steve Gromek scattered eleven hits in a nail-biting 2–1 victory in the second. Don Black, pitching for the A's, gave up only four hits but yielded a solo home run to Paul O'Dea. Despite the sweep the Indians were sitting in last place with a record of 8–13. On Sunday they split two games with Philadelphia, taking the series 3–1 but remaining in the cellar.

The following day, with 5,000 Moline, Illinois, fans looking on, the Great Lakes team played Dizzy Dean's All-Stars. Player-manager Bob Feller went five innings, piling up twelve strikeouts and yielding a single run in a 5–1 victory. Feller had the advantage of veteran catcher Walker Cooper, the Cardinals' three-time All-Star, calling the pitches. Ol' Diz hurled the first two innings, shifted to first base for four more, then sat on the bench, a weary man.

While America took a few steps back to normality, the draft question regarding Major League Baseball persisted in the sporting pages headlines. The selective service announced that men over thirty who were in "useful service" would no longer be eligible for the military. Baseball players were not mentioned specifically, but the general assumption was that they were safe from any government service. The next move was for fans to see soldiers exchange their battle gear for bats and gloves and return to their usual places on the diamond.

At the end of May, Roger Peckinpaugh and the Indians pulled the trigger on a deal to shore up the catching. They sent holdout Buddy Rosar to Philadelphia for veteran receiver Frank Hayes. The new catcher had begun his career in 1933 with the A's, moved to the Browns in 1942, then back to Philadelphia in 1944. Hayes possessed good power for a catcher and was a bona fide iron man behind the plate, catching all 154 games in 1944. Cleveland had improved the second and third base positions, and now the catching was in good hands.

The same day, Jeff Heath let the press know he was on his way to Cleveland for a talk with Peckinpaugh. Whether he was getting low on money or he had the itch to play baseball again, or both, he would be back in a Cleveland uniform, strengthening the outfield the moment he stepped on the playing field.

The timing of Hayes and Heath donning Cleveland uniforms became critical when Boudreau suffered an infection in his cornea that would sideline him for at least ten days. His doctors had him wear sunglasses at the ballpark and off the field. An extended absence for the player-manager was a serious blow to the Indians' attempt to move up in the standings. On June 2, the situation improved a bit when Mel Harder agreed to return to the mound for another season. At thirty-five, he believed his arm had enough left in it to bolster the struggling pitching staff. Gromek and Reynolds were on their way to outstanding seasons, but no other starter had shown any consistency.

Jeff Heath arrived in Cleveland, telling sportswriters his knee had completely recovered from the November surgery. He took a few moments to defend himself against the uninformed Cleveland fans who had accused him of faking the injury and taking it easy. If the fans really wanted to know, he had a lengthy scar running down from his surgically repaired knee for anyone to gaze at. As to why he had held out, "I am not hard to get along with, but I have to protect myself. The club wanted to penalize me and that's where matters stand at present."

The next day the twenty-nine-year-old Heath signed his contract and made a verbal agreement with Peckinpaugh. If he played at a certain level for the rest of the season, extra pay would be added to his salary. Heath may have got his point across, but at what cost to him and the ball club? He had missed playing all of April and May and part of June. His presence in the lineup from the start of the season would have notably strengthened the batting order, giving the Indians a chance at better than a 2–7 start.

On June 7, Cleveland lost to the Tigers 3–2, as Hal Newhouser out pitched Allie Reynolds. It was the Indians' fourteenth one-run game, of which they had lost eight. One player would not have been enough to turn their record around, but losing Keltner to the navy, Rosar and Heath holding out, and having to trade Roy Cullenbine all contributed heavily to their 17–21 record. Thoughts of a pennant were all but gone, but for the balance of the year the Indians would play much better baseball.

Chapter 7

THE BOYS COME HOME

In mid-June, the first Major League Baseball star to be eligible for military discharge was the Tigers' Hank Greenberg. After nearly four years in the army, the game's outstanding first baseman–outfielder clearly deserved it. The hard-hitting Greenberg planned to be back in the Detroit lineup by July 1.

Happy Chandler pledged to help returning soldier-ballplayers get back in the game as quickly as possible. "We have an obligation to give every fellow a job," he announced. "I will use every influence I have on behalf of the players." As a United States senator, Chandler knew the right people in Washington and how to get things pushed through red tape. If anyone could grease the wheels to facilitate the timely returns of numerous ballplayers eager to earn a living, he could. With 500 major leaguers and 5,000 minor leaguers in the military, the logistics of a smooth return to baseball were mind-boggling.

One of the obstacles facing the Major Leagues was a new order from the Office of Defense Transportation. The plan was to move tens of thousands of soldiers, jeeps, trucks, and equipment arriving daily from Europe to their respective military bases. When that mass movement was completed, war veterans were next on the list to be given transportation to their prewar homes. Over the next few months ODT planned to appropriate every available rail car to carry out the task, including lounge, dining, and sleeping cars. Teams were challenged to find the means to move their players from city to city while not interfering with ODT's plans. The Indians could utilize boats to get to Detroit, but other trips had to be carefully planned.

While the Indians' front office studied train schedules, manager Boudreau levied fines on Mickey Rocco, Paul O'Dea, and Dutch Meyer for indiscretions during several games. Boudreau explained, "The fines are a culmination of events that happened on the field. We have been giving too many runs away and the pitchers have been placed under severe handicaps." Fans wondered what the three might have done until Ed McAuley of the *Cleveland News* gave out the inside information. McAuley did not reveal the dollar amounts, but explained the fines were nominal ones given for throwing to the wrong base or failing to communicate on pop flies that fell for base hits. By fining the players, Boudreau sought to get them thinking and cut down on the mental errors.

On June 22, the Indians split a doubleheader with Chicago, winning the first 2–1 and losing the nightcap 3–0. But the big news came from Camp Chanute, where the Great Lakes team overwhelmed the army boys 5–0. Bob Feller had his best game to date, cutting loose with his fastball to whiff fifteen batters. It appeared Feller was getting stronger with each outing while moving closer to his discharge.

A week later, playing a home game at League Park, Jeff Heath hammered a drive 460 feet to dead center field as the Indians pounded Philadelphia 11–0. His knee fully healed, he raced around the bases for an inside-the-park home run. It was one of the longest homers ever hit at the old grounds. The red-hot Heath had gone 11 for 20 over his last six games. As happened every season with Heath, the boos turned into cheers while the outfielder kept bashing out hits at a torrid pace.

With the war in Europe over and soldiers coming home at a rapid pace, the July 4 holiday was extra special. The Yankees were in town, and the Indians were eager to put on a good show for the nearly 25,000 fans. Special scorecards were for sale with a team photo and facsimile player autographs inside. In the top of the seventh in game one, Boudreau put a hard tag on the Yankees' Bud Metheny, resulting in a shoving match at second base. The crowd roared while players raced out of the dugout to pull the combatants apart and break up the scuffle. After order was restored and nobody was thrown out, Steve Gromek finished up another win, his ninth of the season, 4–2. In the bottom of the fourth in game two, New York hurler Al Gettel drilled Frank Hayes behind his ear. Hayes, the iron man who had already caught 225 straight games, left the game dazed, but assured everyone it was just a scratch and he'd be catching again the following day. The next batter, Felix Mackiewicz, singled to tie the game 2–2, but Reynolds gave up a sacrifice fly to former Indian Oscar Grimes in the ninth and the Yankees won the game 3–2. Hayes did return for the next game, and his streak would continue into the next season, finally reaching 312.

The final game of the series, played at League Park, featured a pitcher's duel between Ed Klieman and the Yankees' Ernie Bonham. The score was 1–1 when Jeff Heath led off the bottom of the eleventh. He lined the first pitch from Bonham high over the right field wall, but it curved just foul. While the fans grimaced and shook their collective heads, Heath slammed another one, this time soaring over the right center field wall and onto Lexington Avenue to win the game. The fans gave Heath a rousing ovation for his heroics.

With the war still being fought in the Pacific, Commissioner Chandler stood by his earlier statement and did not reinstate the July All-Star game. Instead, Major League Baseball came up with an attention-grabbing alternative. Exhibition games were scheduled between teams in the same city or state (where possible), with proceeds going to the armed forces. On July 9, the Indians played the Cincinnati Reds at Municipal Stadium before an embarrassing crowd of 6,066 fans. The Reds hit several Cleveland pitchers freely for a 6–0 victory and the mythical championship of Ohio. In front of 41,000 spectators at the Polo Grounds, the Yankees, behind a grand slam by outfielder Hersh Martin, clobbered the Giants 7–1. At Comiskey Park, 47,000 fans witnessed a thriller between the White Sox and Cubs. Tied 4–4 in the ninth, the Sox scored the game winner in the bottom of the inning.

The next day at Sportsman's Park in St. Louis, the Browns shut out the Cardinals 3–0, while the Phillies beat the last-place A's 7–6 at Shibe Park and the Red Sox had no trouble with the Braves at Fenway Park, winning 8–1. The Tigers were to play the Pittsburgh Pirates, but ODT ruled the game out because the travel miles were judged excessive. The real drama took place in Washington, where the Senators matched up against the Dodgers. Taking the mound for Washington was lefty Bert Shepard, a former minor leaguer and wounded veteran. A seasoned pilot in the Air Corps, he was flying his thirty-fourth mission over Germany when antiaircraft fire downed his P-38 fighter plane. Shepard miraculously survived the impact but had part of his right leg amputated in a German hospital. He spent eight months in a POW camp before being exchanged. After much rehabilitation Shepard was able to pitch again. Impressed, Clark Griffith signed him to a contract. It had been a long haul, but all the effort paid off when he walked to the mound to a terrific ovation. It was his first action as a Major Leaguer, and much to the delight of his teammates and everybody in the park, Shephard pitched four strong innings, getting credit for the win as the Senators held off the Dodgers, 4–3.

The exhibition games raised several hundred thousand dollars for the War Relief Fund, including over $100,000 from the games in New York and Philadelphia. Major League officials estimated that from 1942 to 1945 the game had donated $3,000,000 to aid the soldiers and families overseas and at home. The generosity was unparalleled in pro sports to date.

With the All-Star game canceled, newspapermen across the country asked managers who they would have chosen. Among his list, Lou Boudreau picked Frank Hayes for his combined play with Philadelphia and Cleveland, along with pitchers Allie Reynolds and Steve Gromek. Lou modestly left himself off the list; however if there had been a game no doubt he would have been lining up at shortstop.

During the break, *Esquire* did a feature article on Bob Feller. After much prodding, Feller reluctantly showed the writer his seven battle stars and pocketful of ribbons. Still humble after all this time, he preferred to talk about baseball rather than his experiences aboard the USS *Alabama*. Feller expressed concern about regaining his control and, just like a rookie, needing to learn the hitters all over again. He hoped to be in the best possible condition upon his return to the Indians but was unsure if he could get back to Cleveland this year. Whether it happened in 1945 or 1946, the ball club would welcome him back.

With Feller looming in the background, the second half of the season went much better for the Indians. On Thursday, July 12, they beat the Yankees in New York, then followed up on Friday with a seventeen-hit, five-homer barrage. In the top of the first, Jeff Heath launched a towering two-run home run. In the third, Pat Seerey walloped a solo homer, then struck again with a grand slam in the fourth. Heath came up next and blasted another for back-to-back home runs. Three innings later Seerey crushed his third home run, this time with two men on. Seerey added a triple to go along with his three home runs. His fifteen total bases tied him for the all-time Cleveland record with Hal Trosky, Earl Averill, and Ken Keltner, one shy of the league record held by Ty Cobb and Lou Gehrig. Steve Gromek did not hit any out of the park but contributed four hits and three RBIs in the 16–4 pasting of the Yankees.

Though the Yankees were soundly beaten in the series, hopeful news came their way: Joe DiMaggio and Tommy Henrich were eligible for early release, and forty-year-old Red Ruffing would be returning to bolster the pitching staff. As it happened, only Ruffing came home early enough to play. The Senators welcomed outfielder Buddy Lewis back to the lineup. Lewis had one of the most amazing stories to tell. He had graduated from flight school in 1942, taking command of C-47 transport planes in the South Pacific. He flew over three hundred missions for the army air force, ferrying troops from island to island. In 1944, Lewis took part in a harrowing secret mission, flying soldiers to Burma, well behind Japanese lines. Three separate times he landed safely on a makeshift airfield to deliver men for a sneak attack. For all his efforts, Captain Lewis received the Distinguished Flying Cross and a return to the Senators to resume his baseball career.

While the former soldiers trickled back to their ball clubs, the Indians enjoyed their best month of the season, winning eighteen of twenty-nine games. Superb pitching from Steve Gromek and a shutout from Jim Bagby, his fifth victory of the year, helped them win the last seven of eight. Cleveland finished the month at .500, giving eager local fans a reason to start filling the stands.

On July 30, the ball club found time to play an exhibition game at the George Crile Hospital on the west side of town. Named for the founder of the Cleveland Clinic, the hospital opened its doors on Easter Sunday of 1944. Built on a sprawling campus, it had 2,000 beds to treat seriously wounded soldiers back from the war. The staff brought out nearly all the patients in wheelchairs and on cots to watch the Crile team, led by starting pitcher Jim Blackburn, back home after two years in a German prisoner-of-war camp. He went seven innings, but the Indians won 13–9. The Indians players and the entire organization and the Major League umpires who worked the game deserved a world of credit for making the time to cheer up the men who had more than done their duty overseas.

The month of August brought all kinds of twists and turns to the Indians' season. Les Fleming, newly released from his Texas war job, reported to Boudreau ready to play ball. And Mickey Rocco, the stopgap first baseman, started to hit the long ball, joining Seerey and Heath in the home run derby. Playing Chicago at League Park on Thursday, August 2, the Indians loaded the bases in the third inning for Pat Seerey. He drove a pitch fifteen rows up in the left field bleachers for another grand slam. Boudreau had four of the team's seventeen hits as the Indians rolled to a 13–7 triumph.

Back on the road, Cleveland arrived in St. Louis for a six-game series, including two doubleheaders, a byproduct of the early season rainouts. The Browns won three of the first four games. On Monday, August 6, in the first game of the second doubleheader, Pat Seerey launched a tremendous shot high over the left field stands and completely out of the ballpark. The feast-or-famine hitter was feasting right now. The game was tied at 6–6 in the ninth when Frank Hayes delivered a three-run homer, and the Indians held on to win 9–7 and pull back to .500.

In game two, the fireworks continued, with Jeff Heath homering and Mickey Rocco going deep twice. Rocco's second home run, a three-run job in the top of the ninth, sealed the 8–4 win. Allie Reynolds and Steve Gromek were the winning pitchers in the doubleheader. Both still had chances at twenty-win seasons.

Though out of the pennant race, Cleveland was one of the hotter teams in either league. Lou Boudreau had to be pleased at the way his ball club was playing both at home and on the road. They had spent time in last place, but had pulled themselves out of the hole and were now challenging for the first division.

On August 14, the Indians were at home to play Boston. In the top of the second inning, the Red Sox had two men on base with one out. Skeeter Newsome drilled a hard ground ball to second baseman Dutch Meyer, who made a clean pickup and flipped the ball to Boudreau as he came across the bag. Just as Lou released the ball for the relay to first, Dolph Camilli barreled into him, knocking the shortstop up in the air. Boudreau landed painfully on his right ankle and was unable to stand up for several minutes. He limped to the bench and watched Jim Bagby finish shutting out the Red Sox 3–0 before going to see Dr. Castle. X-rays showed a small ankle fracture. The doctor could not be certain if it was an old break or a new one, but Lou would have to sit out for at least ten days before Dr. Castle would take another look.

That same day, August 14, 10,000 fans arrived at the Crile Hospital playing field to see Bob Feller and the Great Lakes team battle the hospital staff. It would be the first time Feller had pitched in town since the August 1942 All-Star–Armed Forces game. The crowd waited and waited for Feller to arrive until an announcement came that his plane was stuck in Illinois.

Japan had surrendered to General Douglas MacArthur, prompting an order to ground all military planes for sixty hours. VJ Day had arrived, and World War II was finally over. President Truman, still doing his on-the-job training, proclaimed that 5 million armed forces personnel would receive their discharges over the next twelve to eighteen months. The navy immediately canceled 6 billion dollars in war contracts, meaning thousands of plants and factories could move back to civilian manufacturing or have to shut their doors.

From the airport where he was stranded, Feller managed to announce his pending departure from the navy. He told the *Canton Repository,* "I want to get back in my uniform before the season ends if possible. With two or three games under my belt, I should be back in top shape." Over five hundred major and minor league players had been released from the services to this point. Commissioner Chandler advised the owners that any man returning from the military was eligible to play in the World Series even if it was after the usual cutoff date of August 31. To help matters along, ODT announced the end of travel restrictions for baseball and all other sports, professional and amateur. The effects of the great world war would be felt for years ahead, but millions of people could begin to pick up the pieces of their lives and look to the future.

The Indians celebrated the news of Feller's imminent return by reeling off seven straight wins, all without Boudreau in the lineup. With a record of 57–51, they still had a fighting chance to finish among the leaders. When Washington came to town to play seven games in four days, including three doubleheaders, it was an opportunity for the Indians to make up some real ground on the second-place Senators. Winning five out of seven would put them just a half game behind Washington with almost half of August and all of September still to play. A difficult proposition for sure, but not impossible. After a mostly lackluster year, some slight hope remained.

The Indians lost the first game of the opening doubleheader, but came back to win the second 9–3 as Allie Reynolds recorded his thirteenth win. But that was the last good news. Cleveland lost the next five to burst the bubble and bring up the familiar cry of "Wait till next year."

With the team back to one game over .500, there was still something to be excited about, though. In short order, Bob Feller would be standing on the mound, throwing his one-of-kind fastball.

On Saturday, August 18, the day before the disastrous series with the Senators began, the newspapers reported that Feller's discharge would be granted within the next seventy-two hours and the former chief specialist would be flying to Cleveland on Thursday the twenty-third. Boudreau was considering starting Feller in one of the weekend games, but would wait until Bob reported before he decided. Almost immediately, the city leaders gathered to plan a fitting welcome for the most popular man in town. A Friday luncheon was scheduled for the classy Rainbow Room at the downtown Hotel Carter. Invites went to Cy Young and to Steve O'Neill, currently the Tigers manager and Feller's first manager in Cleveland, along with many former players and friends of the pitcher. At six that evening, Feller would be a guest on WGAR radio with host Tom Manning. Jack Graney would broadcast the night game at Municipal Stadium, and there would be a special ceremony before game time with Mayor Burke, Tris Speaker, and Lou Boudreau making presentations.

On Thursday Feller arrived in Cleveland in the early afternoon and went straight to League Park for fifteen minutes of throwing, followed by trainer Lefty Weisman working on his pitching arm. For some reason Feller's equipment bag did not arrive with him, but still hidden in his old locker was a musty old glove from 1941, which would have to do.

Reporters flocked to the park to view the workout, eager to get quotes for their papers. After Feller completed his stretching and some exercising, he told them, "They might knock me out in the first inning, but maybe I'll get by although I haven't even looked at pitching under the lights in the Navy." Feller modestly chose not to mention all the work he had gotten in while pitching and managing the Great Lakes team. It might not have been quite equivalent to a Major League spring training, but he would be ready to start Friday evening.

The crowd at the Rainbow Room luncheon just about filled the many tables. Steve O'Neill related several anecdotes about his first meetings with the teenaged star-to-be. Lou Boudreau spoke next, amiably welcoming Bob home from the war, home to Cleveland, and back with the Indians. A telegram from Happy Chandler was read, then Feller told the crowd he had no qualms whatsoever about enlisting in the navy and spending twenty-six months at sea. "I have no regrets and would have not taken ten million dollars to miss that trip," he said. He finished by presenting Franklin Lewis of the *Cleveland Press* a $1,000 check from the Indians to be used towards the *Press*'s memorial fund for World War II veterans.

The luncheon included a prayer from Monsignor John Hagan, representing the Cleveland Catholic schools, who said, "We welcome today our sons and daughters who in the years of peril offered their lives and their all. In the years to come, let not the memory of what we owe them ever grow dim." Now all that remained was to play ball.

That evening at Municipal Stadium the largest crowd of the season, 46,477, fought through the heavy traffic to find parking spaces and hurry to purchase their tickets. The three-year wait to see Bob Feller unleash his patented fastball was only moments away. The pregame ceremony began with a parade to the flagpole by veterans of World War I, followed by the Indians and Tiger players. The flag went steadily up the pole as all in attendance stood for the national anthem. Tris Speaker, always a favorite at the ballpark, awarded a smiling Feller a handy utility jeep for his off-season fishing and hunting expeditions. Tris assured him that ODT had given clearance for unlimited usage. Lou Boudreau spoke to the crowd, then bestowed Feller with a handsome engraved pen-and-pencil set from his Cleveland teammates. Mayor Burke came to the microphone to present Virginia Feller with a dozen fresh-cut red roses. There had been many pregame ceremonies at Municipal Stadium, but none as heartwarming as this one. Photos would show men, women, and children standing up and yelling as loudly as they could for their returning hero.

Detroit was not conceding anything, sending twenty-game winner Hal Newhouser to the mound to oppose Feller. The first-place Tigers featured a strong lineup, with Hank Greenberg and Rudy York supplying the home run power. If Feller wanted a true test, the Tigers would give him one.

In the top of the first, Feller retired the first two batters before Doc Cramer belted a triple to deep right field. Hank Greenberg walked to the plate, ready to resume his classic battles with the Indians ace. While the large crowd yelled encouragement, Feller bore down and struck out the still-dangerous Tiger slugger. In the home half of the first, Al Cihocki, Boudreau's replacement, fanned, but Mickey Rocco singled to center, bringing Pat Seerey to the plate. Seerey promptly sent one of Newhouser's offerings deep into the left field seats for a 2–0 lead.

The score stayed that way until the top of the third inning, when Detroit catcher Paul Richards lined a double and Jimmy Outlaw drew a base on balls. Red Borom and Doc Cramer lashed consecutive singles to tie the game at 2–2. The Indians answered in the bottom half when Mickey Rocco doubled to right field, his second hit of the game. Pat Seerey grounded out, but Rocco was able to advance to third. Newhouser pitched carefully to Jeff Heath, eventually walking him to put runners at first and third. Dutch Meyer hit a ground ball, but the only play was to second base, forcing Heath and scoring Rocco with the go-ahead run.

The Indians added another run in the fifth inning when Jeff Heath doubled and went to third on a Newhouser wild pitch. After Dutch Meyer walked, Don Ross lined a bullet off Newhouser's glove that nobody could field in time to make a play. Heath crossed the plate to give Feller a two-run lead to work with.

The rest of the game was vintage Feller. He did not yield another base hit, striking out twelve for the game, including Greenberg and York twice. The Indians won 4–2, an incredible performance from a man released from the navy one day earlier. The Cleveland fans watched with a pure joy that grew inning by inning. It was a perfect evening for Cleveland, one that helped put more distance from the harsh years of World War II.

The Indians and Tigers were off on Saturday, but Boudreau had an important appointment with Dr. Castle. The leg cast was removed and further X-rays were taken. Dr. Castle ruled out an ankle fracture, but found a broken bone in the heel. Lou's season was likely over, but Dr. Castle agreed to take one more set of X-rays on September 19. Though there was nothing to play for, Lou, ever competitive, still wanted to get back on the field.

In game one of the Sunday doubleheader, Allie Reynolds won his fourteenth game of the season, 3–1. In game two, Steve Gromek had a comfortable 4–1 lead heading into the ninth inning, when Rudy York belted a three-run homer to tie the game at 4–4. The Indians were not to be denied, winning it in the bottom of the ninth when baserunner Gromek beat a relay home for the victory, 5–4. It was Steve's sixteenth win of the year.

A fine crowd of 37,459 saw the doubleheader at Municipal Stadium, pushing Cleveland season attendance to over 500,000 with an entire month remaining on the schedule. Business at Major League ballparks was booming, with three or four teams on pace to draw over a million fans. The Cubs and Dodgers were no great surprise, but the Giants had a shot at an all-time record for their ballpark. The outpouring of fans was threatening to break the all-time record of 10 million plus, set in 1930. This was a remarkable achievement in a time of war and a testament to the popularity of baseball even in the most trying times.

One of the ballplayers who always put people in the seats was of course Bob Feller. On Tuesday, August 28, 27,000 fans flocked to Comiskey Park to see him start against veteran Bill Dietrich of the White Sox. In the fifth inning, the Indians batted around, scoring four runs en route to an 8–2 victory and Feller's second straight win. He did not have command of the strike zone, walking six batters, but had enough stuff to keep the White Sox from any sustained rallies.

On September 1, Feller came back to earth against the Tigers, lasting six and a third innings while being touched for four runs, nine hits, and three walks. Detroit won the game 5–4, but the loss went to reliever Ed Klieman, who gave up the winning run in the ninth inning. Feller had now pitched three games without a defeat.

Two days later the Indians hosted the St. Louis Browns in the Labor Day holiday doubleheader. Jack Graney broadcast the game on WGAR along with a new partner, twenty-nine-year-old Bob Neal doing his first game. Neal left home at the age of seventeen to study voice at the Juilliard School in New York. He joined the army in 1940 but suffered an injury that led to a medical discharge in 1942. Three years later he joined the staff of WGAR and won the assignment to assist Graney on the live broadcasts. Neal would become a fixture in Cleveland radio announcing for years to come.

The 39,000 fans at the stadium were in for a disappointment as the Indians dropped both games to the Browns, 6–3 and 5–4. Nevertheless, it was a great day for people to get out of doors and enjoy their first postwar holiday. According to the newspapers, 17,000 people watched the horses at Randall Park, 42,000 more visited the Cleveland Zoo, and there were huge crowds at Euclid Beach Amusement Park. It had been a long time, but Americans proved they still knew how to celebrate.

On Sunday, September 9, Feller took the mound at Yankee Stadium for the first game of a doubleheader. In the top of the first, Jeff Heath gave him an early lead with a three-run homer, his thirteenth of the year. The Indians knocked war vet Spud Chandler off the mound with seven runs on the way to an easy 10–3 win. The second game was much tighter, but Allie Reynolds pitched well enough to gain win number 17, 4–3. More than 72,000 Yankee fans jammed the park. In the four games he had started since leaving the navy, an astounding 180,455 fans had come out to see him on the mound. Major League Baseball owed a great deal to the Indians pitcher, for his military service and for boosting attendance wherever he played.

The Indians finished their home schedule with two games against Detroit and two against Chicago. On the nineteenth, Feller was at his best, yielding only a pop fly single to Jimmy Outlaw in the fifth. Jeff Heath hit a two-run homer in the third to give Feller all the runs he needed as the Indians won 2–0. The next day Allie Reynolds won his eighteenth, 6–1, with all the Cleveland runs coming in the eighth inning. The two wins over the Tigers must have been gratifying for the Cleveland players. Detroit would end the season in first, but at least they were temporarily stopped by the Indians' pitchers. It was not quite revenge for 1940, when the Tigers denied Cleveland the pennant with three games left on the schedule, but it was close enough.

Steve Gromek continued the team's winning ways, beating the White Sox 2–1 in eleven innings and matching Reynolds for the team lead in victories. Feller, pitching on only three days' rest, came back to win the home finale 8–2, his fifth win in just over a month. With Feller, Gromek, and Reynolds, the Indians appeared to have the makings of a dazzling starting staff for the 1946 season. And with additional help coming from returning war vets and a healthy Lou Boudreau, plus perhaps a full season from Jeff Heath, the Indians had reason to be optimistic.

The season ended as it had begun, with rainouts of the last two games. Cleveland ended the up-and-down year with a record of seventy-three wins versus seventy-two losses and two tie games. Because of the large number of rainouts, they played only 147 of the 154 games scheduled. The Tigers, with old friend Steve O'Neill managing, won the American League pennant by one and a half games over Washington.

Four years of wartime baseball had gone by with mixed results. The quality of play had suffered, owners were rarely certain who would be on the roster, and attendance had waned. But the game had continued without interruption, and despite all the turmoil, baseball had finished strong in 1945. It looked like 1946 would be a banner year.

Chapter 8

HEATH MOVES ON

Although Bob Feller had earned a long rest for his wartime duty and five weeks of great pitching for the Indians, the fireballer was not quite finished. In the first week of October 1945, Feller hastily made plans for a barnstorming tour of the western states. With approval from Happy Chandler, he lined up a series of dates pitching against Satchel Paige in cities including San Diego, Los Angeles, Seattle, Fort Worth, and Salt Lake City. Assuming the role of businessman, Feller estimated he could make about $20,000 over the one month of exhibition games.

Whoever the supporting cast was, it was the Major League's and Negro Leagues' best pitchers going head to head that fans would come out to see. At times Satchel brought the Kansas City Monarchs with him, including star infielder Jackie Robinson. In order to play as many games as possible, Feller would travel by airplane, hopping from one city to another in record time. He planned to pitch five innings each game, some with just a day or two of rest.

On October 3, Feller and Paige hooked up in San Diego before a full house of 9,000 fans. Paige got the better of the matchup, going five complete innings while striking out eleven of the Kent Parker All-Stars. Feller nearly matched Paige with ten strikeouts, but his replacement was hit hard, and Satch's Kansas City Monarchs won the game, 5–0.

Playing in Los Angeles in front of 25,000 excited spectators, Feller's team beat Paige's by a score of 4–2. Once again Satchel outperformed

Bob, pitching six innings with ten strikeouts, two hits, and no bases on balls. Feller managed six strikeouts but walked five and allowed two runs. The tour appeared to be a success for Feller, as he pitched in front of good crowds in each city he appeared in. He may not have earned $20,000, but surely turned a substantial profit in less than a month's work.

While Feller rested a short time, the Major League clubs worked to revamp their rosters and make spring training plans for Florida and the West Coast. Alva Bradley negotiated a return to Clearwater, a favorite spot of his and the players. An ample number of exhibition games would be scheduled for the first normal spring training since 1942.

Commissioner Chandler officially resigned from the Senate on November 1. The commissioner had recently received a vote of confidence from fourteen of the owners, with two abstentions. Chandler had left himself open for criticism at the Detroit-Chicago World Series when he named a personal friend as one of the official scorers. The two abstaining owners, and probably a few more, were concerned about Washington politics entering the commissioner's office.

With the Major League meetings scheduled for early December, the Indians' front office made it known they were actively seeking to trade Jeff Heath. This time there appeared to be a consensus between Bradley, Peckinpaugh, and Boudreau that Heath would have to go no matter what they received in return. Another player sure to be sent packing was Jim Bagby. While Heath could still hit, Bagby had pitched poorly for most of the season. With Feller back, his value to the club was minimal.

The winter meeting took place in Chicago with several issues of note along with a good deal of controversy. The first point of contention involved limiting the powers of Commissioner Chandler. Judge Landis had the ability to veto any legislation or proposals he deemed detrimental to major or minor league baseball, and the owners had no recourse but to accept the verdict. After Landis died, the owners voted to set aside that power and address it again when the new commissioner took office. On the first day of the meetings, the owners voted to permanently remove Landis's absolute power from Chandler's scope of authority. They quickly added a statement that the decision would not "take away authority to investigate, determine, and punish conduct detrimental to baseball." The owners explained that Chandler would continue to operate as Landis had done, but his rulings were subject to an overriding vote. In less than a year, Chandler had lost a significant piece of his authority. He was not a puppet by any means, but he had been knocked down a peg.

In other action, the owners created a AAA classification for three minor leagues, the American Association, the Pacific Coast League, and the International League. The move up settled a beef between the three leagues and the Majors. Any player taken from a AAA roster would now fetch a price of $10,000 instead of the previous $7,500. In turn, the Southern Association and Texas League were elevated to AA and the South Atlantic (Sally League) now received A status.

The Pacific Coast League submitted a proposal to be declared a third Major League, to compete equally with the American and National Leagues. The owners agreed to look over the request and announce a determination at the end of the meetings. The PCL was organized in 1903, just two years after the American League. It featured eight clubs in California, Washington, and Oregon, with franchises in the biggest West Coast cities. The closest Major League teams were the St. Louis franchises. PCL officials believed their teams were staunch enough for a major league and drew enough fans to be on a similar level with the American and National Leagues. The increased popularity of air travel allowed for a schedule to include road trips up and down the West Coast.

At the conclusion of the meetings, the owners rejected the PCL proposal, but acknowledged that cities including Los Angeles, San Francisco, and Seattle were potential MLB territory. They offered to establish a committee to study the issue, but suggested nothing beyond that. The PCL officials left the meeting with a higher classification but little else to celebrate.

The winter meetings always offered a large amount of trade talk, and this year's gathering was no exception. The Indians were at the forefront, moving Jim Bagby to the Boston Red Sox for twenty-five-year-old lefty pitcher Vic Johnson and $5,000 cash. Johnson, who had a lifetime record of 6–7 with Boston, was seemingly a throw-in to the cash transaction. It was addition by subtraction.

A few days later the Jeff Heath era ended in Cleveland when he was traded to Washington for outfielder George Case. Heath had stopped in Chicago while the meetings were going on and let everybody know how much he wanted to leave the Indians. His wish was granted, but not without a parting shot from Boudreau. "I think we got the best of the deal," he told the press. "Case should be of great help. At least we expect Case will report on time to our training camp."

George Case was thirty years old, a nine-year veteran with the Senators. He possessed tremendous speed, leading the American League in steals five straight seasons. He did not hit for power but got on base frequently. Adding Case to the lineup gave the Indians a dimension they had been lacking for many years.

As for Jeff Heath, at times he could be one of the best hitters in baseball, but he was rarely happy playing for Cleveland. He had gone toe to toe with manager Oscar Vitt on several occasions, fought with at least one teammate, and in a fit of anger heaved his bat into the stands, injuring the editor of the *Cleveland Press*. From the beginning, Heath and Boudreau were not a good match. The trade was for the best, though the long home runs and RBIs would definitely be missed.

At the meetings a rumor surfaced that Hollywood actor-singer Bing Crosby had an interest in buying the Cleveland Indians. Alva Bradley immediately quashed the tale, stating he had never met Crosby and had zero interest in selling the team. The story ended there, but it gave impetus to people reflecting on Bradley's nineteen years as the Cleveland owner and maybe reaching the point of moving on.

At the same time, Bob Feller revealed he was planning to conduct a January baseball school in Tampa, Florida, for veterans who had minor league or organized baseball experience. The purpose was to attract as many baseball scouts as possible and get at least a few of the students contracts for the 1946 season. Feller did not expect to see any of his ballplayers signed to a Major League deal but hoped many of them would be playing some class of minor league ball and making a steady income.

The school would run from January 20 to February 9, featuring current and retired Major League personnel. Feller offered free tuition and equipment, courtesy of several sporting goods companies, and hotel rooms at a reduced rate. He planned to put his own money toward the free classes and renting five baseball fields for the students. Will Harridge offered assistance from the American League to help defray costs for the approximately seventy-five students. The school was an enormous gesture from Feller, who had no obligation to do anything except ready himself for spring training.

Applications for the school were to be sent care of the *Sporting News*. Within days requests flowed in from all around the United States,

Canada, and Puerto Rico. Rollie Hemsley, Feller's old catcher, signed on as an instructor, as did Tigers pitcher Tommy Bridges. Though still in the planning stages, the school received national attention, all of it positive for Feller. Alva Bradley noticed the change in his pitcher from shy teenager to assertive adult. "He is not the same fellow he was before the war," Bradley said. "He is, shall I say, much more independent and positive in his views."

Bradley and his counterparts had a lot of work to do before the start of spring training. The American League had 398 players on the active rosters, 230 from 1945 and 168 rookies. That figure did not include 152 players returning from the war, an impressive list that included names like Ted Williams, Joe and Dom DiMaggio, Tommy Henrich, Johnny Pesky, Bobby Doerr, Phil Rizzuto, and Cecil Travis. The owners and general managers had to sort out the numbers and fill out their rosters accordingly.

The big question still to be determined concerned the returning war vets. Would most be able to regain their skills over the course of a spring training, or would more time be needed before they could play at a Major League level? How could their managers be able to decide over a six-week period? To help with the process, owners agreed to open camps on February 20 just for the veterans, then for everybody else on March 1. Each man would have thirty days of training before any decision could be made regarding his status. Baseball was doing the smart thing in trying to give the ex-GI's a fair shake.

In January, salaries became a hot topic for the owners and returning vets. The guys who had been overseas had lost a lot of money during their service and sought to recover as much as they could. Owners had a difficult time saying no and risking negative comments from the press and the fans. Nobody was going to get Babe Ruth money in the $80,000 range, but the *Plain Dealer* reported that Hank Greenberg was getting $55,000, Feller $50,000, Joe DiMaggio $42,500, and Ted Williams $25,000. Salaries were on the rise, and rightfully so for the players who made the sacrifice.

Bob Feller's baseball school opened with seventy-seven players from twenty-six states and additional instructors Dizzy Dean, ex–Indians general manager Cy Slapnicka, Bucky Walters, and Spud Chandler. The students had multiple game films to watch and instructional films to go over after class had finished. Each player was guaranteed a minimum of sixteen innings of game time per day. The only area not addressed was how many of them would end up with professional contracts.

If Feller was not busy enough, he talked about tentative plans to buy a minor league Class A franchise in Denver. He had the idea of restarting the defunct Western League, which might have teams not only in Denver but in Omaha and Lincoln, Nebraska; Sioux City, Iowa; and other nearby states. Feller assured the press this venture would only be a sideline and not get in the way of his Major League career. A big supporter of air travel, Feller planned to use only planes to transport his players in the proposed league. Alva Bradley's earlier comment that Feller was a changed man certainly rang true. A businessman, an entrepreneur, a highly paid ballplayer—those all described the new man wearing number 19 on his Cleveland uniform.

In early February, the Indians announced that thirty-eight players would be going to spring training in Clearwater and thirty-two exhibition games would be played. The first group was scheduled to arrive on February 18 and the bulk of the team on March 1. Reporting with the first group was new pitcher Don Black, acquired off waivers from the Philadelphia Athletics.

A native of Salix, Iowa, Black had played high school basketball, but since there were only twenty boys in his class, there was no baseball team. Based on his impressive sandlot play, Black started his professional career in 1937 pitching for Fairbury in the Nebraska State League. After one season he left the minors and did not return until 1941, signing on with Petersburg of the Virginia League. He had two winning seasons there, resulting in Connie Mack buying his contract for 1943. Black spent three years in Philadelphia, compiling an unimpressive 21–39 record with an ERA of 4.39.

Problems developed between Mack and his pitcher, chiefly concerning Black's excessive use of alcohol. After several suspensions over the years, Mack finally gave up and placed his pitcher on waivers. The Indians signed him off the waiver list. After dealing with catcher Rollie Hemsley's alcoholism, they likely believed they could handle the right-hander and make good use of his better-than-average fastball and curve.

On February 18, the Indians' first caravan departed Cleveland's Union Station, bound for Clearwater and seventy-degree temperatures. On board were Mel Harder, Ray Mack, and former servicemen Gene Woodling and Joe Krakauskas. Upon arrival at the Fort Harrison Hotel, they were met by minor league catcher Sherm Lollar and military vets Bob Lemon and Eddie Robinson.

Bob Feller sent word he would be leaving shortly from Illinois, traveling with his wife and ten-week-old son Stephen. After working out every day at his baseball school, he did not need the extra time afforded the war vets. Also absent were Ken Keltner and Hank Edwards, both hopefully days away from receiving their discharges.

Manager Boudreau arrived in camp, announcing that his right heel was completely recovered and he was ready for workouts. Lou, in a jovial mood, let the players know their practice on the twenty-sixth would be cut short for everybody to catch the charity golf match between stalwarts Byron Nelson and Sam Snead. And Feller sent word that on the twenty-eighth he was taking all the boys for a ride on his twenty-two-foot ocean cruiser. The mood at camp was certainly upbeat, but how would that translate to the regular season?

The Indians' presence in Clearwater was a welcome sight for the city and much of Florida's west coast. The end of the war had brought a steady flow of tourists to the area, transitioning cities like Tampa, St. Petersburg, and Clearwater from retirement areas to sought-after vacation spots. To show its appreciation, the City of Clearwater held a pregame celebration on Sunday, March 10, when the Indians met the Red Sox. All businesses closed at noon, followed by a high school band marching to the playing field. Anticipating a crowd of 4,000 people, the city put up temporary bleachers. The game turned out to be a rousing all-rookie affair, with the Indians holding on for a 5–4 win. The crowd did not quite reach 4,000, but the spectators were treated to an entertaining ball game and music from the Ringling Brothers Circus Band. Sherm Lollar had two base hits while blocking the plate to stop a Boston runner from scoring in the seventh inning. Bob Lemon played third base and Eddie Robinson was at first as Boudreau wanted to keep the veterans rested for another day.

More happy news came on Wednesday when Ken Keltner received his discharge. He expected to be in Clearwater within the next two weeks. Hank Edwards would also be returning soon, bolstering the Indians' roster with two more seasoned veterans. Anticipation of the start of the regular season increased each day with news of more ex-servicemen returning to their teams. The 1946 season promised to be filled with the most excitement Major League Baseball had seen since the beginning of the decade.

Monday, March 18, brought a matchup with the New York Yankees. The phones at the Clearwater baseball park rang nonstop with enthusiastic fans calling for tickets. The highway to the city became jammed with hundreds of cars trying to get to the park before game time. As it happens in Florida, the skies suddenly darkened and a tremendous downpour covered the ballpark and the immediate area. The skeleton crew of groundskeepers only had enough tarp to cover the pitcher's mound and batter's box, leaving the rest of the infield underwater. Reluctantly, the game had to be canceled, turning away record numbers of fans.

The next day the skies were clear, allowing the Indians and Tigers to get their nine innings played. The game marked the spring debut of Lou Boudreau, keen to test his recently mended heel. He played four innings without a problem as training camp star Bob Lemon homered and drove in two runs in a 6–5 win. Enjoyment of the victory was somewhat tempered when the front office learned Ken Keltner had rejected the Indians' contract offer. The third baseman planned to stay in Milwaukee until the club upped the ante. Don Ross was in camp and able to play third, but the Indians sorely needed Keltner's glove and his proven ability to hit home runs.

The first month of Major League spring training had gone efficiently, other than many war veterans pulling up lame with sore muscles. The owners thankfully looked forward to a regular season with capacity crowds and more profits than in quite a while. Their happy dreams were tempered by worry, however. For the past several weeks, the president of the Mexican League, Jorge Pasquel, had been flying around the United States raiding the ball clubs for talent. Pasquel, from Veracruz, had amassed a fortune in the shipping business and was not timid about throwing huge sums of money around to bring American ballplayers to Mexico. In years prior he had signed many of the stars of the Negro League, including Satchel Paige, Josh Gibson, Willie Wells, James "Cool Papa" Bell, Roy Campanella, and Monte Irvin. With these players on board the Mexican League became highly competitive and quite popular south of the border. In 1946, Pasquel aggressively turned his attention to the American and National League, hopeful of signing big names like Bob Feller, Ted Williams, Joe DiMaggio, and Stan Musial. Reportedly, Feller was offered a three-year deal for $100,000 per year.

When none of the stars were interested in jumping their teams and forsaking their lives in the United States, Pasquel focused on lesser-known players like pitchers Max Lanier of the Cardinals, Alex Carrasquel of the White Sox, and Harry Feldman of the Giants. Eyebrows were raised when All-Star shortstop Vern Stephens agreed to play in Mexico, along with another All-Star, catcher Mickey Owen of Brooklyn. Owen would reportedly receive a salary of $15,000 with a signing bonus of $12,500 and a rent-free apartment. Pasquel let the ballplayers know he had deposited $500,000 in an American bank, available to any ballplayers who wanted to sign. Another big move happened when Pasquel signed Giants pitcher Sal Maglie. Though he had appeared only briefly for New York, Maglie had the makings of an outstanding Major League pitcher.

With the huge sums of money available, a great many Major League ballplayers were interested in finding out about playing in Mexico. The contracts offered were generally double what they were currently earning, and the deals extended as long as three years, eliminating the need to negotiate each winter with tight-fisted owners who rarely paid fair market value.

The biggest anxieties about jumping leagues were the language barrier and living in an unfamiliar country. Many of the American ballplayers had families they would want to bring along with them. During road trips the families would have to fend for themselves in cities where they did not understand the customs or way of life. Each player had to carefully weigh the good versus bad prior to deciding. It proved to be quite a dilemma. Many of the players wrote letters to their wives and families, seeking their input before making a life-changing decision.

To compound matters, Commissioner Chandler announced that any ballplayer who jumped his contract to play in Mexico would be subject to an immediate five-year suspension. Chandler left a window open by offering amnesty to any player who returned from Mexico before the regular season began. Vern Stephens hustled back to the States and was allowed to rejoin the St. Louis Browns without penalty. The rest of the defectors, somewhere between eighteen and twenty-seven players, stayed in Mexico, hoping to make the best of it.

Pasquel was not finished by any means, trying to pry away Washington's Stan Spence, Roger Wolff, and Gil Torres. Though he failed, Major League owners were looking over their shoulders, fearing Pasquel was right behind. So much for peace and harmony in 1946.

On the local front, the broadcasting of Indians games was presenting some difficulties. The team had several sponsors lined up, but the

Cleveland stations grumbled about inconsistent starting times through the season. Some games started at 2:00, some at 3:00, and there were twilight doubleheaders and night games. The stations had their regular moneymaking programs and did not want to jumble their schedules to handle the different game times. There were signs of progress, but nothing definite with the regular season approaching.

As the end of March approached, the Indians worked on trimming their roster. Ken Keltner signed his contract and reported to camp, leading to Bob Lemon being switched to center field. After visiting Clearwater to take in the sun and observe how the team was shaping up, Alva Bradley told the papers, "We will have a hustling, harmonious team including one of the best crops of rookies the Indians have had in years." Bradley was referring to the promising trio of Lemon, Lollar, and Woodling.

Tickets for the April 20 home opener went on sale at two locations, League Park and Richmond Brothers Clothing Store downtown. Jack Graney, still off the air and serving as Indians publicity director, reported heavier than usual demand for seats. He predicted that crowds for the first two home games might be the highest seen since before the war. There seemed to be electricity in the air about baseball, as people looked forward to sitting in the stands with a hot dog and a cold beer and worrying about nothing for the next two hours other than how their team fared.

Cleveland broke camp on April 3, taking two days off before embarking on their reestablished barnstorming tour with the New York Giants. The trip was shortened to nine games, with two stops in Jacksonville, Florida, one in Hickory, North Carolina, four different cities in Virginia, then home to Cleveland and League Park for the final two games.

About the same time, one hundred former servicemen were given their release by various teams. The league announced that each of them would receive salaries for the next twelve weeks regardless of where they wound up. It was an admirable gesture toward these men who were eager to latch on to a minor league team; if they did not, they would have to go job hunting with the rest of the population. The ball clubs, pared down to workable roster numbers, started looking ahead to opening day.

On April 9, the Indians and Giants played to a twelve-inning 3–3 tie in Danville, Virginia. A sold-out crowd of 5,500 was on hand to see last year's star Steve Gromek pitch all twelve innings. The two clubs were drawing big numbers at every stop. Boudreau and Feller appeared to be in great shape, ready to start the season at 100 percent.

While the Indians traveled around Virginia, the U.S. State Department chided the Major Leagues for not attempting to find some middle ground with the Mexican League and help alleviate tensions between the two countries. "Baseball is making it tough on us," a department official told the papers. "We try to build up good will and this sort of thing tears it down."

Happy Chandler, a veteran of Washington politics, fired back. "The state department has enough to do without meddling in baseball," he said, adding that he had had no communication with Pasquel or the Mexican League and would not initiate it. He did not officially recognize them, and any overtures would have to be made by Pasquel or a representative. Meanwhile, the American and National League owners were taking the situation seriously, talking about scheduling a meeting in Chicago to figure out ways to stop the poaching.

It seemed the only people with their minds totally on baseball were the fans and the guys wearing the uniforms. On Sunday, April 14, in front of 9,700 noisy spectators, the Indians played the Giants at League Park to wrap up the exhibition season. Boudreau announced his starting lineup for the season opener in Chicago. Lou would be the only returning name from a year ago.

Case lf
Lemon cf
Edwards rf
Fleming 1b
Keltner 3b
Boudreau ss
Hayes c
Mack 2b
Feller p

The lineup featured mostly experienced players, with the exception of Bob Lemon. The speedy Case looked like the ideal leadoff man, while the middle of the order had proven contact hitters who could drive in runs. Catching was in solid shape with Frank Hayes, and the starting pitcher had won a few games in his career. On paper, the Indians looked like a competitive team, one that could stay in ballgames and usually have a chance to win. The bench looked strong with Jim Hegan, Pat Seerey, Eddie Robinson, and others waiting for their chance.

As one would expect on April 16 in Chicago, the temperature struggled to reach thirty-nine degrees, while a chilly wind enveloped the field. The conditions did not bother Feller. Through five scoreless innings, he matched pitches with thirty-six-year-old Bill Dietrich. In the top of the sixth, George Case drew a base on balls, went to second on Bob Lemon's sacrifice, and came around to score on Hank Edwards's base hit. The score was still 1–0 in the bottom of the ninth. Chicago's Bob Kennedy was on second base with one out, ready to dash for home on a base hit. The next batter, Wally Moses, hit a weak pop fly into shallow center field. Bob Lemon came racing in, dived at the last second, and caught the ball. In one motion he got to his feet and rifled the ball to second base, doubling off Kennedy, who had strayed too far. The outstanding play saved the game for the Indians and gave Feller a thrilling 1–0 win. The White Sox hitters managed only three singles while going down on strikes ten times. Dietrich was almost as good, striking out nine and surrendering six hits. One game does not make a season, but the Indians were off to an encouraging start.

The attendance for the eight openers came to 236,000, the highest total since 1931. Many of the ex-soldiers had fine performances, including home runs from Hank Greenberg, Ted Williams, and Joe DiMaggio. Billy Herman, playing for Brooklyn, had four hits to round off a triumphant day for Major League Baseball.

The next day the Indians made it two in a row, rolling over the White Sox behind the five-hit pitching of Allie Reynolds. Ken Keltner powered the attack with a double and two home runs, knocking in four in the 7–1 win. Reynolds had two hits and two RBIs while outpitching Johnny Rigney, another of the returning war veterans.

The opening of the baseball season was just the right thing for Americans still shaking off the effects of the long world war. They could buy a newspaper and read game highlights on the first page again, rather than gruesome war stories to make them shiver. On April 17, among the latest baseball news was a mention of a curious new organization, the American Baseball Guild.

The man behind the proposed player's union was Robert Murphy, a thirty-five-year-old graduate of Harvard Law School. Though not a practicing attorney, Murphy had worked for several years as an examiner for the National Labor Relations Board. Intent upon organizing Major League players into a viable union, Murphy registered the ABG in Suffolk County in Massachusetts.

Murphy was not the first person to attempt a union for ballplayers. In 1890, the Brotherhood, led by John Montgomery Ward, formed a players' league to compete against the players still left in the National League and American Association. The attempt to rebel against the owners failed due to underfunding and the reluctance of the Brotherhood's team owners to continue the fight after one season. Ten years later the Players' Protective Organization was established with Chief Zimmer, the former Cleveland Spiders catcher, as president. Zimmer made some initial progress but resigned in 1901, and the organization soon disappeared.

The Players' Fraternity, the most successful of the unions, was formed in 1912 under the leadership of former Major League outfielder and attorney Dave Fultz. The union had the support of many ballplayers, including prominent stars like Ty Cobb and Christy Mathewson. After winning some initial concessions, Fultz called for a general strike before the 1917 season. At the outset the players were behind him, but as spring training approached they gradually defected, leaving no alternative for Fultz but to call it off. The Fraternity collapsed shortly thereafter.

Murphy's American Baseball Guild had a number of demands to present to the owners, most of them quite reasonable by today's standards. The one issue that elicited a high degree of support concerned establishing a minimum wage for all players. Murphy suggested a figure of $7,500 but was willing to negotiate something less. Another demand the players favored involved a percentage of a player's sale price being given to the player. This had been a dispute for decades.

Another important request involved salary negotiations. The ABG suggested that players be allowed representation when negotiating new contracts. If no salary agreement could be reached, the player should have the right to an arbitrator to settle the impasse. Other points included establishing a uniform bonus plan both owner and player could refer to.

Robert Murphy's plans for the ABG were not radical, nor did they threaten the existence of baseball. Predictably, however, the owners were negative about the entire idea. Alva Bradley cautioned that a union would cause a standardization of salaries, to the detriment of the players. "Who is this guy Murphy and where does he get the authority to start such a thing?" blustered Washington owner Clark Griffith. He insisted a union would wreck baseball and destroy the reserve clause, "the foundation on which the game stands." The reserve clause had given the owners tremendous power over the players for the past sixty-five years. It stated that club owners had the right to sign a certain number of their players to yearly contracts for as long as needed. The ballplayers had no say in the matter; they could either sign or stay home.

At no time did Murphy directly threaten to destroy the reserve clause or wreck the "foundation of baseball." He stressed that the ABG officers would all be current or retired ballplayers, while his role was only an administrative one. The *Sporting News* sided strongly with the owners, expending a large amount of ink denouncing Murphy and the ABG. Their writers sarcastically asked rhetorical questions like, Will all outfielders have to be paid the same? and, What about left-handers?

The Indians came back home on Thursday, April 18, not commenting on the ABG but ready to open the home part of the schedule. Advance ticket sales had reached 50,000, showing that the Cleveland fans had already bought into this year's version of the Indians and were gearing up to support a winner. Projections for the two weekend games went as high as 100,000 depending on the weather.

After an excruciating wait, baseball arrived on Saturday at Municipal Stadium. The temperature was officially fifty-two degrees, but heavy winds off Lake Erie made it feel much colder, and fans arrived sporting heavy coats and earmuffs and carrying blankets. Stadium vendors did a thriving business, selling the 42,775 brave souls at the stadium 500 gallons of coffee and a staggering 5,000 pounds of hot dogs. Sales of ice cream, beer, and soda pop were negligible.

Over the winter months and early spring, the city had done a makeover of Municipal Stadium, applying fresh paint to all the seats, the scoreboard, and the steel framework and cleaning up and painting of all the bathrooms in the concourse. Emil Bossard and the grounds crew had worked for weeks getting the infield and outfield in prime shape to play ball.

Before the game, Cy Young was on the mound to hand the baseball to the city law director, who subbed for Mayor Burke in throwing out the first pitch. Asked about the openers he had pitched, the seventy-nine-year-old said there had been so many he could not remember. He did mention his first game with the Cleveland Spiders in August of 1890 and the joy of stopping the Chicago White Stockings on three hits.

Moments later the Indians took the field in new home uniforms with "Cleveland" across their chests in script. The caps were blue with the bright red brims and button, complemented by red stripes on their stirrup socks. Steve Gromek had the honor of pitching the first game on the lakefront, opposing Detroit's Hal Newhouser. The early innings belonged to the pitchers, with the Tigers leading 1–0 after four. In the top of the sixth, the Tigers blew the game open with four runs, led by Dick Wakefield's two-run triple. Gromek lasted until the seventh before being replaced by Don Black in his first appearance as an Indian. The Tigers greeted Black with two more runs on their way to a 7–0 thrashing. The Indians were helpless against Newhouser, who struck out seven and allowed only two singles.

The next day the Indians tried to even the series with Bob Feller pitching against Frank Overmire. The score was 1–1 heading into the seventh. The Tigers scored in the top half and the Indians answered, and the game went to extra innings at two runs apiece. In the top of the tenth, Eddie Lake walked, Feller's fifth base on balls of the afternoon, and Eddie Mayo dropped a double on the left field line to score Lake with the go-ahead run. Virgil Trucks, pitching in relief, retired the Indians in the bottom of the inning for the Tigers' second win of the afternoon. Despite another quality start, striking out ten batters, Feller took the loss.

The team arrived in New York at the end of April at a game below .500. Their inconsistent hitting and pitching did not bode well for a first-division finish. On Tuesday, April 30, Bob Feller was on the mound facing the Yankees' Floyd "Bill" Bevens. In the bottom of the first, a line shot by George Stirnweiss deflected off Feller's glove and rolled to the left of second base. Lou Boudreau came across the infield in full stride, picked up the ball, and fired to first just ahead of the runner. With Feller having all his pitches working, that was the only thing close to a hit until the eighth inning, when Phil Rizzuto shot a line drive to the left of Ken Keltner. Once again Boudreau made a terrific stop, backhanding the ball on one hop and zipping the ball to first in time to get the speeding Rizzuto. The Yankee fans were astonished at the play, believing their shortstop had broken up Feller's no-hitter.

Bevens held the Indians scoreless, if not hitless, until the top of the ninth, when Frank Hayes sent a pitch deep into the left field seats for a 1–0 lead. In the bottom of the inning, Stirnweiss reached on an error by Hayes and was sacrificed to second by Tommy Henrich. Feller retired Joe DiMaggio on a grounder that advanced Stirnweiss to third, leaving Charlie Keller as the Yankees' last hope. The fans stood as Keller shot a ground ball directly at Ray Mack. The second baseman made the pickup but slipped and fell to the ground. He quickly righted himself and flipped the ball to first for the last out. It had taken 133 pitches, but Bob Feller had his second no-hitter, tying Addie Joss for the Cleveland record. It was the first no-hitter at home against the Yankees since Cleveland's Ray Caldwell threw one in September of 1919.

The New York fans gave Feller a tremendous ovation, with several thousand pouring onto the field trying to shake his hand. Later several more thousand would stand outside the Indians' clubhouse entrance waiting for him to step outside. In the clubhouse, a jubilant Feller visited with reporters. New York writers had been saying he was not looking good and did not resemble the pitcher from before the war. With a broad smile, he told them, "Well I guess that proves I'm all washed up. Soon as I leave here I'm headed to the nearest hospital."

The next day Feller was bombarded with telephone calls to his hotel room. Overwhelmed, he eventually asked the hotel operator to stop all calls at the desk. Since his return from the navy, Feller had enjoyed some moments of privacy, but the no-hitter had vaulted him back to the center of the baseball world. From here out he would rarely have any time for himself, constantly sought after by the media and baseball fans throughout the country.

On Saturday the Indians were in Boston, where Feller made his first start since the no-hitter. The 30,713 Red Sox fans at Fenway Park set a record for Saturday attendance in Boston. This time Feller was hit hard. He scraped by until the sixth inning, when Ted Williams launched a two-run homer into the Indians bullpen. Before getting the hook, he allowed ten hits and five walks while striking out nine in a 6–2 loss. For the Red Sox, Jim Bagby, in his first game against his old team, went the distance for the win.

The Indians had entirely fallen apart after the no-hitter. This was their fourth consecutive loss in a streak that would reach seven and drop them to seventh place. The team was desperately trying to find any type of rhythm. The Jeff Heath–George Case trade had left the Indians without a consistent power-hitting outfielder, as Hank Edwards, Les Fleming, Pat Seerey, and Case were not able to pick up the slack.

Trying to lighten the mood a little, the *Plain Dealer*'s Jim Doyle published one of his famous rhymes:

> I have a hunch that Robert Feller,
> Will keep our club out of the cellar.

Feller's pitching was indeed keeping the Indians out of last place. He ended the losing streak by beating the Athletics 5–2, striking out eleven batters, followed that up by going ten innings with twelve strike-outs to beat the Browns 4–3, then pitching a sparkling 3–0 shutout over Washington. He struck out fourteen Senators to give himself a total of eighty-five K's in just seventy-one innings. With Reynolds and Gromek off to slow starts, only Feller stood out among Indians pitchers.

Feller's shutout of the Senators was the first game of a doubleheader. The Indians lost the second game 9–4. The last six innings were pitched by opening day center fielder Bob Lemon.

Robert Lemon was born on September 22, 1920, in San Bernardino, California. His father, Earl, was a shortstop who had worked his way up to the Pacific Coast League before calling it quits. When Bob was a boy, his dad moved the family to Long Beach, where Earl opened up Pop Lemon's Filling Station. Bob became friends with Vern Stephens when the two future American Leaguers were on a sandlot team managed by Vern's father. The next year Bob starred in American Legion baseball, attracting attention throughout the area.

A modest and friendly person, Bob attended Wilson High School in Long Beach, playing several positions on the baseball team, including pitcher. In 1938, his senior year, he was named Southern California's high school player of the year. Scouts congregated at the Lemon home until Bob chose to sign with the Indians for $100 monthly. He was sent to Springfield to play Class C ball, then quickly moved to Oswego of the Canadian-American League, where he hit .312. Primarily a third baseman, Lemon advanced in 1939 to New Orleans, in 1940 to Wilkes-Barre, where he played for two years, then in 1942 to Baltimore. With the Orioles he batted only .268 but clouted 21 home runs and drove in 80 runs.

In September of 1942, Bob reported to a navy base in San Diego, and later was shipped to the Hawaiian Islands for the duration of the war. There he pitched for a team coached by Yankee great Bill Dickey. Lemon would later remark how surprised he was when he was able to get Major Leaguers out. His discharge in November of 1945 freed him to return to Long Beach and assist his father in running the filling station. In late February, he joined the Indians in Clearwater, intent on winning the third base job.

Ken Keltner's return ended that experiment, and a .180 batting average in center field pushed him to a seat on the bench. Boudreau was unsure what to do, but several conversations with Bill Dickey and other ex-navy men convinced Lou to try Lemon as a relief pitcher. Bob had a good fastball, not overpowering but having a natural sink to it. Along with a good curveball, it made him an intriguing prospect.

Lemon made his pitching debut May 12 against the St. Louis Browns. It was strictly mop-up time, as the Indians were already down by seven runs when he entered the game. Lemon went three innings, allowing one run and fanning three. On May 17, at home against Washington and trailing 8–2 in the fourth inning, Boudreau called on Lemon, who went six strong innings to finish up, allowing only one run and six hits and striking out six. He also walked seven men, but in two relief stints he had shown that he had enough quality stuff to get people out. The club needed help with starting pitching, the bullpen was not doing a first-rate job, and there was an opportunity for a pitcher with a lively young arm.

While the Indians played the Senators, terrible news came from Baltimore. Eddie Robinson's two-year-old daughter, Robbie Anne, had died from an inoperable brain tumor. She had remained unconscious for over a month until passing away at Johns Hopkins Hospital. Robinson had left the Indians in mid-April to be with his wife and daughter, temporarily putting his baseball career on hold. The Indians assigned Robinson's contract to the Orioles to give him as much time as needed at home. For the short term, at least, Les Fleming had the first base job.

On Sunday the Yankees came to town for a doubleheader. The New Yorkers had chartered a United Airlines plane for the short flight from Chicago instead of the usual train ride. The Yankees front office wanted to give their players plenty of time to rest for Sunday. Major League Baseball was not seriously looking at air travel for road trips, but from time to time teams would take advantage of the reduced travel time. The airplane may have cost the Yankees more money, but their players thanked them for it.

The first game matched Allie Reynolds against Spud Chandler, who already sported a record of 5–1. Reynolds had struggled through April and early May, but today he looked like the pitcher of 1945, battling Chandler through eight scoreless innings. He was on first base in the bottom of the eighth when George Case hit a ground ball to the pitcher. As Joe Gordon took the throw at second and threw to first for the double play, Reynolds slid hard into him. Gordon reacted by jumping onto Reynolds and throwing several punches. The two wrestled on the ground while both benches emptied. Their teammates separated the players, but the home crowd of 57,310 stood and shouted approval when a stirred-up Reynolds broke free and charged after Gordon. The umpires stopped him from further damage, and play resumed with neither fighter, surprisingly, getting tossed from the field. The Yankees plated two runs in the next inning to win 2–0, and won game two 7–1. The Indians managed to win on Monday behind Steve Gromek, then evened the series on Tuesday as Bob Feller won his sixth decision.

The homestand ended with two games against Boston. As the Red Sox arrived in town, news circulated of a national rail strike that would likely cease all train traffic indefinitely. Despite President Harry Truman's best efforts, several hundred thousand workers went off the job. Alva Bradley tried to charter a United Airlines flight to St. Louis for the next game, but at the last minute the government announced that all air traffic would be prioritized for vital shipments of mail, food, and other necessities. Teams were essentially banned from flying, leaving them to find their own means of transportation.

The Tigers organized an automobile caravan to drive the 272 miles to Chicago. But it was twice as far from Cleveland to St. Louis, so the Indians chose to rent a bus and have the players endure the long, uncomfortable ride to Missouri. No dining cars and sleeper berths here. The lengthy ride must have unearthed some old memories the players had from their days as minor leaguers. One-hundred- to two-hundred-mile late-night trips were the norm back then rather than the exception. The bus pulled out of Cleveland on Friday, May 24, at 3:00 p.m. and arrived at the hotel in St. Louis late Saturday morning. In a sporting gesture, the Browns changed the afternoon contest to a night game to let the Indians players stretch their legs and clear their lungs.

Betting men who put their money on the Browns beating a thoroughly worn-out Indians team would have been surprised when Allie Reynolds pitched his finest game of the year, fanning nine while shutting out the Browns 1–0. The lone run came in the top of the sixth inning when Pat Seerey hit one of his trademark blasts deep into the left field seats. Fortunately for baseball and the country as a whole, the rail strike was resolved swiftly.

While the club was on the road, several newspapers reported that Bill Veeck, the former owner of the Milwaukee Brewers, had made a bid to acquire the Indians for 1.4 million dollars. Reportedly he had two partners, one being Louis Jacobs, who owned a slew of concessions at minor league parks and several in the Major Leagues. Alva Bradley emphatically denied the rumors, claiming he had not talked to Veeck in years and did not know Mr. Jacobs. Veeck also claimed the talk was false, stating, "I was supposed to be buying the Pittsburgh Pirates. Tomorrow they may have me buying the Philadelphia Phillies. In the first place where could I get any part of that kind of money?"

The denials seemed genuine, but where did the story come from? Bradley had given no impression at any time that he wanted to retire from baseball, and there was no evident reason for his wanting to sell, especially with Feller back and attendance off to a fast start. Possibly his stockholders, many of them the heirs, widows, and attorneys of the original investors, had raised the subject. Or Veeck himself may have been the source of the rumors. In January, he had sold his Milwaukee franchise, which he held for several years, leaving him with little to do. A man with an unusually high energy level, he had spent most of his life in baseball, working with the Chicago Cubs before buying the Brewers. At thirty-two he was much too young to retire.

About the same time, the Cleveland papers reported that Al Sutphin, the owner of the American Hockey League Cleveland Barons and the Cleveland Arena, was considering building a combined baseball-football stadium. The proposed facility would be located adjacent to his property on Euclid Avenue and 40th Street. Sutphin planned to approach the nearby college and Catholic high schools to gauge interest in his ambitious plan, and he explained that he only meant to rent the stadium to the Indians and Browns, not to buy either of those franchises.

Sutphin's plan had some merit to it. League Park needed a major overhaul, and Municipal Stadium was thought to be too large for baseball. A new stadium with reasonable seating and closer to the east side suburbs might have a chance of drawing all the sports there. Certainly the colleges and high schools would be more comfortable playing in a 40,000-seat venue rather than the 79,000 seats available downtown. And Alva Bradley, who was shuttling the Indians between League Park and the stadium, might be induced to scrap League Park and move to the new facility for all home games. All of this was up to Al Sutphin and how willing he was to risk huge sums of money on the venture.

Bob Feller started the first game of the Memorial Day doubleheader against the White Sox. After a moment of silence for those lost during the war, he set down the Chicago hitters in the first. The Indians scored a run in the bottom of the inning, and in the second Frank Hayes clubbed a two-run homer. Feller had all the support he needed, as he fanned six batters, giving him 104 for the season, in tossing another shutout, 3–0. With four months still to play, Feller had an even-money chance to join the exclusive 300-strikeout club. In the second game, the Indians failed to use the momentum Feller had given them, losing 4–0.

Major League Baseball enjoyed another grand attendance day, drawing 276,599 for an average of 34,575 at each of the eight parks. The Yankees led the way, with 60,851 fans watching them easily sweep their doubleheader against the Athletics. In the National League, the Cubs-Reds game at Wrigley Field attracted 45,120 spectators to see the two teams split a twin bill. Money in the coffers was a welcome sight for the owners, who had struggled to keep the lights on during the war years.

On June 3, the Indians were in Philadelphia to play a doubleheader with the A's. They won the first game 6–5, but the fans' and reporters' attention was on the second game and Bob Lemon's first Major League start. After the A's touched him for a run in the first inning, Lemon steadied himself, not allowing another run for the next two innings. But in the bottom of the fourth Philadelphia scored twice more, prompting Boudreau to pull his starter in favor of Don Black. The A's held on to win 3–2. In three and two-thirds innings, Lemon gave up four hits and four bases on balls in addition to the three runs, two of them earned. It was not spectacular, but he had shown enough to earn at least a few more.

The next evening at Washington, Feller came out blazing, striking out the first two Senators he faced before Stan Spence got ahold of a fastball and launched it into the seats for an early 1–0 lead. In the top of the third Feller singled, moved to second on a sacrifice, and scored on Les Fleming's base hit. Later that same inning, with two runners on, Pat Seerey homered to increase the lead to 4–1. The Indians broke the game open in the top of the eighth when Frank Hayes doubled with the bases full for a 9–1 margin. Feller posted fourteen strikeouts and only one walk in a lopsided 10–2 win.

Jorge Pasquel and the Mexican League made the news again in June when they poached several more players from the Majors, this time from the St. Louis Cardinals. Pasquel was crisscrossing the baseball cities and flashing dollar signs to any player willing to listen. The Mexican League continued to be worrisome for the owners, but players were not defecting in large numbers. The idea of leaving the country and Commissioner

Chandler's threat of a long-term suspension were effective deterrents for most players.

More concerning for the owners was the American Baseball Guild. The papers reported that the Pittsburgh Pirates were considering a strike vote as early as June 5, before their home game with Brooklyn. The Major Leagues were refusing to meet with Murphy or allow him to visit most of the clubhouses, and he had chosen the Pirates as his test case due to the strong union presence in Pittsburgh.

The Pirates players opted to hold off on the vote until Murphy met with Pirates owner William Benswanger, who initially refused but finally agreed to talk on Friday, June 7. In the meantime, Murphy addressed a meeting of the Steel City Industrial Union Council in Pittsburgh, which boasted a membership of 200,000 workers. Anthony Federoff, the regional director of the Congress of Industrial Workers, supported the ABG, warning, "No red-blooded American man or woman carrying a union card will go to a ballgame while there is a strike of the players."

The meeting took place before the Friday night game with the New York Giants. Details were not released, but word filtered out that it was hardly a friendly get-together. Murphy left the meeting with nothing accomplished, giving the players the motivation for a strike vote. A strike would require a three-quarters majority. Leaving batting and fielding practice unattended, the players discussed the pros and cons behind the closed doors of the Pirates' clubhouse.

The baseball community nervously waited for the result. A strike vote would turn the game upside down, demonstrating to the owners that the players in Pittsburgh were behind the ABG and building the framework for additional strikes and calls for equitable relations. The owners were hoping the players would not have the nerve to finally call out the men in charge.

After what seemed an eternity, the doors opened and the players walked towards the field. Though many voted to strike, they did not reach the three-quarters majority, ending the controversy for the moment. Robert Murphy, understandably let down, told reporters, "The fight to organize baseball has hardly begun. All baseball players recognize the necessity to have a representative to deal with club owners so that they have some say in overturning the one-sided picture in baseball." Murphy was subtly referring to the reserve clause, the thorny issue that had frustrated Major League players for an eternity. The ABG had suffered a critical blow, but was not ready to give up the fight.

Les Fleming, ca. 1942. Brought in to replace Hal Trosky, Fleming had a good season in 1942 but left the team for a war job. He did not return until 1945. *Author's collection.*

The Army-Navy All-Stars at Cleveland Municipal Stadium, July 1942.
Bruce Milla Collection.

Allie Reynolds, 1942. In 1943, Allie led the American League in strikeouts with 151. Traded to the Yankees in 1946 for Joe Gordon, he became a five-time All-Star and threw two no-hitters in one season. *Author's collection.*

Women working at Goodyear aircraft plant, 1942. Two women install rivets on an airplane wing. Goodyear and many other northeast Ohio plants employed thousands of women during the war. *Cleveland Press Collection–Michael Schwartz Library, Cleveland State University.*

Mel Harder, May 1944. Mel is congratulated by Lou Boudreau for winning his two hundredth game. One of Cleveland's greatest pitchers, he would retire in 1948 and become the Indians' first pitching coach. *Author's collection.*

Lou Boudreau, ca. 1944. Player-manager Lou Boudreau is flanked by coaches Del Baker and Burt Shotten. Lou, one of the best shortstops in the game, led the Indians to the world championship in 1948. *Bruce Milla collection.*

Pat Seerey, ca. 1945. "The People's Choice" Seerey was a crowd favorite, either slamming a long home run or striking out. In 1948, Cleveland traded him to Chicago, where he hit four home runs in one game. *Author's collection.*

Jeff Heath, Steve Gromek, and Pat Seerey, July 1945. The Indians pounded the Yankees 16–4, with Jeff Heath belting two home runs and Pat Seerey three, with eight RBIs. Steve Gromek had four hits and was the winning pitcher.
Author's collection.

Bob Feller, navy discharge, August 1945. Feller prepares to leave the navy and rejoin the Indians. A day later he beat the Tigers 4–2, pitching nine strong innings.
Cleveland Press Collection–Michael Schwartz Library, Cleveland State University.

Dale Mitchell, ca. 1947. A left-handed hitter, Mitchell had a career batting average over .300. In 1948, he had a lifetime best of .336 and 204 hits in helping the Indians to the pennant. *Author's collection.*

Bill Veeck and Hank Greenberg, March 1948. Greenberg joined the Indians as a vice president only, despite Veeck wanting him to continue as a player. Veeck would sell the club in 1949, but Greenberg stayed on, becoming general manager through most of the 1950s. *Cleveland Press Collection–Michael Schwartz Library, Cleveland State University.*

Larry Doby and Satchel Paige, July 1948. Doby and Paige receive portable radios from a local store in Washington, DC. Doby was already having an excellent season, while Paige pitched brilliantly down the stretch. *Cleveland Press Collection–Michael Schwartz Library, Cleveland State University.*

Jim Hegan, July 1948. Hegan (second from right) celebrates with teammates after hitting a grand slam to beat New York, 12–8. From left, Ken Keltner, Joe Gordon, Hegan, and Walt Judnich. *Author's collection.*

Russ Christopher, 1948. Notice the thin frame on the 6'3" pitcher. Christopher had serious heart issues that cost him his life at age thirty-seven. Nevertheless, he pitched effectively, recording seventeen saves in 1948. *Author's Collection.*

Don Black, September 14, 1948. Black is being helped off the field by trainer Lefty Weisman and Bob Lemon. Seconds later he collapsed in front of the dugout with a cerebral hemorrhage. Black recovered but had to retire from baseball. Jim Hegan is at left. *Author's collection.*

Eddie Robinson, October 1948. Despite having a good season and World Series, Robinson was abruptly traded before the start of the 1949 season. He went on to be a four-time All-Star and one of the better first basemen in the American League. *Author's collection.*

Bob Lemon, ca. 1948. Lemon became the backbone of the Indians pitching staff, winning twenty games during the 1948 season and two more in the World Series. Lemon would win 207 games and have seven twenty-win seasons on his way to the Hall of Fame. *Bruce Milla collection.*

Clubhouse scene after playoff win over Boston, October 4, 1948. The Indians celebrate the 8–3 victory and the opportunity to face the Boston Braves in the 1948 World Series. Ken Keltner can be seen (second from left), as well as coaches Mel Harder and Bill McKechnie (center, arms around each other) and Dale Mitchell (second from right, in front of mirror). *Bruce Milla collection.*

Crowd at World Series game five, October 10, 1948. A record crowd of 86,288
packed Cleveland Municipal Stadium for game five. The Indians lost 11–5
in what turned out to be Bob Feller's last chance to win a World Series game.
Author's collection.

1948 World Series champs. Portrait of the Cleveland Indians following their championship season. In the photo are six Hall of Famers: Bob Feller, Bob Lemon, Satchel Paige, Larry Doby, Lou Boudreau, and Joe Gordon. *Author's collection.*

Chapter 9

A CHANGE AT THE TOP

June began with a thirteen-game eastern road trip for the Indians, who managed to lose eight times while winning only five. In spite of the team's losing ways, Bob Feller continued his mastery over the American League hitters, piling up the wins and strikeouts. In Boston he beat the Red Sox 7–2, fanning ten and not walking a single batter. Pat Seerey hit a two-run homer in the first, followed by a second-inning solo blast from Ken Keltner. The Red Sox were scoreless until the top of the sixth, when Ted Williams hit his fourteenth home run of the year with no one on base. Old friend Jim Bagby started for Boston, lasting until the fourth inning before being removed.

On the trip, Bob Lemon picked up his first Major League win against New York. Lemon entered the game in the sixth inning in relief of starter Don Black and blanked the Yanks for an inning and two-thirds before Boudreau went to Tom Ferrick to finish the 9–5 victory. It was a happy moment for Lemon, who had made the transition from third base to center field to the pitcher's mound in a matter of three months. The Indians returned home with a mark of 22–31, staying out of the cellar (as Jim Doyle had written) because of Bob Feller.

During the homestand that followed, the front-page news had it that American League president Will Harridge believed the Indians were about to be sold. He named Bill Veeck and partner Harry Grabiner, who had recently retired from the Chicago White Sox after a forty-year career there.

Grabiner started work under Charles Comiskey as a scorecard vendor, moving up the ladder to secretary and later vice president. He was in the front office when the Black Sox World Series scandal broke. But despite the scandal, his many years of experience in running a baseball team appealed to Veeck, who needed a partner and friend he could lean on for advice.

Starting on June 19, the newspapers published many details of Veeck's life, including his years working in the Chicago Cubs front office and his 1941 purchase of the Milwaukee Brewers of the American Association. Veeck, at the young age of twenty-seven, began building a miserable last-place team into a winning franchise. He gained considerable notoriety by staging wild promotional nights where he gave away an assortment of oddities, including codfish, white mice, blocks of ice, a duck, and a basket of peaches. The recipient of the peaches went home and baked a two-pound pie, which she delivered to the Brewers' offices the next morning. The promotions won the heart of the Milwaukee fans and significantly increased attendance. In the middle of his efforts he left baseball for the military, enlisting in 1943 as a marine with the intent of seeing combat.

While he was serving as an antiaircraft gunner in the South Pacific, a heavy machine gun broke loose and fell on top of him, crushing his right ankle. After a long convalescence, he received his discharge and returned to guiding the Brewers. Always short on cash, Veeck each year routinely sold players to the Major Leagues for up to $75,000, using the money to finance his organization. With his experience in the Chicago Cubs front office, Veeck built the team into a pennant winner three consecutive seasons while breaking attendance records. The papers reported that Veeck had raised about $700,000, roughly half of the Indians' listed sale price.

Alva Bradley claimed all these reports were false, as did the team's largest shareholders, John Sherwin Jr. and his brother Francis. When Bradley's group first acquired the Indians, John Sherwin Sr., one of Cleveland's most prominent bankers, went in with Bradley to raise about half the purchase price between them. Sherwin remained the largest shareholder up until the time of his death, when his investment in the team passed to his widow and two sons. The family had no interest in baseball, staying on the sidelines along with the other shareholders and letting Bradley, a minority owner, run the team with little input. In all the rumors there was no mention or even speculation that Bradley and Veeck had spoken to each other. If the rumors had any truth in them, it seemed that Veeck was trying to woo the other shareholders behind Bradley's back. That would mean gaining the support of the Sherwin family. Once they agreed, the other shareholders would likely fall in line and yield their shares.

In his autobiography, *Veeck—as in Wreck*, Veeck claimed to have quietly traveled to Cleveland and registered at the Hotel Cleveland under an assumed name. After canvassing the city, talking to as many people as possible about the state of the Indians, he became convinced the franchise was viable and sought out the Sherwin family to determine their interest in a sale. Apparently they were quickly on board. After several days, Veeck let it be known that he was staying at the Hotel Cleveland, ready and willing to talk with reporters. He admitted he was looking at buying the Indians for an extended time, preferring to acquire the team before the June 15 trading deadline since wholesale changes would be more difficult afterwards. He told reporters, "It wouldn't be truthful to say I hadn't studied the Indians roster before I made a bid for the club. The Indians have the best pitcher in Bob Feller, but the team will have to be bolstered in other departments."

For the acquisition to happen, the vote of the stockholders would have to be unanimous. Bradley, still unaware of the probable sale, would never consent to it unless he was the only one opposed. The situation was akin to a hostile takeover, though one of the two principals was unaware of the maneuvering. Veeck was ruthless in his plan, forgoing any courtesy that Bradley might have deserved. "All's fair in love and war," the saying goes, and apparently to Veeck that applied to baseball too. Veeck's actions were unethical, to say the least.

To raise the money to buy the Indians, Veeck called on numerous people he was familiar with in the banking industry and elsewhere. His plan was to get a million dollars in bank financing, then beg, borrow, and steal whatever money he could to cover the rest. His own capital was said to be only $200,000, but Veeck found friends willing to put up the rest of the money in exchange for shares in the ball club. One of those keen on buying in was Bob Hope, the world-famous comedian and former Cleveland resident. With a bank loan approved and the cash from his friends, Veeck gathered his assets and made his move.

With Veeck's plans now out in the open, a stunned Alva Bradley called a meeting of his board of directors for Saturday morning, June 22. Bradley had been blindsided, shocked that after nineteen years not a single shareholder warned him what was going to happen. The only option left to him was a final appeal to his fellow shareholders.

There are no known documents to confirm this, but it was believed Bradley owned about 25 percent of the shares. Though not the majority owner, he had run the franchise from the beginning, making the major decisions without pressure from any board members. He had hired and fired the managers and general managers and represented the team at all the winter meetings. Bradley chose the spring training sites and negotiated the Municipal Stadium leases and the radio and advertising contracts. In 1938, he alone pressed the other American League owners to allow him to install lights at the stadium to play night baseball. He was the sole individual responsible for keeping the franchise running.

Perhaps Bradley was out of touch with most of his stockholders and had no inkling they wished to have their shares bought out. He may have been guilty of not communicating and of assuming all was well if he wanted it to be. Bradley was aware that John Sherwin's sons had little interest in the team, but at no time did he approach them about selling their shares to him or lining up a friendly buyer.

The meeting began at 11:00 a.m. at the Union Commerce Building, with attorneys present. Bradley presented a hastily formed plan to allow him to purchase all the outstanding shares of the Cleveland Baseball Club. He asked to be allowed several months to raise the necessary capital. The directors apparently hesitated a bit, but decided to decline his offer. Though Bradley had been the man to run the organization for its entirety, the shareholders chose to accept Veeck's instant cash. Had Bradley come to them sooner the outcome might have been different, but he did not, and money won out over years of loyalty. Bradley was done and Bill Veeck officially owned the Cleveland Indians.

With the ownership came League Park, worth about $150,000. Veeck, a man who always thought big, had little interest in playing games there, preferring to play all the home games at Municipal Stadium. He would have to wait until the 1947 season to make the change, but the proud old ballpark was about to become a relic of the past. Al Sutphin's plans for a new midtown stadium quietly disappeared.

Bradley and his general manager, Roger Peckinpaugh, did not leave Veeck a starving franchise with little talent. Bob Feller was the most talented pitcher in the game, while Lou Boudreau ranked as one of the great shortstops. Ken Keltner was a five-time All-Star at third base and in line for another appearance. Jim Hegan had not yet become the starting catcher but was working his way toward a long stay behind the plate. Pitcher Allie Reynolds already had an eighteen-win season behind him, Bob Lemon was a prized prospect, and the Indians' minor league clubs had high-level talent, including Eddie Robinson, outfielder Dale Mitchell, third baseman Al Rosen, and pitcher Mike Garcia. Veeck would have work to do in shaping his new club into a pennant contender, but he had a solid base to build on.

The change in ownership had no outward effect on the Indians. The night before Veeck took over, they were at home against the Red Sox. Bob Feller, seeking his sixth straight win, was matching pitches with Boston's Tex Hughson. The crowd of 36,676 saw a tremendous pitcher's battle. In the top of the second inning, Bobby Doerr tripled and scored on Rudy York's sacrifice fly. That was all the scoring in the ballgame as Feller lost 1–0.

Alva Bradley was seen at the game the next day, sitting in his customary seat behind the home team dugout. Reporters said he looked shaken, keeping his eyes on the playing field and nowhere else. Bill Veeck arrived a short time later, wearing his usual open-necked shirt without a jacket or tie. He and his party found seats in the vicinity of Bradley while reporters crowded around the new owner, looking for Sunday's headlines. In between cheering for the Indians, Veeck outlined his plans for the immediate future. Ladies Day would be resumed, and the starting time for all afternoon games would be 1:30. He wanted the games back on radio as soon as possible and said he intended to get to know all the players on and off the field.

Veeck wanted to liven things up at the ballpark with various promotions and entertainment to lure families out of their living rooms. Veeck told the reporters, "Baseball has generally been too grim, too serious, it should be fun, and I hope to make it fun for everyone around here." His idea of fun included strolling musicians, clowns, acrobats, and fireworks. Giveaways were his specialty, though he did not go into detail about what bizarre items he planned to give away to the Cleveland fans.

The game itself must have seemed like an afterthought, with the fans more interested in seeing the excited new owner jump up and down and talk to the newspapermen. But with the Indians trailing Boston 3–2 in the bottom of the eighth, Hank Edwards caught the fans' attention when he smacked a two-run homer to give Cleveland the lead and the victory, 4–3. The come-from-behind win ended an incredible day for Veeck, who later claimed he had solved his financing for the sale just before the 11:00 a.m. deadline. Whether or not this was true, it became part of the fast-growing lore surrounding him.

The Cleveland fans knew there were going to be some radical changes taking place but were utterly stunned when the rumor surfaced that Jimmy Dykes was coming to Cleveland to replace Lou Boudreau as manager. Veeck did not deny that Dykes was meeting with him. "You can't say point blank that Boudreau will be the manager for the rest of the year," he said. "Sometimes things happen to make a change in management desirable."

Veeck was a great fan of Boudreau as a player but did not believe he was competent enough as a manager to lead the Indians to a pennant. The new owner had the right to fire employees he believed were underperforming, but he failed to understand how popular Lou was in Cleveland and that he had had the backing of most fans and newspapermen since 1942. Several days later Veeck changed his mind, stating that Boudreau would manage the rest of the year but not committing to anything beyond that. There was already enough upheaval in Cleveland with the new ownership and the 180-degree turn in thinking. To replace Boudreau with a new manager and expect him to play shortstop without a grudge would have been too much. Veeck was apparently savvy enough not to immediately alienate the fan base.

While the Indians lost their next three games, scoring a total of one run, the new front office was busy implementing new directives. Veeck, always a whirlwind of activity, met with several radio stations about getting the home games back on the air. He scheduled a meeting with Mayor Burke about dropping League Park and playing exclusively in 1947 at Municipal Stadium. With phone company reps he drew up plans to install a switchboard and operator at Municipal Stadium so fans could call there directly for tickets. The next day he made his first player transaction, sending Mickey Rocco to Nashville in return for outfielder Heinz Becker, a player he knew from his tenure in Milwaukee. The first Ladies Day of the season would take place on July 3 at League Park.

Veeck proved he knew how to get things done swiftly, securing deals with several radio stations to carry games the rest of the season. Standard Oil once again stepped up to sponsor the broadcasts. Under the somewhat complicated plan, WJW and WGAR would carry road games, re-created in the studio by Jack Graney and Bob Neal. WTAM radio agreed to broadcast live from Municipal Stadium with Tom Manning, the Indians' first-ever announcer, who had been doing their games since 1928. WHK negotiated with Veeck to handle night and weekend broadcasts, along with sister station WXUB, FM radio 107.1. FM (for frequency modulation) was a relatively new medium, able to deliver high-quality sound without static or interference. Retail stores did not stock many FM receivers yet, but would be rapidly expanding their inventory for the expected surge of customers. Less expensive converters were available that could be easily attached to a standard AM receiver.

Working at a frenzied pace, Veeck signed two more veterans, forty-one-year-old pitcher Joe Berry and veteran infielder Jimmy Wasdell. The trading deadline had passed, leaving Veeck with the choice of picking up players via waivers or buying their contracts from minor league clubs. The players he added were stopgap measures, not expected to help much beyond the current season. Once the schedule was played out, Veeck was looking to accomplish a flurry of trades designed to transform the ball club.

The first Ladies Day game in the Bill Veeck era drew nearly 3,400 animated women to League Park. As promised, the game between the Indians and St. Louis Browns started at 1:30, with Bob Feller facing ex-Indian Denny Galehouse. Cleveland scored three runs in the fourth inning, then came back with three more in the sixth to go up 6–0, the big hit a bases-loaded single by Feller. The Browns, like most teams in the American League, could do nothing against the Cleveland fireballer, getting shut out 6–0. Feller struck out 10 batters to raise his eye-popping total to 184 for the year. If he continued at this pace, he now had an excellent chance to top the 300-strikeout mark and threaten the American League record of 343 held by Rube Waddell. (Later, researchers found Waddell's correct total to be 349, but in 1945 the 343 number was considered official.)

Feller already had ambitious plans for the off-season. He lined up a sixteen-game barnstorming tour, with five games in Hawaii and eleven more below the border in Mexico and Venezuela. The current rules allowed for only ten-day trips and permission from Happy Chandler for any extensions. Feller would use airplanes exclusively and play against Satchel Paige and his group of all-stars. Major League players, including Hal Newhouser, Spud Chandler, Charlie Keller, Phil Rizzuto, and Jeff Heath, were mentioned as probable members of Feller's traveling party. Several Cleveland players would help round out the roster.

On July 9, Feller participated in the 1946 All-Star game held at Fenway Park in Boston. Joining him on the American League squad were teammates Ken Keltner and Frank Hayes and many players back for their first full seasons after their time in the military. For the American League those included Ted Williams, Dom and Joe DiMaggio, Bobby Doerr, Johnny Pesky, and Bill Dickey, while the Nationals had Stan Musial, Pee Wee Reese (who was injured), Pete Reiser, and Enos Slaughter.

The afternoon game got off to a rousing start in the bottom half of the first inning when the Yankees' Charlie Keller hit a two-run homer off the Cubs' Claude Passeau. The American League continued to pour it on as Ted Williams came through with four hits, two of them home runs, and five RBIs. Feller started the game and pitched three shutout innings with three strikeouts. He now held the record for most All-Star game strikeouts with twelve. Hal Newhouser and the Browns' Jack Kramer continued the scoreless string as the Americans went on to rout the Nationals 12–0. Members of the winning team each received a $50 bond, while the losers had to settle for diamond-studded cigarette cases with lighters.

After the short break, the Indians opened the second half of the season at New York. Pitching on one day's rest against a well-rested Spud Chandler, Feller surrendered two runs in the first and a two-run homer by Aaron Robinson in the fourth. An inning later the Yankees loaded the bases with one out for Robinson, who connected again. Feller finished the inning, but his night was over. The decision to pitch after just one day off fell on the shoulders of manager Boudreau. Carried away by Feller's astounding season, he may have forgotten that even the best pitchers need rest. In his five innings pitched, Feller allowed eleven hits and nine earned runs, by far his poorest start of the season.

While the Indians were in New York, stories circulated that the Yankees' Joe Gordon and manager Bill Dickey were not seeing eye to eye and the second baseman would be available in a trade in the off-season. Gordon, though named to the All-Star team, was not having a typical season, with his batting average and home run and RBI totals well off previous years. At thirty-one, he seemed to be on the downside of a fine career and no longer in the Yankees' future.

In another surprise move, Indians catcher Frank Hayes was placed on waivers, paving the way for Jim Hegan to claim the starting catcher's job. Hegan's defensive abilities were first-rate, but questions persisted about his ability to hit Major League pitching. With a new regime in place, it seemed logical to see whether Hegan could handle playing every day. Waiving Hayes did leave the Indians thin at catcher, but Veeck was probably conceding that this team would not reach .500 and was more concerned with finding out who could play now and in the future.

After salvaging the final game of the series against the Yankees 3–2 behind Allie Reynolds, the Indians moved on to Boston for three games, starting with a Sunday doubleheader. The 31,508 fans were rewarded with a thrilling afternoon. In game one, the Indians jumped out to a first-inning lead, powered by a Lou Boudreau three-run homer. The Red Sox answered in the third when Ted Williams belted the first of his three home runs for the game, giving him twenty-six for the season. Williams had eight RBIs and four hits to just about win the game himself. Cleveland pitchers Steve Gromek, Don Black, and Joe Berry were hammered unmercifully. Boudreau had a fabulous game himself with five hits, including four doubles to go with the home run, but the Red Sox scored three in the eighth to win 11–10.

In game two, Boudreau had a surprise in store. When Williams came to bat in the third, already having hit a double to help Boston to a 3–0 lead, Boudreau called time, then motioned for left fielder George Case to move to the shortstop position and Keltner to move over to behind second base. Boudreau himself stood about ten feet to Keltner's left, while Jack Conway, the rookie second baseman, backpedaled to short right field, completing the "Boudreau shift." Third base and left field were uncovered. The Boston fans watched the unorthodox moves with curiosity, then broke out laughing. Williams laughed too. He was a lefty who almost exclusively pulled the ball, and Boudreau had had enough of him lining singles and doubles through the right side of the infield and resolved to challenge him to hit the baseball to the opposite field. Though most fans had not seen it before, this type of strategy had been tried several times in the past, including by the Indians in the 1920s against Babe Ruth and in 1926 by several National League teams against the Phillies' power-hitting outfielder Cy Williams.

Williams grounded a pitch from Red Embree to near second base. It probably would have been a base hit under normal conditions, but Boudreau was there to scoop up the ball and throw Williams out at first. In two more trips to the plate Ted walked twice, making the shift moot for the time being. The Red Sox added three more runs to take the game

6–4. Still laughing afterwards, Williams told reporters, "If everybody plays me like that, I'll have to turn around and hit 'em righthanded." The next day fans from around the country read about the "Boudreau shift" and wondered if it was the future of baseball or just a crazy stunt.

On Tuesday the teams played in front of 33,534 fans, the second-largest crowd in Red Sox history. With Bob Feller pitching, the Boston front office reported turning down an additional 22,000 requests for tickets. Ken Keltner helped spoil the fans' afternoon by hitting two solo home runs, while Pat Seerey launched his fourteenth with a man on. Jim Hegan, eager to impress the folks in his home base, added two big hits, including a triple. Feller was not at his best but went the distance for his twentieth complete game. He had seven strikeouts to increase his total for the year to 202, a number most pitchers would accept for a full season. Cleveland won the game 6–3 to stop Boston's win streak at seven.

The Indians' number one fan, Bill Veeck, spent the weekend at Cleveland's Lakeside Hospital, troubled by an infection in his still-bothersome right leg. Even lying in a hospital bed, Veeck was working nonstop on his latest changes for his team and fans. Two more Ladies Days were scheduled for July 25 and August 1. He decided to give children a break, lowering the cost of bleacher tickets for them to sixty cents beginning July 23. Veeck planned to add ticket offices in Akron and several other cities to allow out-of-town fans to pick up their tickets and load up their cars before traveling to Municipal Stadium. In the works was a major re-decoration of both ballparks, including adding National League results to the scoreboards.

In the meantime, the owners met on July 19 to discuss ways to eliminate the ongoing irritation of the American Baseball Guild. Larry MacPhail, part owner of the Yankees, was named to head a new committee to improve relations between the owners and players. The owners decided to throw a few bones to the players in hopes of cooling off their interest in unionizing. They proposed allowing each ball club a player representative, who would be responsible for listening to grievances and reporting them. Three reps from each league would be accepted at the winter meetings to speak directly with the club heads and Commissioner Chandler. A date of August 5 was selected for teams to have their reps elected and meet with MacPhail's committee and the two league presidents.

MacPhail was a maverick among the owners. He advocated the abolition of the ten-day release-notification rule and was in favor of a minimum salary for all players. He called the ten-day rule, which meant a club was not required to inform a player until ten days before his release, "inequitable as hell." He still believed the reserve clause should stay as it was, however.

July 29 was set as the date for all player representatives to meet in Chicago to iron out their resolutions. That did not give them the proper time before the August committee meeting, but they were still eager to put their ideas on paper and discuss them with their fellow delegates. The clubs quickly elected their reps, hoping they could put together several plans to bring to Chicago. Mel Harder was easily elected by the Cleveland players and was also a shoo-in for the three-man committee that would attend the winter meetings. The players and reps discussed a wide range of ideas, including weekly allowances for spring training and payment for every exhibition game, higher meal allowances when traveling, and, the most compelling of all, a pension plan. With less than ten days to formalize their blueprints and with ballgames to play at the same time, the new reps had a big task ahead.

The Indians moved on to Philadelphia, one team they had no difficulty beating. After winning the first two games going away, on July 19 they rolled over the A's again, with Mel Harder winning his second game of the season. Mel's turns in the rotation had been cut back significantly, but on this day he breezed through the Philadelphia hitters, scattering eight hits and surrendering a single run. In the top of the fifth inning, Cleveland loaded the bases for Pat Seerey, and he did not disappoint, blasting a majestic grand slam home run. "The People's Choice" was not done for the day, leading off the eighth with a tremendous shot high over the left field pavilion and clear out of the park. The distance to the roof was 331 feet, but to clear the top it had to reach a height of more than one hundred feet. Reporters at the game could remember only one player, Jimmie Foxx, accomplishing the feat, and noted that Seerey's rocket shot was still on its way up when it left the grounds. The final score stood at 6–1, with Pat driving in all but one of the Indians' runs.

July was usually a winning month for the Indians, and this time around was no exception. Back home on the twenty-third, they beat up on the hapless A's again. Allie Reynolds tossed a three-hit shutout for his fourth straight win, 2–0. Reynolds seemed to have a custom of starting slowly each season and picking up the pace by July to finish strongly. A few years later he would be diagnosed with a thyroid condition that caused him to gain weight during the winter, hampering him through spring training and the early months of the season. Medication eased the problem, freeing him up to become a complete pitcher for the rest of his career.

The next afternoon a scalding-hot Bob Feller was on the mound against Philadelphia's Bob Savage, winner of one game in nine decisions. The game was scoreless until the fourth inning, when Hank Edwards belted a solo home run. Savage pitched one of his better games, but Feller could not be touched, winning number 18, 1–0. Feller added nine more strikeouts to raise his season total to 220, miles ahead of any other pitcher in the American League. He now had seven shutouts in less than four months. Feller's work of art lifted the Indians to within four games of .500.

Throughout the ballgame the Cleveland fans were entertained by the "Melo-Makers" band, hired by Bill Veeck to play at all the home games. At one of their first games they played "Three Blind Mice" at the start of the game when the umpires gathered at home plate. After that, for obvious reasons, the song was deleted from their playlist. The musicians were dressed in Native American costumes, complete with war bonnets, and had a newly built wigwam standing behind the center field wall. The costumes and wigwam represented Native American stereotypes and would be protested in the years ahead.

The next day both teams' hitters, tired of the good pitching, combined for thirty-two hits and seventeen runs. A timely ninth-inning single by Heinz Becker gave the Indians a 9–8 victory, bringing the season win-loss total to 44–47, the high-water mark since the first weeks of the season. Among the afternoon Ladies Day crowd were 3,930 women and 1,500 children, the kids taking advantage of the sixty-cent grandstand admission. With the Melo-Makers and the new promotions, Veeck was putting his personal stamp on Cleveland baseball. Everyone who knew him was aware that this was just the beginning.

After the game, Mel Harder met with his teammates to finalize their points to be debated in the Chicago player rep meetings. These were the seven issues:

> Modify the reserve clause.
> Set minimum salary to be no less than $5,000.
> Establish a pension fund with contributions from players, owners, and the league offices.
> Provide $5 allowances each day at spring training in addition to room and board.
> Remove all restrictions on barnstorming (probably Feller's idea).

In all sale or waiver deals, players should receive 10 percent of the sale price.

Salary should be paid out on a twelve-month basis.

Any modification of the reserve clause would assuredly not happen. The owners would fight to the death on that one. Commissioner Chandler would likely nix the plan for unlimited barnstorming, while it was unlikely the owners would pay the ballplayers year-round. Otherwise the players' requests might at least be open for discussion. The August 5 meeting promised to be noteworthy if not groundbreaking.

Harder met his fellow representatives in Chicago on the twenty-ninth to formalize a single list of items for the owners' committee to address. The consensus was to take a moderate approach rather than come on like firebrands and push the owners to their limit. Any ideas about the reserve clause were tabled, along with the percentage on sales price or waivers. The minimum salary stayed on the list, as did the pension plan and daily allowance at spring training. New requests concerned player contracts being mailed no later than thirty days prior to the start of spring training and improved conditions in the clubhouses. The three American League reps wanted their positions to be made permanent and, lastly, a modified plan to allow thirty days each year for barnstorming.

The National League reps had similar proposals but advocated sixty days' severance pay upon termination of contracts. More than their counterparts, the Nationals emphasized the importance of a pension plan. The reps consulted with five insurance companies to gather information about setting up retirement plans and mulled over a set of games in early July where all receipts would be targeted for the fund. With the agenda set, the player reps eagerly awaited their initial session with the owners in one week's time.

At the end of July the Red Sox came to town. It had been the Indians' first winning month of the season, and attendance was growing at a rapid pace. On July 30 they were shut out at home, 4–0, but 56,000 fans poured into Municipal Stadium to see Red Sox ace Dave Ferriss win his seventeenth game of the year, beating Steve Gromek. Ted Williams smacked his twenty-eighth home run.

Bob Feller finished off the month with one of the top performances of his stellar season. In the home half of the second inning, Don Ross and Jim Hegan singled and scored on Feller's triple. Rookie Jack Conway singled in Feller, giving him all the cushion he needed. Feller won his twentieth game by pitching his seventh career one-hitter, tying the Naps' Addie Joss for the most by any Cleveland pitcher. Addie, who died at age thirty-one in 1911, did not hold many Cleveland pitching records, and he was now in danger of losing them all to the Indians phenom.

The next Ladies Day was held on August 1 at Municipal Stadium. By 11:00 a.m. Cleveland women, attracted by Bill Veeck's promise to personally hand out 503 pairs of free nylons, began lining up three deep at the ticket windows. The odd figure came about because Larry MacPhail had recently given away 500 stockings at Yankee Stadium, prompting Veeck the showman to top him by adding three more. At game time many women were still in line for tickets. Margaret Reed wrote a vivid description of the event for the *Plain Dealer.* "Gorgeous blondes wearing chic sports clothes rubbed elbows with hopeful barelegged bobbie soxers, tailored suits, rolled up jeans and sweat suits that were in vogue." On several foul balls to the seats, Reed wrote, some of the women ducked while others stood their ground and tried for the catch. All told there were 21,371 ladies at the stadium, the most since late September 1940, when the Indians battled the Tigers for the pennant.

During the game a smiling Veeck strolled through the stands talking to as many fans as possible while yelling encouragement to his players. The fans could not help but warm to him for creating a hugely entertaining atmosphere at the park. Veeck, wearing his customary shirt unbuttoned at the top and no jacket, became something like a pied piper in front of crowds sometimes reaching upwards of 50,000. The hottest place in town was Municipal Stadium, with fireworks, bands, barbershop quartets, and more promised with seemingly every game. If you lived in Cleveland and had a few dollars to spend, you drove or rode the bus to the stadium to see what Bill Veeck was going to put on.

If anyone noticed, Mel Harder pitched brilliantly, winning his 215th game, 2–1, over the Red Sox. After a quick clubhouse celebration, instead of going out on the town with the boys or stopping by Joe Cavoli's restaurant, the Indians' hangout, Mel hurried home. He had promised his two young daughters a late afternoon at the movies. He missed another spectacle: when the other players left the locker room, they found several thousand fervent ladies hovering by the gate, begging them for autographs. Despite the prospect of a losing season, the fans, with a big assist from Veeck, were in love with their Indians once more.

The Friday night game against the Yankees at the stadium drew 35,863 fans. There were no less than five radio stations broadcasting the game, including one from New York. Veeck had set up a genuine carnival, with jugglers, the Paxton Brothers acrobats, two cowboys who did tricks with a whip, and a display of fireworks. Allie Reynolds was on the mound for the Indians, facing New York's Ernie Bonham. George Case led off the bottom of the first with a well-placed bunt between the mound and first. Yankees first baseman Steve Souchock fielded the ball but threw it into short right field. George Stirnweiss chased the ball down, turned, and fired wildly past second. Case, with the best wheels in baseball, reached third base standing up. Jack Conway flied out to short right field, but Case, again using his great speed, scored ahead of Tommy Henrich's throw. A bit shaken up, Bonham walked Pat Seerey and gave up a 460-foot triple to Heinz Becker, making the score 2–0. Three innings later Becker singled, went to second on a sacrifice, and crossed the plate on Don Ross's single. The rest of the game was all Reynolds, who fanned the side in the sixth inning on his way to a two-hit shutout. He had won six in a row, teaming up with Feller to give the Indians two starters capable of winning each time out. The attendance boosted the season's total to a remarkable 713,024. Since Veeck took over on June 22, the Indians had drawn over 500,000 fans, an average of 22,800 per game. They still had a chance to top the million mark.

The Indians had Saturday off, then resumed play on Sunday against the visiting Yanks. The crowd of 75,529 was the second-highest in team history, second only to the 80,104 on July 31, 1932, the inaugural game played at the new Municipal Stadium. The newspapers wanted to praise Veeck for the great attendance, but the owner would not have it, saying, "No gentlemen, this is a tribute to the newspapers and radio stations. After all, I couldn't contact all those folks personally to tell them about the attractions."

Bob Feller started for Cleveland, seeking his twenty-first win of the year. Bill Bevens opposed Feller in what developed into a pitcher's duel. The game was still scoreless with two out in the top of the seventh when Feller, after delivering a pitch, grimaced with pain in the lower back. After some consultation he left the game, replaced by Bob Lemon, who got the final out of the inning. The Yankees broke the scoreless tie in the top of the ninth to win the game for Bevens, 2–0. In the clubhouse, a quick exam by Dr. Castle revealed a minor pulled muscle that thankfully would not keep him out of the lineup for more than a few days.

The Indians and most of the teams had a day off on Monday, but their club representatives were hard at work, meeting in New York with the owners' committee. The two sides met for six hours, discussing all the points presented by the reps. At the end, a visibly tired Larry MacPhail told the newsmen, "Players and owners views were thoroughly discussed and as far as the committee's recommendations are concerned, mutual agreement in principle was reached in all matters discussed." MacPhail added that a joint meeting of all the owners was scheduled for August 27 in Chicago.

The owners were eager to come to an agreement and incorporate any changes into the 1947 standard players' contract. Jorge Pasquel and the Mexican League still troubled them, and they wanted new contracts mailed by early winter, giving Pasquel less time to solicit players while they were in limbo between contracts. Chandler's mandate of a five-year suspension still remained in effect once a player signed his new agreement.

On Thursday, August 8, Bob Feller took the mound for the first time since having to leave the game early against the Yankees. His back gave him no trouble as he pitched the eighth one-hitter of his career to set a new Cleveland record. The 5–0 win over the White Sox gave Feller his ninth shutout of the year and twenty-first victory.

Before Bill Veeck purchased the Indians, the front office had been planning to honor team trainer Lefty Weisman for his twenty-five years of service with the ball club. Weisman lacked formal training when he got the job in 1921. Fortunately for him, Joe Evans, one of the Indians outfielders, was a doctor and loaned several of his physiology books to Lefty. He brought the volumes with him on the road trips until he knew the human body as well as if he'd gone to school. He would become one of the best medical men in the game, and was a gifted singer, an all-around good guy, and one of the most popular men in the game. When Veeck learned about the Indians' plans, he salivated at the chance to add his personal touch.

The first order of business was to hire Max Patkin, the official clown of Major League Baseball, to perform. Patkin, a former minor league pitcher, had a wide variety of skits and mimicry that kept fans entertained. He dressed in a baggy uniform and always had a comical expression on his face while he poked fun at himself, the players, and the umpires. A lot of it was schlock, but he usually went over big.

Veeck also hired another comic performer, Jackie Price. Price's act involved doing unusual stunts like riding in a jeep and catching batted balls on the fly. Price was a genuine ballplayer, skilled enough that Veeck added him to the roster to back up the infield when needed.

On Tuesday evening, August 13, nearly 66,000 people were in the stands to witness the Veeck spectacular. Shortly after eight o'clock the Jackie Price show began with Price standing on the mound and firing two pitches home at the same time, caught by two catchers. Another catcher came to the plate and somehow Price threw three balls simultaneously. He wrapped up his short performance by hanging upside down on a bar extended over the plate, catching several balls before batting a few around the diamond. Max Patkin jitterbugged around the field, clowning his heart out.

Next came fireworks, followed by a parade of fire engines circling the field with Weisman's longtime friend Tris Speaker and Steve O'Neill riding in the back. The two former Indians spoke briefly, followed by the Yachtsman's Barbershop Quartet singing several numbers. Lefty joined in, singing "I Want a Girl" then wowing the fans with the always popular "Mother Machree." The moment Weisman finished the song, a Brink's truck appeared in the outfield, blowing its horn and escorted by several men on motorcycles. As the truck came to a stop in the infield, Mel Harder jumped out, carrying a heavy moneybag over his shoulder. The grounds crew rolled a wheelbarrow out to home plate and Harder emptied the bag, filled with four hundred glittering silver dollars, into it. Speaker handed a check for $6,000 to his friend, a gift from scores of businessmen and friends from around Cleveland. The newsmen and fans had never seen a show like this before, which built on Veeck's several years of entertaining crowds at the Milwaukee Brewers games. The people in the stands happily realized this was just the beginning of what to expect from baseball's master of entertainment.

As the season wore on, the Indians wore down, losing more often than they won. On Saturday, August 17, they were at home at the stadium, playing the White Sox. For the umpteenth time, Bob Feller was pitching shutout ball, blanking Chicago through seven innings while nursing a 1–0 lead. But three Cleveland errors let in four unearned runs, and the White Sox won 4–1. The game did have a bright spot, as 30,519 fans braved intermittent rain to break the Indians' all-time attendance mark of 912,382, recorded during the magical 1920 pennant-winning season. The record would of course be topped at every remaining home game on the schedule. It was a significant accomplishment for a second-division team.

Only three Major League games were scheduled for Monday, but the national spotlight was on one of the teams that had the day off, the Pittsburgh Pirates. The Pirates, smack in the middle of a city with prominent labor organizations, were holding a vote to decide whether to join the American Baseball Guild or stay in the dark ages. The vote, sanctioned by the National Labor Relations Board, would serve as a referendum for all professional baseball. Robert Murphy stood by, anxiously waiting to see if his efforts to change baseball for the better would come to fruition. Twenty-eight players cast their votes, and the final tally showed three yes votes, fifteen no, and ten players refusing to cast a vote either way.

As one would expect, Murphy was bitterly disappointed by the results, blaming the owners and their recently formed committee to hear player demands. "This loss constitutes a setback for the guild," he said. "These illegal committees, set up as a smoke screen by the owners, are both a sham and a farce." Murphy was mostly correct in his assessment of the owners' committee. The group came to be only because of the ABG and the chance it might succeed. Certainly there was a strong correlation between its formation and the activities of the guild. The owners co-opted several of the union's more moderate ideas and legitimized them to pacify the ballplayers and keep them at arm's length. Once again, the people who ran baseball had averted a crisis that would have lessened their control of the game.

With the American Baseball Guild fading sadly out of sight, baseball turned its attention to more pressing matters, such as attempting to determine the actual speed of Bob Feller's fastball. Before a game at Griffith Stadium in Washington, a capacity crowd of 30,052 was on hand to witness a test of how hard Feller could throw. The army brought in their sky screen chronograph, a contraption used for measuring the velocity of shells launched from big guns. Feller would throw six pitches into the machine, which would measure the speed. Feller's fifth pitch was a tad wild, breaking three pieces of wood off the machine. The results showed him throwing at 145 feet per second, or 98.6 miles per hour. The experiment proved what everybody already believed: Feller threw more swiftly than most pitchers on the planet.

Feller lost the game by a score of 5–4, hurt by his own throwing error and, surprisingly, two more by Lou Boudreau. Four days later he shook off the bad outing, beating the Athletics 5–0 for his twenty-second win and raising his strikeout total to a remarkable 280. Reaching 300 seemed assured, but fans were concerned Feller was tiring, putting too much effort into chasing Rube Waddell's record. Since winning his twentieth game on July 31, he had won only two more, with August practically gone. Add in the scheduled barnstorming tour in October and it seemed that Feller might be exceeding the amount of stress his right arm could handle for now and the future.

On August 27 the Major League owners met in New York to decide whether to ratify the demands of the player representatives. All present agreed to form yet another committee, named the executive council. It would have seven members: Commissioner Chandler, Ford Frick, Will Harridge, Larry MacPhail, Warren Giles, and one player rep from each league. The 5–2 advantage of management over players left serious doubt as to how much influence the player reps would have. In a better world, the committee might have included Robert Murphy or one of his delegates from the ABG. Without a union behind them, the players lacked real power to negotiate any major reforms.

As expected, the owners approved quickly a standard minimum wage of $5,000. A total of thirty days for barnstorming was sanctioned beginning in October. The pension plan and modification (note that word rather than "removal") of the ten-day rule were accepted along with the $25 weekly allowance for spring training. Details of the pension plan were not spelled out, nor was the modified ten-day rule. No time frames were set up to hammer out the details of those proposals, which were probably tabled until the winter meetings.

It is difficult to say that the players were successful in their demands. Certainly they won some concessions from the owners, but in the end it was just some well-planned manipulation to keep them from unionizing. Collective bargaining remained a distant dream, as did the abolition of the reserve clause. It seemed the players settled for the quick fix instead of a real fight for long-term gains. The years ahead would determine if the player reps had any kind of leverage on the executive council or if they would receive a nice piece of candy and a pat on the back for good behavior.

On September 7, with the Indians' season a washout save for the tremendous attendance, the front office bought the contract of outfielder Dale Mitchell from Oklahoma City. In 108 games, Mitchell had batted .337 with

140 base hits. Cleveland, starving for an above-average hitter in the outfield, pinned their hopes on the twenty-five-year-old ex-military man.

Loren Dale Mitchell was born August 23, 1921, in the tiny agricultural community of Colony, Oklahoma. The town, situated in the southwest part of the state, had fewer than five hundred people when Dale grew up there. His father, John, bought his left-handed son a first baseman's mitt to play catch in the fields of the Mitchell farm.

When Dale was ten years old, he was crossing one of the narrow roads outside Colony when he was struck by an automobile. He suffered a broken collarbone and numerous ugly cuts and bruises, but, as young healthy children often do, he recovered quickly and returned within a few months to his daily routine of playing any sports available.

As a teenager, Dale attended Cloud Chief High School, where the student body was approximately 160. He excelled at every sport offered, including track, where in the hundred-yard dash he broke the state record with a time of 9.8 seconds. That achievement and his ability to hit a baseball brought Major League scouts to Colony.

With the blessing of his parents, Mitchell signed a contract with the Indians while still in high school. Though that was prohibited by Major League Baseball, the deal was kept secret, enabling Dale to continue playing amateur sports despite being a professional. With both parties keeping silent, the plan was to finish high school then report to Fargo-Moorhead. To entice the Mitchells into approving the contract (the Indians were good at that), the Cleveland scout had promised immediate payments to the family, but they were never sent. In turn, Mitchell did not honor his side of the agreement, failing to report to the minor league club. Instead he enrolled at the University of Oklahoma, arriving in Norman with his new bride, Margaret Emerson, whom he had met while they were students together at Cloud Chief High.

Not revealing his contract with the Indians, which should have made him ineligible to play baseball, he earned a starting spot on the baseball squad as a sophomore and batted an impressive .420. Drafted soon after, he entered the army in 1942 and saw three years of duty in Europe. At the end of the war he returned to Norman and rejoined the baseball team, batting a spectacular .507.

Now, with a wife and young son to support, Mitchell made the difficult decision to contact the Oklahoma City club for a job. He revealed his status with Cleveland, specifically why he had not fulfilled his 1939 contract. The club got in touch with the Cleveland front office, explaining Mitchell's unusual situation. Apparently Bradley and Peckinpaugh were sympathetic, officially assigning his contract to Oklahoma City. It is interesting to guess what might have gone down if Judge Landis was still alive and got wind of what happened. He might have slammed the Indians for tampering with a high schooler and declared Mitchell a free agent. But that was then and this was now, and nobody seemed concerned about the uncommon circumstances.

Mitchell, relieved to get the opportunity, played great baseball at Oklahoma City, where his .337 average won the batting title. In early September, the Indians called him up, and, after a seven-year wait interrupted by the military, Dale finally became a Major Leaguer. Inserted into the starting lineup for the last two weeks of the season, he produced nineteen hits and batted .432.

While Mitchell was on his way from Oklahoma, the Indians were home for a Sunday doubleheader with the St. Louis Browns. Bob Feller would be pitching the second game, but the big draw was a match race between former Olympic champion Jesse Owens and Cleveland's George Case. The 100-yard dash was part of a field events day set up by Veeck, in which the Indians and Browns competed in race walking, a wheelbarrow race, and fungo hitting and long throwing. Owens, thirty-two years old and ten years removed from his spectacular four gold medals in Berlin, wore a Cincinnati Reds uniform complete with baseball spikes on his shoes. He led from the start and won with a time of 9.9 seconds, handing Case one of his rare defeats and showing he could still fly after all those years.

The Indians dominated the field events, winning the silly race walk, in which the coaches, in four-man teams, circled the bases; the throwing contest, in which Gene Woodling, standing at home plate, hurled a baseball 308 feet to the outfield; and the fungo hitting, in which Steve Gromek tossed a ball in the air and whacked it 348 feet. The only Cleveland setback came in the action-packed wheelbarrow race, when Jeff Heath (now with the Browns) carried teammate Johnny Berardino across the finish line ahead of the Indians' entry.

After a few minutes of rest, the Indians took the field. Cleveland fans were not too upset when the team lost the first game 4–1, since the great majority of them were there to watch the second game, in which Feller needed 7 strikeouts to reach 300. His fastball was not overpowering that day, but he mixed in his curveball to keep the Browns hitters guessing. The score was tied at two runs apiece in the bottom of the seventh when Don Ross took advantage of some rare playing time to belt a solo home run. Feller retired the side in order in the eighth and ninth and won the game 3–2. His strikeout of Johnny Berardino in the eighth gave him 300 on the year, and he added one more for good measure in the ninth. Only Walter Johnson and Rube Waddell had reached that plateau in American League history. Boudreau told reporters Feller could get in as many as six more starts, giving him a shot at Rube's all-time record.

The next landmark event in this out-of-the ordinary season would take place between games of the Sunday doubleheader on September 15, when the Cleveland Touchdown Club would honor Boudreau as Man of the Year. The club, set up primarily to promote Cleveland football, was recognizing Boudreau for all his contributions to professional sports and all the goodwill he brought to the city. Mayer Burke issued a proclamation declaring Sunday Lou Boudreau Day in Cleveland: "His conduct both as a player and manager has made him an outstanding member of the great sport and nationally known as a sportsman and gentleman."

The Athletics came to town on Sunday. In attendance were Governor Frank Lausche and several other public officials. Bill Veeck, intending to outdo Lefty Weisman night, had placed big advertisements in the newspapers to help bring out an appropriate crowd for Lou. The final count was 29,395, not a huge number but enough for the Indians to pass the 1 million mark for the first time in their history. An exuberant Veeck decided to honor the fans with free admission for the final home game of the year. He had accomplished a near-impossible feat, buying a lower-division team and boosting attendance to unheard-of numbers. Veeck's triumph brought up the fascinating question of what he could do with a winning team.

The day got off to a fast start with Bob Lemon tossing a five-hitter to beat the Athletics 8–1. Moments later Governor Lausche opened the Boudreau ceremony, telling Lou, "Those of you that play ball know the burden of being a manager. You are in addition to being a fine ballplayer, a wholesome clean-living man." Connie Mack, still spry at eighty-three, spoke next, calling Lou "the greatest shortstop the American League has ever seen."

After the speeches an old rusty jalopy unsteadily motored its way across the field to near home plate. At the wheel was Lou's uncle and in

162

the passenger seat was his aunt. Behind them came a truck filled with gifts, including a refrigerator and stove courtesy of Bill Veeck, a radio from the stadium band, and a clock with chimes from the ballplayers. The coaches gave him a fancy wristwatch, and the Junior Chamber of Commerce brought a scroll naming Lou the outstanding Cleveland athlete for 1946. The highlight of the presentation was a shiny new four-door Lincoln with the personalized license plate L2B, filled with a group of bathing beauties, who each gave the embarrassed Boudreau a generous hug.

To end the program, Lou stepped to the microphone with a speech direct from the heart. "This without a doubt is the proudest moment of my life," he said. "I can't thank everyone, but I want to mention those friends of mine in Harvey, Illinois and the sportswriters and radio men who have given me the kind of support any manager would want." The fans stood and raised the rafters in honor of one of the most popular players and managers ever to wear a Cleveland uniform. While there were many people involved in making Lou Boudreau Day a success, the program had Bill Veeck's handwriting all over it. The jalopy, the pretty women, and the appliances were undoubtably his idea, mixing class with entertainment to give the folks a show like none other. And the best was yet to come.

Bob Feller started game two. Despite losing 2–0, he managed to get seven strikeouts for a total of 315, enough to pass Walter Johnson for second place behind Waddell. He would need 29 more to pass Rube's 343 and claim the record for himself. With four or five starts still to go, his chances for the record looked good.

Dale Mitchell made his Indians debut in the doubleheader, playing center field and collecting the first three hits of his career in eight at bats. With his great speed, the Indians touted him as their center fielder of the future. Whether he could hold down the job would be determined the following spring.

Despite the Indians' losing record, a feeling of goodwill hovered around the club and its dynamic owner. Mayor Burke believed the time was right to approach Veeck about a new lease for the stadium. One of the mayor's chief concerns was the 1946 arrival of the Cleveland Browns and the All-American Football Conference. The Browns' owner, Mickey McBride, saw access to Municipal Stadium beginning every September as essential. Under the current agreement, the Indians had exclusive rights to the facility through October 1. Burke proposed a new lease to both owners, with provision for the Browns to play several home games in September.

Present at the meeting were Mayor Burke, Veeck, McBride, both teams' lawyers, city officials, and the mayor's advisory committee on the stadium. The tone of the meeting was positive, with Veeck agreeing to waive his exclusivity rights in September. That allowed the Browns two home games during the month and a game on Labor Day weekend, provided it was not scheduled for Monday. Veeck retained the right to schedule World Series games at the stadium on any dates in October. College football games would be allowed, but only after October 15. The new agreement would stand for five years, but did not address other concerns such as rental fees, concessions, parking fees, and percentages of the gate, which would be reviewed at a later date. Though the results of the meeting pleased all parties, Veeck had managed to maintain key provisions drawn up in 1944 that heavily favored his ball club. Still in place was the old World Series arrangement calling for the city to receive just $60 per 1,000 spectators. Veeck was in no hurry to revisit the clause anytime soon.

On September 19, Bob Feller's march to the strikeout record resumed against the Washington Senators. In the second inning, he walked in a run with the bases loaded, then slammed the door, retiring eighteen straight Senators. The score stayed at 1–0 until the bottom of the eighth, when doubles by recent call-up Eddie Robinson and Hank Edwards evened the count. Two walks, a fielder's choice, and two singles along with a throwing error and a balk raised the Indians' lead to 5–1, the eventual final score. Feller had five strikeouts to raise his season total to 320. He would need 24 more to pass Waddell.

Intent on pursuing the record, Feller agreed to pitch on Sunday on only two days' rest. His opponent would be the Tigers' Hal Newhouser, like Feller a 25-game winner and more than up for the challenge. The Cleveland fans were ready too, with 38,103 in the seats before game time. Newhouser demonstrated why many fans and writers believed him to be an even better pitcher than his opponent. The Indians were helpless against the Detroit ace, with only Jim Hegan and Heinz Becker able to hit safely and no Indians runner reaching second base. Feller allowed two runs in the fourth inning and one more in the sixth and lost 3–0. He did fan seven Detroit batters to reach 327 strikeouts.

Wednesday, September 25, brought the last home game of the season. Veeck, true to his word, made admission at Municipal Stadium free for seats anywhere in the ballpark, though the fans did have to pay the sales tax of thirty-five cents. A total of 12,800 fans, a good crowd for the middle of the week, went through the turnstiles, put down a dime and a quarter, and raced for the best seats in the house. Bob Feller was at it again, taking the mound on two days' rest and firing mostly fastballs to the White Sox. He racked up 10 more to give him 337 and a fighting chance at the record. Few noticed that the Indians lost the game, 4–1.

In the clubhouse, Boudreau announced an unusual pitching rotation to give Feller the best opportunity to break the record. On Friday he would pitch four innings against the Tigers, then come back on Sunday to start. Meanwhile, the American League office had received an interesting query about what the strikeout record actually was. The *Philadelphia Inquirer* claimed they had reviewed the box score of every game Waddell had pitched in 1904 and discovered several inaccuracies, boosting Waddell's total to 348. To settle the matter, the league office turned to George Moreland's widely used 1914 book *Balldom,* judged to be an accurate account of baseball's historical records. Without much thought, they confirmed the number to beat was 343. Feller would still have to come up with just seven strikeouts in two games, surely an easy task for the fireballer.

On Friday night, September 27, Feller entered the game in the bottom of the fifth inning with the Indians leading 6–4. Though he did not have his best stuff, he managed to shut the Tigers down for four innings. In the bottom of the ninth, he struck out leadoff batter Jimmy Outlaw for number 343, tying Waddell. The next batter singled, and then the dangerous Hank Greenberg worked the count to two balls and two strikes. Hank swung at Feller's next delivery and barely tipped the baseball. Jim Hegan had it in his glove for an instant but could not hold on, giving Greenberg new life. He wound up getting a base on balls, starting a rally that left the Tigers a run short, losing 9–8. Feller remained tied with Waddell. Almost unnoticed were Pat Seerey's two home runs, his 25th and 26th of the season, tying Ken Keltner and early 1930s first baseman Eddie Morgan for the Indians' record for a right-handed batter.

On Sunday, September 29, 47,876 fans in heavy overcoats braved the cold in Detroit to bear witness to the new strikeout record. It was the final game of the season, and Feller was matched up once more against

Hal Newhouser. The Tigers hitters, all determined not to be the guy, avoided any strikeouts for the first four innings. In the bottom of the fifth, Newhouser became the unwanted footnote to history, going into the books as Feller's 344th strikeout. Jim Hegan sprinted to the mound to give the special ball to his elite pitcher, while the Detroit fans gave Feller a terrific ovation. The relieved Feller acknowledged the crowd and turned his concentration to winning the ballgame. Over the next four innings he added four more strikeouts to his total, finishing the season with 348. The final score read Cleveland 4, Detroit 1.

The new strikeout king had had a season for the ages. His 48 appearances, 36 complete games, 10 shutouts, and 371 1/3 innings pitched were personal bests and led the American League. His ERA of 2.18 was also a career best. He accomplished all of this just one year removed from his long service in the South Pacific.

Not one to rest on his laurels, or to rest at all, Feller immediately left Detroit to start his barnstorming tour. The first game was played at Forbes Field in Pittsburgh, with the Satchel Paige All-Stars defeating Feller's squad 3–1. Both star pitchers went three innings before turning over the pitching duties. The next afternoon the two teams met in Youngstown for an afternoon game, then hurried to Cleveland for a night contest at the stadium. The temperatures dropped below the low fifties at game time, but 8,000 fans paid to see some of the finest players in all of baseball, including Feller, Paige, Sam Jethroe, Buck O'Neil, Phil Rizzuto, Mickey Vernon, and Hank Thompson. The Major League stars won 5–0 behind home runs by Jeff Heath, Johnny Berardino, and Spud Chandler.

Squeezing in thirty games to gross as much money as possible, Feller rented two DC-3 airplanes for the entire trip, taking the players to the East Coast, Midwest, and as far as California. At the end of the tour, Feller, with Spud Chandler and Charlie Keller, flew to Hawaii for a brief exhibition tour. Counting the Bob Feller school last January, he had been playing baseball for eleven months straight. Unless his arm was made of steel, it brought up a good question: How many pitches were left in it?

Chapter 10

BUILDING A WINNER

For Bill Veeck, the end of the regular season signaled the beginning of his attempts to transform his sixth-place ball club into a pennant contender. He told sportswriters the only untouchables on his team were Lou Boudreau and Bob Feller. "I cannot tell you who is to remain and who is going to leave. But I certainly don't intend to stand for a sixth-place club." Veeck indicated he wanted fast men and line-drive hitters who could take advantage of the huge outfield at the stadium. Specifically, he was interested in acquiring two outfielders, two infielders, and several new pitchers. Besides Boudreau and Feller, Veeck was fond of Pat Seerey's ability to hit home runs and believed Bob Lemon and Eddie Robinson were destined for solid if not great careers.

At the World Series between Boston and St. Louis, Veeck, eager to complete his first trade as Indians boss, sought out every available general manager. Finding Larry MacPhail interested in picking up a quality starting pitcher, he offered Red Embree in exchange for Joe Gordon. A few years earlier that trade would have been ridiculed, but Gordon was coming off his poorest season as a Yankee. The All-Star second baseman had career lows in home runs, RBIs, and batting average. Certain the thirty-one-year-old Gordon had seen his better days, MacPhail was open to moving him. Embree was not the quality pitcher the Yankees lacked, and before agreeing to anything, MacPhail consulted with Joe DiMaggio, who advised him to refuse Embree and ask for Allie Reynolds. Joe

D. had difficulty with Reynolds's fastball and believed he could help the Yankees a lot more than Embree.

MacPhail made the counteroffer and Veeck accepted, provided that minor league third baseman Eddie Bockman be thrown into the deal. On October 11, the trade went through: Joe Gordon and Eddie Bockman for Allie Reynolds. Bill Veeck gambled on this transaction, believing a change of scenery would benefit Gordon and he could return to his place as one of the premier second basemen in the game, a big upgrade over Ray Mack and several others tried at the position. If he was correct, Gordon and Boudreau would be the top shortstop–second base combination in the American League.

From the Yankees' point of view, they were receiving a pitcher who in four years had compiled a record of 51–47 with an ERA of 3.34 and 9 career shutouts. Reynolds had won 18 games in 1945 and pitched extremely well in the second half of the 1946 season. The Yankees had an exceptional power-hitting ball club, which was ideal for a pitcher who allowed a little more than three runs per game. This was a trade that might benefit both teams.

Several days later Veeck called his new second baseman at his home in Eugene, Oregon. Gordon told Veeck he was already working out, losing weight, and utterly happy to be joining the Indians. The phone call demonstrated how much Veeck, serving as his own general manager, wanted his first trade to work out. He was a hands-on guy in all aspects of his ball club, forgoing sleep to work on club business.

Acquiring key ballplayers was only part of the strategy to improve the Indians. Bill McKechnie agreed to join the club as a coach and assistant to Boudreau. McKechnie, now sixty years old, had managed four different National League clubs since 1922, winning four pennants and two World Series while compiling a winning lifetime record. He was reputed to be a great handler of pitchers, something the ball club needed to be successful. Veeck believed Boudreau was a tremendous shortstop but no more than an average manager. Having a veteran like McKechnie on board would give Lou a confidant who could help him fine-tune his managerial skills. In a wise statement to reporters, McKechnie advised that he had no further ambitions to manage, wanting only to aid Boudreau in winning a pennant.

With one significant trade and one large upgrade in the coaching staff, Veeck had accomplished a great deal in less than a month. It seemed like nothing could slow him down. But on October 25, when he checked into the Cleveland Clinic for more examinations of his injured right leg, the doctors advised him that it was still not healing properly and the best option would be to amputate it. The leg would be removed about seven inches below the knee, after which he would be fitted for a wooden leg and have to be on crutches for a long period. After thinking it over for a few days, Veeck approved the surgery.

The operation, on November 1, was successful. Within three days, despite being confined to his hospital bed, Veeck resumed his nonstop appointment schedule. Bob Hope came by for a visit, followed by Boudreau for a lengthy meeting about the Joe Gordon trade and the ramifications of the McKechnie hiring. Thousands of cards and flowers poured into the hospital room.

Two and a half weeks after the surgery, Veeck left the hospital and moved to a downtown hotel suite. His doctors must have warned him he needed to rest, but time was wasting. Veeck made plans to travel to Chicago, then on to the winter meetings in California. Three days after his release he held a dinner for his stockholders, now numbering twenty, at the Hollenden Hotel. Accompanied by Bob Feller, who was in Cleveland for a visit, he also attended the annual Plain Dealer Charities football game at the stadium, hobbling on his crutches through the mass of fans. The game attracted over 70,000 fans to see the best two high school teams meet for the city championship, and the money raised provided Thanksgiving dinners for thousands who could not afford them. It was something he wouldn't dream of missing.

The December winter meetings were held in Los Angeles. One of the first trades to take place was Ray Mack and young catcher Sherman Lollar to the Yankees for outfielder Hal Peck and pitchers Al Gettel and minor leaguer Gene Bearden. Now that Veeck had Joe Gordon starting at second, Mack, one of the longest-tenured Indians, had become expendable. Lollar had some talent, but Veeck apparently believed he had enough catchers that he could spare him.

On the Yankees' side, Peck was a bench player at best, with Joe DiMaggio, Tommy Henrich, Johnny Lindell, and Charlie Keller ahead of him. Al Gettel was a .500 pitcher, but in 1946 he had boasted an impressive ERA of 2.97. The wild card in the deal was Gene Bearden, a knuckleball-throwing lefty who had won fifteen games for the Oakland Oaks of the Pacific Coast League. In his autobiography, Veeck writes that Casey Stengel, then the manager for Oakland, advised him that Gene Bearden was the best pitcher on the roster and if he had the chance, he should grab him. Apparently Larry MacPhail did not object to losing Bearden or knew little about him, and agreed to deal him.

Gene Bearden was born in the tiny burg of Lexa, Arkansas, on September 5, 1920. The town of approximately two hundred residents was situated in the southeastern part of the state. Gene's father, Henry, a former minor league catcher, worked as a mechanic for the Missouri Pacific Railroad. Being a railroad man meant numerous changes in location for him and his family. Bearden attended Technical High School in Memphis, Tennessee, where he played football and basketball, broad jumped for the track team, and somehow fit in baseball, alternating between pitcher and first base. In the summers, he pitched American Legion ball, later attending a baseball school in Greenbriar, Arkansas. Henry Bearden advanced the $50 needed for tuition and room and board. Gene would remember driving the team bus with little or no brakes. Most of the towns where they played baseball were deep in the country, usually at the bottom of a hill. Bearden delighted in pointing the bus down the hills, then holding tight as it gathered speed, shocking the townspeople as it shot past them before the level ground slowed it down.

In 1939, a Phillies scout signed Bearden to a contract. The Phillies assigned him to Class D Miami Beach, Florida. He pitched two seasons there before advancing to Savannah of the Sally League and being acquired by the Yankees. Any further movement halted when Gene entered the United States Navy.

Bearden rose to the rank of machinist's mate second class while assigned to the light cruiser *Helena*, patrolling in the South Pacific. While engaged in battle the *Helena* was badly damaged by a Japanese torpedo, resulting in a frantic order to abandon ship. Bearden, with only minutes to spare, scrambled down a ladder trying to reach several buddies trapped below deck. On his way back up, another torpedo slammed the ship, flinging Bearden headfirst against the steel deck. He lay unconscious until one of the last officers leaving the rapidly sinking ship spotted him. The officer dragged the seriously injured sailor over the side and onto a life raft below. Bearden drifted for two days on the raft before a rescue ship steamed by and he was carried to the onboard medical facilities.

The doctors found Gene in a terrible state, with a crushed left knee and his skull split open. He would undergo multiple hazardous operations, in which surgeons installed aluminum plates in his head and knee. A long recovery period followed before he was well enough to leave the navy hospital, walking under his own power. For all that happened at the attack of the *Helena*, a Purple Heart was awarded to him.

A return to baseball at any level seemed improbable, but Bearden was determined to try again. He asked the Yankees for a minor league assignment, and they sent him to Binghamton, where he made an unbelievable comeback, winning 15 games, pitching 179 innings, and posting an ERA of 2.41.

In 1946, he earned a promotion to Oakland, managed by Casey Stengel. Bearden would credit Stengel and his coach Muddy Ruel for helping him become a complete ballplayer, even allowing him to take regular turns at batting practice. He won another fifteen games, convincing Stengel his new lefty had a chance for the Major Leagues. The trade to Cleveland gave Bearden the chance to show Boudreau and Veeck what strength and resilience were really about.

At the winter meetings Veeck announced that the Indians' spring training site would move to Tucson, Arizona, and the team would play an ambitious thirty-seven-game exhibition schedule. To make the switch possible, Veeck convinced New York Giants owner Horace Stoneham to move to Arizona with him, setting up facilities in Phoenix. Veeck planned to rent a DC-3 to fly the ball club back and forth to Phoenix and to Southern California to play against the Chicago Cubs and White Sox. Veeck hired Rogers Hornsby and Tris Speaker as instructors who would work specifically with Pat Seerey on cutting down on his strikeouts and with Jim Hegan on his hitting in general. The four would report to Tucson on January 23, a month before spring training officially began.

On the heels of those announcements, Veeck pulled the trigger on another trade. Outfielder Gene Woodling went to the Pittsburgh Pirates for veteran catcher Al Lopez. Woodling was only twenty-four years old and had played sixty-one games with the Indians the year before while batting a lowly .188. Lopez was an ancient thirty-eight and entering his eighteenth year in the Majors. He could hit for a fair average but lacked power and the ability to drive in runs.

Veeck knew that to build a ball club for the long term, one had to give younger players an extended look, permitting them time to develop. With Woodling and Lollar he did the opposite, trading potential for proven experience. Veeck wanted to win now, rather than take time to assemble a contender. His roster was dotted with players on the wrong side of thirty.

Working at a frenetic pace, the Indians boss offered Ken Keltner and George Case to the Washington Senators for three-time All-Star center fielder Stan Spence. In Spence, the Indians would be getting a good-hitting outfielder with home run power, while Keltner and Case, though younger than Spence, were perceived to be on the downside of their careers. On the other hand, trading Keltner, still an excellent defensive third baseman, would give the starting job to untested rookie Eddie Bockman. In the end, the Senators refused the offer and Spence remained in Washington.

At the meetings one of the biggest issues discussed was the pension plan and the means to fund it. The owners nominated Jack Zeller, general manager of the Tigers, and Earl Nelson from the Boston Braves to work on the plan and make it operational. Ideas suggested included having each ball club contribute $250 per player per year and the ballplayers match that amount, and adding in the money earned from the World Series radio rights. The owners were also in favor of donating the net proceeds from the All-Star game to the players' retirement. From all these sources, total amount would be in the neighborhood of $400,000. To qualify for a pension, a player would need to have ten years in the Major Leagues and be at least forty-five years old. Initial payments would start at $100 a month and be paid through the retired player's lifetime. The money was nowhere near enough for a single or married person to live on, but more of a supplement.

In further talks, the owners bowed to the power of night games, agreeing to let teams play in the evenings without any limitations. They also agreed that a player could be placed on waivers three times during a season. The club could withdraw him from the list the first two times, but not the third, and would collect $10,000 if the player was claimed by another club. Once again the Pacific Coast League, the host of the meetings, made noise about becoming a third Major League. This time the league gained a little support from several American League owners, but in the end the league was judged to lack MLB caliber.

The new player representatives scored a small victory when the owners agreed to their request to ban doubleheaders the day after a night game. It appeared the reps still favored treading lightly instead of confronting the owners with anything controversial. On that note of newfound harmony, the meeting adjourned with the selection of Chicago's Wrigley Field as the site of the 1947 All-Star game.

Bill Veeck returned to Cleveland ready to execute plans for the upcoming season. Ticket sales were already at a robust 169,000, with plenty of room to grow. Mel Harder temporarily joined the front office to assist in selling tickets to businesses and individuals. It must have been awfully difficult for potential buyers to say no to one of the Indians' most easygoing and admired ballplayers.

Veeck and his staff were sure they could draw another million fans to the stadium, possibly improving on last year's record of 1,057,289. A winning season and a good marketing campaign might push the numbers to the 1,500,000 range and put them in competition with the Yankees and other high-drawing teams.

January was typically a slow month for the Cleveland front office, but with the new ownership downtime became a thing of the past. Veeck arranged a stockholders' meeting in Chicago as well as a conference with manager Boudreau. He also got Feller to agree to stop in Cleveland later in the month to negotiate his 1947 contract.

Veeck had one important signed contract from second baseman Joe Gordon. The new Indian planned to report early to Tucson to get himself in top condition by the start of training camp. A spiked left finger in March of 1946 hindered Gordon throughout the rest of Yankee camp and into the start of the regular season and may have been partly responsible for his subpar season. Joe had spent previous off-seasons hunting and tending to his several businesses, but this time it was all about baseball and regaining his old form.

Several weeks later Bob Feller arrived in Cleveland to hammer out a contract with Veeck. After his record-breaking performance the previous season, he was due a monster deal. The two men talked at length before agreeing to a new deal of approximately $80,000 plus an attendance bonus. It was believed to be the highest salary in baseball since Babe Ruth commanded a similar amount in 1930. If Feller turned in another season like he did in 1946, and if the Indians moved up a notch or two in the standings, the bonus was just about guaranteed. Despite Feller's salary taking up 20 percent of the Indians' total payroll, Veeck was a shrewd bargainer, knowing his ace brought thousands more fans to the stadium. A happy Feller translated to significant extra revenue for the ball club.

With his ace pitcher signed, Veeck looked to beef up the front office. He hired Tris Speaker to do public speaking on behalf of the team, and former general manager Cy Slapnicka to do scouting around the country. Both men had over twenty years' experience with the club in various capacities. Their expertise in different areas supplemented the organizational structure that Veeck was assembling. Soon the Yankees and Red Sox would be scrambling for cover.

With much of the Indians' business handled, Veeck decided to throw a party at the upscale Hollenden Hotel in honor of his new artificial leg. On Tuesday night, January 28, three hundred of his closest friends were amazed to see Veeck toss his crutches aside and dance waltzes, rhumbas, and sambas into the evening. They must have been worried he might do further damage to what remained of his leg.

Early February brought Boudreau to Tucson to work on strengthening his arthritic ankles. He joined Pat Seerey and Jim Hegan, still at work on adding points to their batting averages. Lou told reporters he believed Feller could win thirty games if the hitting improved. He was eager for Joe Gordon to arrive so they could work on relays and double plays. Veeck's never-ending optimism seemed to be filtering down to his manager and ballplayers. The Indians needed more than positive thoughts to play competitive baseball, but for the first time in a while most of them appeared to be on the same page.

Back home in Cleveland the *Plain Dealer* and Veeck announced a contest to choose the team batboy for 1947. The winner had to be between the ages of eight and fifteen and would receive a $1,000 scholarship toward a college education, a trip to the All-Star game in Chicago, and season passes for his parents to all home games. Veeck remarked to the paper, "I want a boy whose grades in school are good and who is liked and admired by the other kids in his neighborhood and school." Each applicant was required to submit an essay on why he should be hired, and the finalists would be interviewed by a committee. It was anticipated that several thousand boys would apply for the job.

In the middle of February, Joe Gordon reported to Tucson in terrific shape, saying he was being given a new lease on life. Boudreau stated happily, "He's already shown his old-time form." If the Indians were going to improve themselves in the standings, the push would come from the shortstop and second baseman.

Dale Mitchell arrived several days later to work with Speaker on the ins and outs of playing center field. Boudreau already had an idea of his starting lineup, with himself, Gordon, Keltner, and Robinson in the infield and Mitchell, Seerey and Edwards in the outfield. Add in Jim Hegan doing the majority of the catching and Boudreau would have his first set lineup since he became player-manager in 1942.

February 24 marked the official opening of spring training, with twenty-five players going through drills in the eighty-four-degree heat. Nobody seemed to mind the weather, especially Eddie Robinson, who launched three shots far over the right field wall. Gene Bearden looked impressive, throwing strikes in his first genuine chance to stick in the big leagues. At this point only Feller was a lock on the starting rotation, with Steve Gromek, Al Gettel, and Bob Lemon competing for spots. Veeck had given Boudreau a good number of players to study in shaping his roster for the season.

A few days later, pitcher Don Black reported, telling sportswriters he was a changed man. During the winter he had had a heart-to-heart talk with the front office about his difficulties with alcohol. After some persuasion he agreed to join Alcoholics Anonymous, the second Indian to do so since catcher Rollie Hemsley in 1939. Black had quietly moved to Cleveland and attended meetings without the press or anyone outside the Indians organization hearing about it. He arrived at spring training totally sober and determined to stay that way for the rest of his life. But it would be hard work, and Boudreau was keeping a close watch on him, especially off the field. "I've made a lot of mistakes," Black said, "and I think it was swell of Bill Veeck and Lou Boudreau to give me another chance. This is it." He said he intended to observe all training rules in trying to win at least a place on the roster, if not in the starting rotation. He had considerable ground to make up, but for the first time in many years early returns were encouraging.

Just a week into training camp, Veeck made still another trade, sending outfielder George Case back to Washington for pitcher Roger Wolff. The knuckleballer had won twenty games in 1945 but with injuries had fallen back significantly the past season. Case, similarly hampered by injuries, had not hit well for the Indians. If Wolff regained his form of two years ago, the trade would be a big win. At any rate, Veeck was adding more depth to the current staff.

On Saturday, March 8, the Indians' exhibition season began in Tucson with their neighbors the New York Giants. A crowd of 5,000 people was on hand to welcome Major League Baseball to Arizona. Bob Lemon pitched extremely well, while Hank Edwards and Eddie Robinson drove in two early runs toward the 3–1 win. For the next ten days the two teams would zigzag between Tucson and Phoenix before the Indians left for Southern California to play the Chicago teams as well as several from the Pacific Coast League.

On Tuesday afternoon, just a few games into the exhibition schedule, serious injuries struck both teams. In the bottom of the second inning, Bob Feller belted a line drive that struck Giants pitcher Larry Jansen on the left side of the face, fracturing his cheekbone and damaging his left eye. Doctors, fearing he might have also suffered a skull fracture, rushed Jansen to the hospital for X-rays and a likely extended stay. As it turned out, Jansen recovered from his injuries and went on to win 21 games for the Giants in his first Major League season.

In the top of the third inning, Willard Marshall of the Giants lifted a pop fly to short left field. Hank Edwards sprinted in and made a last-second dive to snare the ball before it hit the ground, but landed awkwardly on his right arm, dislocating his shoulder. The prognosis was that he would be out of action for at least six weeks, missing the opener and most of April. In fact, he ended up making his first appearance on May 18. Since George Case had been traded, Veeck went back on the phones to secure another outfielder for the short term.

In late March, the Indians flew to Southern California. Their first stop was Los Angeles, where Boudreau and Feller took time off to appear on Bob Hope's popular syndicated radio show. The players spoke from a script that set up the master comedian for his trademark one-liners. Companies lined up to sponsor his show to the point that he plowed his way through forty-seven live commercials during the broadcast. Everything from toothpaste to automobiles to movies received a quick mention, while Hope kept his audience chuckling throughout. Buying stock in the Indians only increased Hope's visibility and allowed him more opportunities to expand his comedy empire.

After several days, the Indians took the train to San Diego. Jackie Price, the part-time player and pregame stunt man, brought along two of his favorite snakes to keep him company. Price routinely carried snakes with him, usually hiding them inside his shirt and pants. His teammates' reactions were mixed. Someone in the Indians' traveling party noticed that a group of seventy-five women from the American Bowling

Congress was traveling in an adjacent car, and a scheme was hatched. Price nonchalantly strolled through the bowlers' car and dropped the snakes on the floor. Within seconds ear-piercing screams were heard as ladies fled the car or jumped up onto their seats. After a while Price casually returned to gather up his slithering friends.

Once Bill Veeck received word of the incident, he summoned Price all the way to Cleveland. Price admitted he had let the snakes go on a dare from a teammate, but refused to name him. Told that either he or the snakes would have to go, pick one, Price returned hurriedly to San Diego and donated his pals to the San Diego Zoo. The snake incident was history, but it made great copy for newspapers around the country.

At the beginning of April, Veeck cut a deal to buy the contract of Red Sox outfielder George Metkovich. The twenty-six-year-old left-hander had played four seasons with Boston, his best year being 1944, when he batted .277. Primarily a singles hitter, Metkovich was expected to be the temporary replacement for Hank Edwards. With the start of the regular season two weeks away, the outfield was still uncertain, with rookie Dale Mitchell, Pat Seerey, Hal Peck, and Metkovich to juggle around.

On April 3, the Indians closed training camp and prepared to barnstorm through the Southwest with the Giants. The Cleveland players and staff had come away with a favorable impression of Arizona, and the team had already decided to return in 1948. Most of the players were pleased with the dry climate, except for Bob Feller, who complained that it caused tightness in his right shoulder. If so, he recovered quickly, three days later pitching seven innings in a 2–1 win in Oklahoma City. An overflow crowd of 11,157 watched the game, a large part of them standing behind ropes in deep center field. The following day 7,000 fans crammed the ballpark in Fort Smith, Arkansas, bringing the two-day total to 18,157. Since the first exhibition game at Tucson the Indians had drawn a spectacular 125,000 fans.

A 1947 *Baseball Digest* article gives an idea of what a team's expenses for spring training amounted to. Transportation alone could run as high as $12,000, while hotels were estimated at $10,000. Another $1,000 went toward laundry, buses, baseballs, and uniforms. Meals provided for players came to about $3,000. All that totaled about $26,000, but the Indians' heavy exhibition schedule had enabled the team to come out ahead.

While the Indians and Giants moved slowly toward the east, the winner of the Indians' batboy contest was announced. Jack Flanagan, a fifteen-year-old student at St. Ignatius High School, had won the job and the college scholarship that went with it. Veeck, deeply impressed by the applications and essays, awarded the runner-up the job of visiting team batboy and gave the next five finishers season tickets. In typical Veeck style, the owner had successfully raised the prestige of the batboy jobs along with just about every area of the Indians organization. Now it was up to the team on the field to catch up.

One of the few issues that did not find an adequate solution was the proposed lease agreement with Mayor Burke and the City of Cleveland. Other than letting the Browns use the stadium in September, Veeck kept the mayor at arm's length, finding fault with several of the city's new suggestions. He let it be known that his reluctance to sign stemmed from the Cleveland Concessions Company retaining food and drink rights indefinitely. Veeck obviously wanted his old friend Lou Jacobs to obtain the rights, using his generosity with the Browns to try and gain leverage with the city.

As far as the other proposals, Veeck probably would have compromised over a guarantee of $50,000 for rent (Veeck wanted to pay $35,000) and the city asking him to pay the cleanup bill for the stadium after the games. Attendance had reached such a level that cleaning crews had to work overtime in 1946, picking up stale popcorn, ice cream spills, and candy wrappers by the thousands. For now, Veeck would cordially meet with Mayor Burke about the new lease but would not be signing anything.

On opening day, Tuesday, April 15, Cleveland fans rolled out of their warm beds and checked the nearest window to see what the weather had brought. They were relieved to see sunshine and blue skies without any hint of rain. The weather bureau advised no rain for the day but "coolish" conditions throughout the afternoon. By the three o'clock start time, temperatures had fallen closer to the mid-thirties.

The Indians' bullpen pitchers, courtesy of Wilson Sporting Goods, had thick new blankets with the team logo blazoned on the front. Bob Feller, the opening day starter, wore a specially designed jacket with heated electric wires inside. The players were ready to handle the chill, but the record-breaking opening day crowd of 55,000 made a mental note to remember that the weatherman's word "coolish" was open to interpretation.

An hour before game time, the *Cleveland News* photographer snapped a photo of the massive wall of people trying to squeeze down the steps of the "Ox Cart Bridge," which spanned the railroad tracks on the way to the ballpark. The temporary wooden bridge dated all the way back to 1931 and the opening of Municipal Stadium. It had been slated to be rebuilt by the city numerous times over the last sixteen years, and as recently as 1945 the city had announced plans for a large two-deck iron and metal bridge, but due to changes in office, political bickering, and money issues, fans would have to continue stepping cautiously over the wobbly planks.

While the Indians and White Sox took their pregame warmups, fans succumbed to the spell of hot buttered popcorn, warm roasted peanuts, and hot dogs. Vendors could not keep up with the demand, hurrying back to the stockrooms to reload as fast as possible. The hot dog buns, piled to the ceilings an hour earlier, steadily shrank to floor level as the game went on.

Fans and reporters were surprised to find the pregame ceremonies quite close to what they had seen in the past. There were military figures marching to the flagpole, several bands playing, and floral arrangements for the managers. Veeck told reporters he was saving the spectacular shows for later in the season. He promised some great ones, including one in particular that he said made him laugh out loud whenever he thought about it.

Feller would be opposed on the mound by Chicago's Eddie Lopat, whose mastery of the curveball, screwball, and several off-speed pitches had earned him a 9–1 record against the Indians over the past three seasons. So it was no surprise when the game was scoreless after three innings. In the top of the fourth, Pat Seerey misplayed a liner by Bob Kennedy into a triple. The next hitter grounded out to Eddie Robinson, with Kennedy holding at third; then Don Kolloway lofted a medium fly ball to left. In his haste to throw home, Seerey dropped the baseball for an error, letting in the first White Sox run. They added another in the sixth and led 2–0 going into the bottom of the ninth. With two out and the fans moving towards the exits, Seerey drove a ringing double to left field. Ken Keltner then shot a sinking line drive to right, but Kennedy raced in and snagged the ball off his shoe tops. Despite a good performance by Feller, the White Sox took the Indians' home opener 2–0.

Rain washed away the next day's game but gave the Cleveland players a chance to meet with insurance men to learn about the new pension plan and what they needed to do to become eligible. The players had broken new ground in starting the plan, which over the years would become a valuable asset for those with qualified service time.

Thursday night was reserved for the Cleveland baseball writers to honor Bill Veeck as Man of the Year. The $10 a plate dinner took place at the Hollenden Hotel with six hundred guests packing the room, including most of the Indians players, who paid to get in. Notable attendees included Commissioner Chandler, league president Will Harridge, a marine commander to honor Veeck for his service, and the large cast of Cleveland sportswriters: Gordon Cobbledick and Alex Zirin from the *Plain Dealer,* Ed Bang from the *News,* and Ed McAuley and Franklin Lewis from the *Cleveland Press.* There were loads of speeches, a fine dinner, and gifts for Veeck that used up most of the proceeds, including a combination record player and radio, a portable bar, three pieces of luggage, a portable radio, and menus signed by the Indians and writers. Veeck, for once, was taken aback by the praise and gifts and unable to speak without becoming emotional.

The most touching moment of the evening concerned a local restauranteur who purchased an entire table and brought with him six boys from two of the Cleveland orphanages. The boys had stars in their eyes, meeting some of the players and dining in an expensive hotel for the first time in their young lives. After the program, a special cab waited to take each of them back to their homes. Kindness and charity were alive and thriving in Cleveland.

In other news, Veeck announced that within ten days permanent outfield fences would be installed at Municipal Stadium. Left and right center would be brought in from 435 feet to an inviting 365 feet, center field would be brought in from 470 to 410 feet, a reasonable poke for a long-ball hitter, and the foul lines would stay at 320 feet. It was hoped that cutting down the size of the outfield would finally give a fair chance to the hitters. The 420-foot shots that had been long doubles or outs for power hitters like Earl Averill and Hal Trosky in the past would now be legitimate home runs for current Indians sluggers like Ken Keltner, Joe Gordon, and Pat Seerey. The fences would be five feet, three inches high and topped with flexible wires to ease any collisions with the outfielders. The new dimensions would help outfielders as well, greatly reducing the possibility of an inside-the-park home run. They would also aid visiting players like Joe DiMaggio and Ted Williams, but the excitement for fans witnessing a barrage of home runs would be worth it. Pitchers would certainly have to bear down, knowing a 410-foot mistake would be a double off the wall or a home run instead of a long out.

The Indians opened their road schedule with a Friday afternoon game at Detroit. Red Embree pitched well, but solo homers from ex-Indian Ray Cullenbine and outfielder Pat Mullin were enough for Virgil Trucks in a three-hit, 2–0 shutout. The 46,111 Tiger fans watched the Indians hitters stretch their scoreless streak to eighteen innings.

On Saturday, Don Black was on the mound against the Tigers' Freddie Hutchinson. In the top of the fourth, Pat Seerey smashed a two-run homer to give Black an early lead. Two innings later, with the score tied 3–3, Boudreau, Les Fleming, and Joe Gordon each doubled for two more runs. With another lead to work with, Black shut down the Tigers over the last four innings for the 5–3 win. It was only one win, but the Indians pitcher was starting to make believers out of his teammates and American League fans. Boudreau indicated he would be using a rotation of Feller, Black, and Red Embree for the time being.

The Indians were back home Tuesday for a two-game series with St. Louis. Temperatures peaked in the mid-forties. Bob Feller must have been wearing his electric jacket, because the Browns saw an abundance of heat throughout the game. Feller mowed down the first nineteen batters he faced before surrendering a base hit to right fielder Al Zarilla. An inning earlier Joe Gordon stroked his first home run as an Indian. The three-run blast gave Feller all the support he needed in a 5–0 victory. The one-hitter was the ninth of Feller's storied career. He struck out ten hitters and walked only one, in the ninth inning. The timing could not have been better, as Feller's new book, *Strikeout Story,* had just hit the newsstands and other retail outlets. Sales forecasts were excellent, promising another stream of income for the one-man entrepreneur. Feller did book signings at the downtown Cleveland bookstores and department stores, with one appearance selling an unbelievable 2,000 books.

After another victory over the Browns, putting them near the top of the early standings, the Indians moved on to Chicago. Don Black started the first game there, seeking his second win of the season. Cleveland got on the scoreboard first in the top of the second inning when Pat Seerey hit a solo home run to the left field seats. Black made the lone tally stand up, yielding only four hits and a walk in a 1–0 shutout. The season was much too young to draw any conclusions, but the Indians' starting pitchers were taking care of the opposition with relative ease. Boudreau had had a phone installed in the stadium dugout for calling the bullpen, but he had not yet had a reason to use it.

Back home in Cleveland after a loss to Chicago, Feller faced the Tigers and Hal Newhouser before a nice crowd of 40,925. The Saturday numbers were swelled by the first Ladies Day of the year, adding over 20,000 female rooters to a surprising total for late April. Veeck, showman that he was, wanted to debut the fences by stopping the game after three innings and having the grounds crew quickly install them. Will Harridge advised him there were no rules against it, but he needed permission from the Tigers. Veeck asked manager Steve O'Neill, who vigorously shook his head no. The fences would have to be installed after the game.

With the fence plan thwarted, Pat Seerey showed he could reach the seats without one when he hit a home run into the upper deck in left field. Jim Hegan added two triples and two RBIs to help Feller coast to another shutout, 6–0. Newhouser lost his sixth decision in eight tries to the Cleveland ace, throwing cold water on the idea that the Detroit star was the top pitcher in the American League. Though he had only pitched three games, Feller was off to a torrid start, on pace to equal or better his tremendous season of a year ago.

Sunday was designated throughout the Major Leagues as Babe Ruth Day to honor the Sultan of Swat for all he had done for baseball. Each home team would give free admission to large numbers of orphans, who were always close to the Babe's heart. Unfortunately, it rained in Cleveland, but overall the day was a triumph for Ruth and his kids. He appeared at Yankee Stadium looking gaunt and weak after a long stay in a New York hospital, where he had undergone a serious neck operation for throat cancer. Standing before the microphones wearing his fashionable camel hair coat and cap, he told the crowd, and thousands of children and adults across the United States, "The only real game in the world is baseball. In this game you have got to start way down at the bottom if you're going to be successful." After a thunderous round of applause from the Yankee fans, the Babe accepted a bronze plaque from the American League offices, which read, "In honor of and in appreciation of Babe Ruth, whose contribution to baseball will live forever." Even suffering from an incurable illness, the Babe still commanded attention across the country which few if any baseball players or anyone else could equal.

The next day the skies cleared enough for the Indians and Tigers to finish their brief series. The new fences were in place. Ken Keltner lifted a drive to the 365-foot sign in left center. Dick Wakefield glided back and stretched his 6'4" frame over the fence to haul in the ball, and Keltner jogged back to the dugout wondering what he had to do to get a home run. The Indians lost the game 3–0 to Dizzy Trout, who homered and knocked in two runs to help his own cause.

After a loss to the A's in a two-game series abbreviated to one by rain, the Boston Red Sox were next to visit Municipal Stadium, given the unenviable task of trying to cool off Bob Feller. In the top of the first inning, Johnny Pesky rapped a base hit, but that was all Boston could muster. Joe Gordon homered to help Feller rack up his third shutout in a row and tenth one-hitter of his career, 2–0. He fanned ten batters and lowered his season ERA to a microscopic 0.26. After the game, an army of newspaper photographers swarmed Feller, snapping pictures for fifteen minutes.

Every day at the stadium seemed to bring a new level of excitement. Ladies Day on Saturday, May 3, included 3,441 enthusiastic females to cheer on the home team. In the bottom of the first, George Metkovich, Pat Seerey, and Joe Gordon brought the fans to their feet with home runs. Two innings later a burst of rain stopped the contest for nearly half an hour. The crowd watched with interest as Emil Bossard's crack grounds crew unrolled and spread the tarp over the infield in a shade under four minutes. Their swift response kept the infield playable enough for the umpires to signal game on when the rain ceased.

In the bottom of the fourth inning, the Indians loaded the bases with Joe Gordon coming to bat. The former Yankee made an impact in style, slamming a home run over the shortened left field fence. Red Embree breezed through the formidable Boston lineup to win 9–3. So far Bill Veeck's fences were considerably assisting Indians hitters. Over the course of the season the numbers would even out some, but early in the schedule the Indians were becoming home run champs.

With interest in the ball club growing every day, the publicity department began issuing *Indians News,* a smart four-page newsletter. Published every other month and available at newsstands around northeast Ohio or packed inside the ten-cent scorecard, it offered stories and features about the team and individual players. Game action shots were highlighted along with previews of opponents and updated roster summaries. The front page carried a schedule of upcoming home games with notations for Ladies Days. It was one way in which the Indians' front office continued to break new ground in promotion techniques. Other owners and general managers who wanted to keep pace would need to change their ways of doing business.

The next day Cleveland played Washington in front of 43,340 spectators. In nine home games, mostly in April, the Indians had drawn 163,107 fans, a remarkable figure given the rain and cold temperatures for most of the contests. With the more hospitable summer weather still to come, a new attendance record seemed a certainty. Cleveland led 3–2 heading into the top of the seventh when Boudreau used his dugout telephone to summon Bob Feller to the mound. His scoreless streak of twenty-nine innings came to an abrupt halt as the Senators pounded him for four runs. After Feller's one inning, Bob Lemon finished out the last two frames. Washington won the ballgame, 6–3, giving Feller the loss and bringing him back down to earth.

The Wednesday, May 7, game against the Yankees was postponed due to thirty-six-degree temperatures and light snow, complicating matters for Veeck, who had planned a special afternoon for seven hundred members of the Youngstown school safety program who were on their way to see the game. Rather than forwarding his apologies to the children and sending them back home, Veeck dispatched Boudreau and Feller to meet the train and talk with the students, and he bought seven hundred tickets at the downtown Palace Theatre so the students could have an afternoon at the pictures. It was an excellent public relations move, but it was also a demonstration of Veeck's real fondness for children and his commitment to doing acts of kindness.

A week later, Veeck again showed his deep affection for children. Glenwood Brann Jr., an eleven-year-old boy from Malden, Massachusetts, had lost both his legs in a freak accident while horsing around with some pals. Veeck sent a long letter to the boy with an Indians cap and a team-autographed ball. He wrote about his own injury as a marine, telling the boy about his amputation and how he fought back and overcame the loss. Veeck then embellished the truth a little by telling him that Major League scouts had seen Glenwood playing second base at school and been impressed by his play.

Cheered by the letter and the gifts, the boy let his nurses and doctors know everything would be okay. It did not hurt that the previous day Ted Williams, after promising to hit a home run for him, belted not one but two. Veeck had gone out of his way to brighten the life of a child who had little to do with his Cleveland team or publicity. He was probably making himself a strong candidate for a second Man of the Year award.

The City of Cleveland was pondering ways to improve revenue at the stadium. Since a new lease was blocked by the Indians, the city searched for events that might put a little more in the coffers. The sport of midget car racing, on tracks as short as a quarter mile, had been popular since the 1930s all across the United States and over to England and Australia. Noticing the money to be made from it, the city decided to join the craze and build a dirt track outside the foul lines and far into the corners of the outfield. This would require tearing up ground and hastily covering it over when the Indians played at home. Veeck hated the idea but had no way to stop it.

Construction on the track was not yet completed when the Indians returned to Cleveland on Thursday, May 22, for their next homestand. Several days of nonstop rain and the ditches from the unfinished track left the playing field a quagmire. The American League sent a representative to examine the swamped infield. His decision would determine if the Friday night game with St. Louis would have to be forfeited or changed to an afternoon game at League Park. Emil Bossard's grounds crew worked around the clock, attempting to get the field into playable condition. Mayor Burke, no doubt having second thoughts about auto racing, sent a hundred city workers to aid Bossard. The improvised crew worked into early Friday morning, and in the end the rep approved the field. This was the Indians' first night game of the season, and Veeck's plans included fireworks, a barbershop quartet, and Bob Hope doing a live comedy routine over WGAR radio. If the game had been canceled or hastily moved to League Park, Veeck stood to lose a small fortune. Fortunately, in front of a gigantic crowd of 61,227, everything went off as planned. After all that work to make it happen, the game went to extra innings tied at 3–3. Indians reliever Bryan Stephens, in relief of Feller, held off the Browns until the top of the twelfth, when they scored two runs to win 5–3. The near-disaster did nothing to help relations between Mayor Burke and Veeck, though things might have been even worse if the rep had given a thumbs down to playing.

A week earlier the Indians had cut their roster to the mandatory twenty-five, sending Gene Bearden to Baltimore and Dale Mitchell back to Oklahoma City. Both moves caused trouble. Mitchell refused to report to the minor league club, while Bearden announced he would not play at Baltimore, preferring to go to California, where his family lived, and pitch again for Oakland. Though Bearden had no real leverage, and the Oaks were not affiliated with Cleveland, Veeck yielded, working out a deal to loan Bearden to the Oaks for the season.

Mitchell was batting a measly .143 with the Indians, but he felt that because injuries had caused him to play at less than 100 percent the demotion was not warranted. A stalemate began that lasted for two weeks. The Indians were the ones to cave in, sending outfielder Ted Sepkowski to the Yankees on waivers to make room for Mitchell's return. Soon he would prove the club had made a serious mistake by trying to send him down.

The end of May found the Indians in third place with a record of 16–14, four games behind the league-leading Tigers. The first two months of the season had brought a series of ups and downs, a large number of rainouts and crowds (when weather permitted) of spectacular proportions. After starting the season on pace to break every conceivable pitching record, Bob Feller began having difficulty with his control and with completing games. Pat Seerey went on a home run binge, followed by a severe slump that finally placed him on the trading block. On the bright side, Joe Gordon proved to be far from done, hitting the long ball and driving in runs as in the old days. Boudreau turned to Bill Veeck for assistance in finding a player or players to help turn the season around before the June 15 trading deadline.

Chapter 11

LARRY DOBY ARRIVES

In June, Bill Veeck received a petition, signed by a hundred fans, asking that the new fences be adjusted. At the left and right field corners, instead of curving back right away from 320 feet at the foul lines to 365 in left and right center, they jutted out for ten feet or so before they began to curve, so that the distance was still 320 feet even well off the lines. Visiting clubs had been taking advantage of this, hitting home runs that should not have been, and the fans asked Veeck to move the fences to a more reasonable angle. Veeck agreed, and gave the order to do it.

Another question that was not so easy to resolve concerned the lease negotiations. It was learned that the city had violated the old agreement. The city was required to choose a food company by February 1. Since it had waited until after that date to choose Cleveland Concessions for the 1947 season, the Indians should have had the option to choose for themselves. Veeck sent his attorneys to City Hall, demanding a new concession agreement. It was no secret that Veeck's buddy Lou Jacobs was ready to load his trucks in Buffalo with peanuts and popcorn and drive them straight to Municipal Stadium. Despite Veeck seeming to have a good case, the court declined to resolve the stalemate.

On Friday night, June 7, for the eighteenth time that year, the game was canceled by rain. The unusual number of rainouts meant that more doubleheaders would have to be squeezed into the already busy schedule. According to the new agreement with the player reps, double-headers could not be played after night games, which left fewer options for scheduling them. Some would have to be played back-to-back or during the week.

Three days later, on a hot, dry evening, the Indians took on the Boston Red Sox in front of close to 50,000 fans. Outside the stadium forty-eight chartered buses from New York, Pennsylvania, and all around Ohio were parked. Max Axelrod, the beleaguered owner of Cleveland Concessions, almost exhausted his supply of soft drinks and beer. He told reporters enough drinks were sold to fill a good-sized ship. After losing 3–2, the Indians could have used a few of those beers.

The next day at the stadium was designated Cy Young Day to honor the old Cleveland Spider and Nap, who had turned eighty back in March. Veeck had attended Cy's birthday party in Newcomerstown, Ohio, where he had presented him with a new automobile, and had invited the entire community to see the afternoon game on June 11 at no charge. Cy and 4,800 friends from Tuscawaras County took advantage of the offer. The Hall of Famer had lunch at the ballpark with some of the Cleveland Naps players of forty years ago, including Bill Bradley, Elmer Flick, Terry Turner, and Paddy Livingston, and before the ballgame he received presents of a set of luggage and a heater and radio for his new car. The Red Sox spoiled the party again, blanking the Indians 3–0.

On Friday night at the stadium, midget racing took the spotlight. More than 21,000 racing fans were in attendance. Twelve cars navigated thirty laps around the outside of the diamond, splattering the fans in the front rows with mud. Though it was a financial success, the damage done by the cars gave the city reason to reconsider having the races there.

The Indians were on the road, where they won six of twelve games. A much-improved Jim Hegan took the hitting honors, as his extended spring training began to pay dividends. In a game against Boston, Hegan homered and singled to drive in all the Cleveland runs in the 3–2 victory. His proud hometown of Lynn, Massachusetts, presented their guy with a new Buick, a refrigerator, a radio, and a check for $1,000. His torrid hitting continued when the Indians returned home. At one point he connected for eight straight hits before making an out. In the midst of Jim's hot hitting, four-year-old Mike Hegan and his mom visited the clubhouse, rummaging through Dad's locker and trying on his spikes. Reporters asked the blue-eyed, blond-haired little boy what he thought of his father's play of late. Mike responded wisely, "Dad is hitting pretty good."

At the end of June, the All-Star teams' starting lineups were announced, based on voting by the fans nationwide. Boudreau led American League shortstops with 748,153 votes, finishing third overall behind Joe DiMaggio and Ted Williams. Lou had an injured ankle again, leaving his status for the game undetermined. Joe Gordon also made the lineup, edging out Boston's Bobby Doerr for the second base starting job. Pitchers and reserves would be named later, but Bob Feller, with ten victories, seemed to be a certainty, while Jim Hegan and his hot bat stood a chance of joining the reserves.

The Tigers were in town for a four-game series beginning July 2. The first game featured another Bill Veeck spectacular at the stadium, a night to honor Mel Harder. Harder was still on the roster, but had pitched only a handful of times. In front of 56,359 fans, the ceremony began with the largest fireworks display of the season, followed by a presentation of a $4,000 check from Veeck, $200 for each of his twenty years as a member of the Indians. Next came a brand-new Buick courtesy of Veeck, who had likely worked out an advertising tradeoff with a local dealer. Tris Speaker himself drove the car to the infield. There were telegrams from Happy Chandler, Will Harridge, old friend Mel Ott, and former teammate Joe Vosmik. A tan puppy was handed to Mel along with 221 red carnations to signify his career win total. It was a fitting night for a great pitcher who was near the end as a ballplayer but still at the forefront of Cleveland baseball. The Indians dropped the game 6–5.

While the Tigers were still in town, Bill Veeck dropped a bombshell. He had bought the contract of twenty-three-year-old infielder Larry Doby, from the Negro League's Newark Eagles. Veeck intended for Doby to join the team on July 5 in Chicago at the start of a western swing. Pressed for comment by reporters from all three Cleveland papers, Veeck stated, "[Jackie] Robinson has proved to be a real big leaguer, so I wanted to get the best available negro boy while the getting was good." Veeck was probably being paternalistic in using the word "boy," but nonetheless could have phrased the quote differently. Veeck saw to it the color barrier was broken in the American League, and would become a lifelong friend of Doby, yet his language here echoed some of the worst parts of American history and exhibited some of the ubiquitous prejudice in America at the time. The White newspapers freely circulated the comment without any thoughts to its racial nature.

Jackie Robinson became the first Black man to break the modern Major League color barrier when he started at first base for the Brooklyn Dodgers on April 15, 1947. Veeck's move was not made on a whim. For a few months he waited to see how things developed with the Dodgers and Robinson. When the sky did not fall, he asked around to get a consensus on which Negro League ballplayer was on par with Robinson. The name he got back was Larry Doby. Veeck assigned Cleveland scout Bill Killefer, who had been a Major League catcher for thirteen years, to watch Doby play. Killefer's scouting report came indicating that Doby had the ability to play for Cleveland. With the trading deadline already past, the traditional options were to check the waiver wire or buy or promote a prospect from a minor league club. Veeck chose another option. He knew that after Robinson and Doby there were more talented ballplayers to be found playing in the Negro Leagues.

Larry Doby was born on December 12, 1923, in Camden, South Carolina. His father, David, a semipro baseball player, died when Larry was a small boy, leaving the boy to be raised by his grandmother. At twelve years old Larry moved north to Paterson, New Jersey, to reunite with his mother. He got his start in baseball playing for the Smart Sets, one of the first-class Black teams in the city.

In 1938, he entered Eastside High, where he played basketball and baseball. Within the next two years he added football and track. In his junior and senior years, he became an All-State performer in baseball and basketball, and as a halfback led the football team to the New Jersey state championship. By the time he graduated he had earned ten letters in four sports and was one of the greatest athletes in Eastside High School history.

In the fall of 1942, Doby entered Long Island University with the intention of playing varsity sports, but soon a draft notice took him out of school and into the navy. He was assigned to the Great Lakes Naval Training Station and went on to play on the touring Black baseball team. It was then that he would play for the first time at Cleveland Municipal Stadium. Soon the order came to ship out to the South Pacific and join the naval base on Guam. He remained on the island until the end of the war, serving as an athletic instructor.

Upon his return home, Doby had to consider his future. He settled on playing professional baseball. He signed with the Newark Eagles in 1946 and had a terrific season, batting .342 with 9 home runs. That winter he played for a Puerto Rican baseball club in Latin America. In a short season there he found his power stroke, belting 14 home runs. In the spring he reported to Newark, and in just three months of the regular season collected 10 doubles, 8 home runs, and 41 RBIs.

Convinced he had the right guy, Bill Veeck contacted Eagles owner Effie Manley to make an offer for their best player. At the time he would not reveal how much he had paid for Doby, saying only that he handed over a good chunk of change. Ms. Manley would later claim that with few options she had accepted much less than he was worth; the amount Veeck paid is believed to be $15,000.

At 7:00 a.m., home after a game in Wilmington the day before, Doby picked up the telephone to find Effie Manley on the line, telling him the Cleveland Indians had purchased his contract. A few hours later the phone rang again. This time it was Louis Jones, the only Black member of the Cleveland front office. Jones said he would arrive in New Jersey the next day and accompany him to Chicago, where he would get acquainted with Veeck.

News of the historic acquisition quickly reached the newspapers, and reporters planted themselves on his doorstep. Larry politely answered their rapid-fire questions. "It's a big jump from our league to the majors," he said, "but I think I can make it. If I fail it won't be because I did not try." The reporters described him as soft-spoken, a nonsmoker, and looking younger than his twenty-three years. The stories printed were favorable, piquing the interest of fans across the country.

Doby had just enough time to throw together a suitcase, take a deep breath, and say good-bye to his new wife, Helyn. The young couple had been high school sweethearts and were destined to be together for over fifty years. During their time at high school, he had wanted her to see him play baseball, but, with nine brothers and sisters, she had nonstop babysitting duties. Fortunately, Helyn could spare a few hours to cheer on her boyfriend at football games on the weekends. The two of them had been suddenly thrust into the limelight with no time to prepare themselves.

Louis Jones arrived in the morning to take Larry to the train for the long journey to Chicago. It is not known what they talked about while the rail car sped along, but Jones's mission was to reassure Doby and deliver him safely to the ball club.

Mixed in with all the stories about Doby was an editorial in the *Sporting News* advising caution about the direction baseball was taking. The editorial quoted an unnamed ballplayer, an All-Star. The player claimed he had no objection to playing alongside a Negro, and that he felt it would be wrong for baseball not to accept Black ballplayers and the game should yield to the wave of the future. However, he revealed some bitterness that others might have shared. "I fought my way through the minors for five years and I rode buses all night," he said. "If we are to have Negroes in the majors let them go through the same preparation that the white player is forced to undergo." Robinson had joined the Dodgers after one year at Montreal, and Doby had had no experience at all in White organized baseball, and this player saw their quick promotion to the Major Leagues as a kind of reverse discrimination.

The argument failed to note that Robinson and Doby were two of the best players anywhere and did not need a long period of seasoning in the minor leagues. When it came to talent, men like Veeck and Brooklyn's Branch Rickey were color-blind, willing to sign any player, Black or White, who could potentially help their teams right away. Bob Feller skipped the minors entirely, while Tris Speaker, Ty Cobb, and Babe Ruth spent little time there. Even Cleveland players such as Ken Keltner, Mel Harder, and manager Boudreau made the Indians' roster after only short stints in the minors. Most Hall of Fame players tend to reach the Majors sooner than those who are destined to be .260 lifetime hitters or .500 pitchers. The *Sporting News* editorial, along with the unnamed player, was well off the mark.

In Chicago, Doby and Jones met Bill Veeck at the team hotel. In front of representatives of all the Cleveland newspapers, including the *Call and Post*, Cleveland's Black paper, Doby signed his 1947 contract. He hurried from there to Comiskey Park, where he was welcomed in the locker room by Boudreau, who told him to suit up. Moments later the manager and player emerged from the dugout and played catch, followed by infield practice, where Doby worked at second with Joe Gordon.

Boudreau was faced with the problem of where to play the rookie. Gordon was anchored at second base, Keltner at third, and the shortstop position was definitely not available. Doby had played outfield for

Newark on a limited basis, but he lacked the experience to try it for Cleveland. Veeck usually did his homework well, but this time he had not thought through on where his new acquisition might break into the lineup. He left the challenging issue up to Boudreau to figure out.

Larry Doby made his Major League debut that afternoon as a pinch hitter for pitcher Bryan Stephens in the top of the seventh inning. Wearing number 14, the left-hander hit the ball sharply down the left field line, just a few inches foul. With the count at 2–2, he took another heavy swing but missed badly. Sitting in the dugout were two men in suits, Chicago plainclothes detectives assigned to protect Doby in case of any incidents. The hometown fans seemed more interested in the runs on the scoreboard than in the historic occasion, as their White Sox beat the Indians 6–5.

After losing the first game of the doubleheader on Sunday, Boudreau made the hard decision to start Doby at first base in the nightcap. This did not sit well with Eddie Robinson, who reportedly refused to let go of his first baseman's glove. After arguing heatedly with several club officials, he reluctantly gave it up, but not directly to Doby. There are conflicting explanations for Robinson's behavior. A biography of Doby claims his motivation was purely racial: for a man from a small town in Texas, having to loan his glove to a Black man was an affront. Robinson would claim in his autobiography, however, that race was not a factor. Two days earlier, in the first game of a doubleheader against the Tigers, Robinson had hit two home runs and batted in five. He seemed to be hitting his stride as a power-hitting first baseman and had recently received a vote of confidence from manager Boudreau. But when the Indians signed Doby, Robinson did the math, figuring that the only position for Doby was first base. Veeck would not have paid "a good chunk of cash" for the new player to warm the bench, Robinson assumed. And being benched for Doby only confirmed that thought, infuriating him to the point where he considered quitting the team and going home. We will probably never know for sure, but after the All-Star break Eddie Robinson was back at first base on a regular basis. Doby would have to play another position, but where?

The *Call and Post* reported that several Chicago Black churches let their members out early to allow them time to head to Comiskey and buy their tickets for the doubleheader. Entire families came with picnic baskets and bottled water to sit out the long afternoon in hopes of seeing the first Black player in the American League take the field. Doby handled eight throws without any difficulty and in four trips to the plate had one single, a high chopper in the infield that he legged out for his first Major League base hit. Though the ball did not go past the pitcher's mound, it did score Dale Mitchell from third, helping the Indians to a 5–1 victory.

The game brought an end to the first half of the season. The players not chosen for the All-Star game scattered in different directions to spend a few days with family and friends. Doby went to Cleveland, where he was greeted at the Majestic Hotel by leading members of the Black community, including W. O. Walker, editor of the *Call and Post*, Cleveland Browns star fullback Marion Motley, and members of the Cleveland Buckeyes baseball team. Motley and Doby knew each other from their time at the Great Lakes Naval Training Center.

Doby would have a few friends on the Indians, such as Steve Gromek and Jim Hegan, who would kid around with him in the locker room. Sometimes when the clubhouse phone rang Gromek or Hegan would yell to him that it was Lena Horne, the gorgeous Black singer-actress, looking for him. The other players were mostly standoffish, unsure how to act around him. In the western cities, restaurants and hotels were often segregated, causing some of the players to leave Doby out when they went on the town. They feared that when they took him to a nightspot the maître de or concierge would inevitably refuse admittance.

Doby, like Jackie Robinson, possessed great inner strength and was intent on ignoring the racial slights and concentrating on setting a good example for owners and general managers to observe. Their behavior paved the way for more Black ballplayers in Major League Baseball. Doby would face untold insults from opposing players and fans around the league, but he never responded, looking ahead to the day when equality would be the norm.

On Thursday, July 10, the Indians began the second half of the baseball schedule with a twilight doubleheader against the Athletics. Though they were a game under .500, 47,871 fans came out to the stadium. Don Black started the first game and immediately got in trouble by walking Eddie Joost and Barney McCosky on eight pitches, but made it through the inning without any hits or runs scored. After a forty-five-minute rain delay, the Indians scored three times in the bottom of the second on singles by Robinson, Gordon, Hegan, and Metkovich along with a perfectly executed squeeze bunt by Black to take the lead, 3–0. In the top of the third inning, the A's Elmer Valo lifted a pop fly into shallow right field. Joe Gordon, with his back turned to the infield, sloshed towards no-man's-land and caught up with the ball at the last possible moment. The crowd applauded the difficult running catch.

The score remained 3–0 through the middle innings as fans began to realize the Athletics had not recorded a single base hit. Black remained wild, but his fastball and slider kept the hitters guessing. The A's were still hitless in the top of the ninth inning when Sam Chapman came to bat with two out. The fans were standing, ready to explode. Black delivered and Chapman hit a bouncing ball to the pitcher's mound. Though nervous and sweating profusely, Black fielded the baseball and threw to Eddie Robinson for the final out. Don Black had just pitched the tenth no-hitter in Cleveland Indians history. His teammates raced to the mound, grabbing and hugging him. The moment was even sweeter for him after the long way he had come since his days of out-of-control drinking.

On his way to the clubhouse, Black was cornered by Jack Graney for a radio interview. He said all the right things, complimenting Jim Hegan, Joe Gordon, and the rest of the players for all their help in preserving the special game. In the clubhouse, the reporters surrounded him, wanting to know every detail. Black answered their questions, then pulled aside Alex Zirin from the *Plain Dealer* and asked for a big favor. Though he had been in Cleveland since April, he could not find a reasonable apartment or house to rent for his wife, Joyce, and two daughters. Knowing that readers would be reading all about him in Friday's sport pages, he asked Zirin to put a note in for him about needing a place to live. Even after he had just enjoyed his finest moment in baseball, Black was thinking of his family first and how much he wanted them there.

The second game was a scoreless duel between Bob Feller and Philadelphia's Dick Fowler until the Athletics got a run in the top of the sixth. In the Indians' half of the seventh, Dale Mitchell singled and Hank Edwards homered to give them the lead. Feller developed a blister on his finger in the top of the ninth, but Ed Klieman finished the game for a 2–1 win and a sweep of the doubleheader.

For the rest of July, even with better-than-average pitching, the Indians plodded along, failing to make any kind of move to raise themselves in the American League standings. Larry Doby mostly sat on the bench, occasionally pinch-hitting but seeing little time on the field. The club did not seem to know what to do with him. The starting infield played well, with Joe Gordon chasing a thirty–home run season, Keltner driving in runs, Robinson continuing to improve, and Boudreau immovable at shortstop. Perhaps a demotion to Oklahoma City, where he could play every day, would have been the best option for Doby, but the front office did nothing.

Near the end of July, Bill Veeck underwent further surgery on his partially amputated leg. Because of his always-on-the-go lifestyle, the leg had never fully healed after the first operation, leading to an additional infection. The doctors removed another two inches of leg and warned Veeck sternly to allow ample healing time before he did any more ballroom dancing. This time he followed orders.

On August 8, the Indians reached an attendance milestone, going over 1,000,000 for the second straight year. The millionth customer, a startled eighteen-year-old waitress, received special mention in the newspapers along with two season passes for the 1948 season. Their 1946 record was only 44,000 fans away. With some luck and some good weather, the team was on track to hit the 1.5 million mark, a tremendous accomplishment for a club struggling to stay above .500.

Three days later, Bob Feller drew some unwanted attention when he announced his fall barnstorming tour. He neglected to run the itinerary by Veeck, who would have advised him against the scheduled stopover in Cuba, where Feller planned to pitch five games for the Almendoras club in regular season play. Not pleased, Commissioner Chandler issued a statement banning any Major League player from playing games in the Cuban baseball league. "Major League baseball players shall not play as members of the Cuban Winter League during the 1947–48 season. Players may play during the barnstorming period outside of the continental United States if their schedules are approved by the commissioner and they do not play with or against ineligible players," he said. Chandler believed there were ballplayers in Cuba that he did not want his guys mixing with. The commissioner also believed it would be wrong for a Major League player to participate in league games in a foreign league. There was no issue, he said, if Feller wanted to play in exhibition games with picked squads, but at no time could he take part in the Cuban league official schedule.

Surprised by the backlash, Feller asked reporters, "Players are permitted to conduct barnstorming tours in other places outside the U.S., why should Cuba be the exception?" Feller went on to say his contract stipulated that he would not face any players who were banned in the United States. Feller's disagreement with the ruling made headlines. He told Ed McAuley, writing for the *Cleveland News* and nationally for the *Sporting News,* that "no employer should be able to tell his men how much they can earn, or where they can earn it once they've fulfilled their contract obligation for the season." Feller also commented on the owners' decision at a July 7 meeting to delay the start of the barnstorming season until October 8. Feller knew the biggest crowds turned out in the first week of the month and dwindled later due to football games and cold weather. In 1946, he said, the early October crowds added up to about 150,000 fans, which accounted for a large share of the barnstorming revenue.

Writers around the country took turns blasting Feller for his pursuit of the almighty dollar. Robert L. Burns, a columnist for the *St. Louis Globe-Democrat,* wrote, "For a while it might be a good idea for him to quit worrying about how many thousands of dollars he will make during the barnstorming period and do something about earning that $90,000 President Bill Veeck of the Indians is paying him." Feller was making more money than the president of the United States, Burns stated, and he should stop lining up business ventures while in the middle of a season. The $90,000 figure may have been a tad high, though the fantastic gate numbers in Cleveland meant Feller was about to cash in on his attendance bonus.

Cleveland fans wrote numerous letters to the local papers, most of them asking Feller to concentrate on pitching and nothing else. His record at the time was 14–9, good for most pitchers but not up to Bob Feller standards. He had been lit up in a recent start in Chicago, surrendering eight runs on twelve hits, two of them home runs, and striking out only two batters. A year ago he was burning up the American League; in 1947, not so much.

Veeck summoned Feller to his hospital room for a private chat. Afterwards Veeck told newsmen, "Feller knows his main job is to pitch winning baseball for the Cleveland Indians. I've been worrying quite a lot about him, but I feel a whole lot better now." That evening Feller pitched the second game of a home twilight doubleheader against the Yankees. When he stepped to the mound, many of the 52,105 fans booed him loudly, but as the game progressed the boos turned to cheers as Feller pitched a four-hitter, giving up only one unearned run in a 6–1 victory.

Bob Lemon won the first game 4–3, making excellent progress in his bid to become the number two starter.

The next afternoon against New York, Eddie Robinson came to bat in the bottom of the third inning against ex-Indian Allie Reynolds. The pitch came and Eddie fouled a ball off his right ankle. For several minutes he tried to walk it off, but limped to the bench unable to continue. X-rays revealed a small bone fracture in the ankle, sidelining him for the rest of the season. The loss of Robinson left a vacancy at the first base position. It could have been an opportunity for Larry Doby to show what he could do, but Boudreau and Veeck chose to insert Les Fleming in Robinson's place. Fleming did have years of experience at first, but did not figure in the Indians' long-range plans.

Going into September, the Indians were still hovering around the .500 mark. Recently discharged from the hospital, Bill Veeck planned a classic night out, though it had nothing to do with baseball. He had been invited to a movie-themed party by friends in Shaker Heights, an affluent eastside suburb. Inspired by the 1923 silent film *The Covered Wagon*, Veeck somehow managed to rent a covered wagon and six mules to pull it and loaded them all on a large flatbed truck. The truck arrived at the party, but the mules were not about to jump off it. Veeck, always the quick thinker, drove to the Shaker Heights fire station and borrowed several long planks to coax the mules down. By then it was already 11:00 in the evening, but that did not bother Veeck as he made his grand entrance to the party with half the neighborhood standing outside gawking.

The Indians ended the season in fourth place with a record of 80–74, much improved from a year ago, when they won only 68. Individually the players put up some good numbers. Joe Gordon hit 29 home runs, breaking the previous record for Cleveland right-handers by three. Dale Mitchell batted an impressive .316 to finish sixth among all American League hitters. Lou Boudreau hit .307 while leading the league with 45 doubles. Bob Feller was the strikeout king once again with 196, though that was far below his record 348 in 1946, and won 20 games. The Indians' front office, however, expected much more from him.

Feller would get permission to stage another barnstorming tour, renting a DC-3 and covering as much of the United States as he could squeeze into his schedule. With him on the tour were teammates Hegan, Lemon, and Keltner, along with Jeff Heath, Ralph Kiner, and several others. Max Patkin and Jackie Price were hired to provide entertainment at the exhibitions. Some bad weather hampered the schedule, but during a late-October trip to Mexico they played in front of sellout crowds in several cities, likely recouping any losses.

Bob Lemon had a fine second half of the season and ended up winning 11 games and losing only 5. He had earned the chance to be at least the number three starter and possibly number two. Don Black recorded 10 wins, including the no-hitter, and Al Gettel, staying under the radar, won 11. Veeck would need one more starter, either by a trade or from the minors, to contribute in 1948.

Larry Doby remained a fixture on the bench, even in September when the Indians called up several prospects for a look. Though they had nothing at stake, the Indians continued to use Les Fleming exclusively at first base despite his .245 season average. Doby, used only as an occasional pinch hitter, appeared in twenty-nine games, totaling only 32 at bats, 5 hits, and 2 RBIs for an average of .156. What plans the organization had for him were yet to be determined. He would report in the spring to Tucson as a man without a set position.

The attendance for the year was a phenomenal 1,521,978, fourth in the Major Leagues behind the three New York teams. Cleveland averaged nearly 20,000 fans per game, a tribute to Veeck and his staff for an amazing job of tirelessly promoting the team across northeast Ohio. Veeck knew, however, that the fans would not keep coming if the team failed to improve further. The off-season would be filled with trade talk, innuendos, and rumors about most of the players on the roster, setting the scene for an intriguing year to come.

Chapter 12

THE BOUDREAU CONTROVERSY

The 1947 World Series was an all–New York affair pitting the Yankees against the cross-town Brooklyn Dodgers. Bill Veeck was in the stands networking round the clock with just about every Major League executive. Usually his manager was with him, but Boudreau skipped the series and went directly home to Harvey, Illinois. Before the season ended, Veeck had revealed a lack of confidence in his player-manager by letting his contract expire without serious negotiations. All he offered was a one-year player contract at $50,000. It was no secret that Veeck thought highly of Lou's playing ability, but not of how he ran the ball club. Boudreau saw little reason to spend any of his off-season time with his boss.

On Friday, October 3, fans were startled to read a bold-type front-page headline of the *Cleveland News* that said, "Boudreau Through with Indians." Ed McAuley broke the story, citing a fellow reporter with a Chicago newspaper. According to the source, Veeck wanted to trade Boudreau for St. Louis Browns shortstop Vern Stephens. The deal, being negotiated with Browns general manager Bill DeWitt, included the Indians' Red Embree and George Metkovich. In return, the Browns would send Stephens along with pitcher Jack Kramer and outfielder Paul Lehner.

McAuley contacted Veeck, advising him that Cleveland fans would hate the trade and he would lose the strong relationship he had built up with them. Veeck seemed resigned to that, believing the deal would strengthen the ball club and place them in position to win a pennant. Stephens could not match Boudreau on the defensive side, but he could provide a lot of home runs and RBIs. Kramer, a veteran right-hander, would add stability to the pitching staff to go along with Feller and Lemon, while Lehner was a young outfielder with potential. On paper it looked like a trade that would benefit the Indians, but on the emotional side it looked like a disaster. Boudreau, a stalwart in the lineup since 1939, was loved by the fans. For years his clutch hitting and sensational plays from his shortstop position had made him an icon. The fans' admiration for him only increased when he accepted the player-manager job at age twenty-four and became the face of Cleveland baseball along with Bob Feller.

McAuley advised fans to prepare themselves for Boudreau not being with the 1948 edition of the team. Boudreau said little to the reporters, only claiming that missing the World Series meant nothing; he simply wanted to be home earlier with his wife and children. Given the opportunity to criticize Veeck, he took the high road and waited for things to play out.

Boudreau would not necessarily be the manager in St. Louis. The Browns would have to fire their skipper, Muddy Ruel, to make room for Lou. As for who would manage the Indians, Veeck was a huge fan of Charlie Grimm, the Chicago Cubs manager, who was currently signed to a five-year contract. They had worked together with the Milwaukee Brewers in the early 1940s when Veeck owned the club and Grimm was the field boss. McAuley believed Veeck would attempt to pry Grimm away from Chicago with an offer far and above his current deal, a move that most owners would not entertain.

Immediately after the *News* headline, Cleveland fans bombarded the papers and the Indians' front office with letters and postcards regarding the pending trade. Realizing what a storm he had created, Veeck left the World Series and returned to Cleveland. He walked the downtown streets, stopping in bars and restaurants to plead his case with the fans there. He explained to them why he believed Lou was starting to slip as a ballplayer and the time was right to move him. The fans disagreed. Of the 4,000 to 5,000 letters he received, roughly 90 percent were against the trade. One postcard came right to the point in four words: "Mr. Veeck—Drop Dead!" Most of the letters were more thoughtful, but they emphasized how important Lou was to Cleveland, the best ballplayer and manager the team had seen in decades.

Holding up the trade was the Cleveland front office's refusal to allow Bill DeWitt to speak with Boudreau about salary demands and how he would feel about being a player only. Without that information, and afraid that it would take long-drawn-out negotiations to sign Boudreau, DeWitt found it difficult to justify agreeing to the deal.

While the trade hung in limbo, State Auto Sales, on Cleveland's Euclid Avenue, posted signs in its windows reading, "Keep Boudreau Headquarters—Drive In—Sign Your Petition Here." It was a clever advertising ploy, since some of the people who came in to sign the petition might be persuaded to buy a car while they were there. The ledgers full of signatures were turned over to the Indians' office, adding to the waist-deep piles of letters. Even with the negative publicity, Veeck seemed calm with all the uproar. He told reporters, "I think anyone who takes the time to write us a letter certainly has the interest of the club in mind and should get an answer." How he could find the time to reply to all the letters is difficult to imagine, but this was not an ordinary man. In the middle of the ruckus, Veeck found a moment to announce that Mel Harder would serve as Indians pitching coach and minor league instructor. He would have a free hand to work with the young pitchers as long as necessary while moving from place to place at his discretion. The salary was reported at $14,000, high for a coach. Mel was pleased with the job, accepting that his pitching days were behind him. It was a win-win situation for both him and the team.

Throughout October and into November, the Cleveland fans anxiously scanned the papers in hopes of seeing a resolution to the Boudreau situation. On November 17, the stalemate abruptly ended when the Browns traded Vern Stephens and Jack Kramer to the Boston Red Sox for a beyond-belief seven players and $300,000. A few days later the Indians made a trade with St. Louis, sending Bryan Stephens, two minor league players, and $25,000 to the Browns for outfielder Walt Judnich and pitcher Bob Muncrief. Both newly acquired players were over thirty years old, fitting in with Veeck's win-now strategy. Judnich, who had spent three years in the armed forces, had some long-ball power, hitting 18 home runs the previous season. Muncrief was a bit surprising. He had pitched well during the war, but had an 11–26 record over the past two years, with an ERA close to 5.00. Either Veeck desperately wanted more veterans or he was simply eager to make a trade. Either way, this did not look like a move that would push the Indians much closer to being a contender. Not by itself.

On the Monday of Thanksgiving week, Boudreau came to Cleveland for a sit-down with Veeck. Over nearly the last two months, the owner had tried and tried to deal away his shortstop and manager. The winter meetings were just around the corner and quality shortstops were unavailable, forcing Veeck to bring Boudreau to town. They talked for six hours until they had hammered out a contract. Lou got a guaranteed deal keeping him as player-manager through 1949. The multiyear term was necessary because it indicated Veeck's renewed confidence in Boudreau's ability to run the ball club. A single-year contract could have been interpreted as showing that Veeck had backed himself into a corner and would either have to sign Boudreau or manage the team himself. Veeck had done the best he could to save face.

The victorious Boudreau spoke to reporters afterwards, appearing pleased and relieved. He promised a tougher spring training with a major emphasis on conditioning and fundamentals. He intended to bring a pitching machine to the Tucson camp and have the grounds crew dig out a large sliding pit. Bunting and base stealing were going to be a top priority for the 1948 Indians and their energized manager.

With everybody happy, Mayor Burke figured the timing was right to try and pin down Veeck on a long-term stadium lease. In 1947, for the seventy-seven home dates, the Indians paid the city $91,000, while the Cleveland Browns paid out $60,000 for just seven games. Veeck responded that he was interested in a new lease, but would need to print tickets and schedule his promotions first. In the meantime, the old agreement, which was still good for another season, would remain in force. Like Alva Bradley before him, Veeck held most of the cards, keeping the city at bay while paying them as little as possible.

On the eve of the winter meetings, Veeck received another blow when the Senators dealt coveted outfielder Stan Spence to Boston. Earlier, he had offered Washington Jim Hegan, three unnamed players, and cash for Spence, but Clark Griffith declined. Veeck turned his attention back to St. Louis, trading George Metkovich and $50,000 for infielder and aspiring Hollywood actor Johnny Berardino. The former Brown could play all the infield positions, making him a valuable utility player.

Later in the month Veeck would have to fly to Hollywood to meet with a studio producer to obtain permission for Johnny Berardino, who had a contractual obligation to film several movies, to play ball from March through September. Berardino had a reputation as a hustling player, something Veeck very much wanted on his team.

Veeck still had more wheeling and dealing to do. The next day he acquired outfielder Allie Clark from the Yankees in exchange for Red Embree. Clark was an interesting proposition. He had appeared in twenty-three games the previous season with 25 hits and 14 RBIs, and in the World Series he had swatted an RBI single in game seven to give New York a 4–2 lead and an eventual series win. The right-handed batter was only twenty-four, bucking Veeck's trend of going for veteran ballplayers. If nothing else, he was stocking up on outfielders, hoping to find at least a couple more guys to pair up with Dale Mitchell.

The winter meetings in New York passed without any sensational stories. The owners did agree to allow barnstorming players the right to participate without penalty in the 1948–49 Cuban baseball league. The Pacific Coast League tried again for Major League status, but the owners, still kicking around plans to expand to Southern California, would not consider the request.

Veeck paused his trading frenzy momentarily to announce in-season exhibition games with the Brooklyn Dodgers. Scheduled for June 14 in New York and July 24 in Cleveland, the games would benefit amateur baseball in both cities. Specifically, Veeck would turn over 100 percent of the ticket sales at the stadium to the Cleveland Baseball Federation, a worthy gesture.

Despite Veeck's hyperactive off-season, he was unable to secure an All-Star performer as he had in 1946 with Joe Gordon. He added a lot of pieces and parts, but nobody with the ability to lift the club in the standings. In a couple of months, the squad would assemble at Tucson, where hopefuls, including Gene Bearden, a still untested Larry Doby, and highly regarded minor leaguer Al Rosen, would all get extended looks. The Indians were optimistic that one or two from that group might be able to help the team's chances.

Contracts were mailed out on January 1, with many of the players receiving generous raises. Bob Lemon, working at his father's California service station, saw his pay double to $15,000. Dale Mitchell got a good raise, as did Ken Keltner, who had a bonus tacked onto it. Bob Feller would not receive quite as much as last year, but his contract still had an attendance bonus, which kicked in when attendance reached 1,000,000 fans, up from the previous year's 750,000. Based on the last two years, getting it was a certainty. Feller had no problem with the money, succinctly telling reporters, "Shucks, I signed didn't I?"

Many contracts were quickly returned with signatures, allowing the front office time to concentrate on marketing and ticket sales. Oversized photos of most of the players were printed and placed in various downtown store windows. Eddie Robinson, his ankle healed, joined the ticket sales team along with Don Black and holdover Mel Harder. Veeck bought a new, modern tarp for the field. Made of spun glass and costing $5,000, it weighed half as much as the old one and could be rolled out by the grounds crew in record time.

Near the end of January Veeck met with Hank Greenberg in New York to talk over possibilities for the upcoming season. Greenberg, now a free agent after one year in Pittsburgh, wanted to start a new career, preferably in a front office position. Veeck tried to persuade him to accept a coaching position that would also include pinch-hitting and playing part-time at first base and in the outfield. They did not reach an agreement, but Greenberg assured Veeck he would think the offer over.

Before the month was over, Veeck got the urge to trade again, this time acquiring center fielder Thurman Tucker from the White Sox for a minor leaguer. A fine defensive outfielder, the thirty-year-old Tucker gave Boudreau yet more options in the outfield. The team was still light on talent in the infield and would be counting on Boudreau, Gordon, and Keltner to stay healthy.

While the Indians seemed to be on track for the season, Jim Hegan unexpectedly refused to sign his 1948 pact. After he returned four contracts unsigned, the club assumed he wanted more money, but there was more to the story. In early February the newspapers reported Hegan was still upset about the 1947 season, when Boudreau decided to call pitches himself rather than letting Hegan do it. Boudreau's explanation was that he wanted to take pressure off Hegan and let him concentrate on his batting, but Hegan took it as a slight and stewed about it for the rest of the season. Hegan certainly wanted more money, but the incident with Boudreau added to the stalemate.

In early February, Hank Greenberg visited Cleveland to attend the sportswriters' "Ribs and Roasts" dinner honoring manager Boudreau. He spoke briefly, apologizing for taking any of the spotlight from Lou. After the dinner, he told reporters, "I haven't signed yet and before I take such a step I want to make sure that my association won't be just a one-year proposition. I'm looking for something more permanent."

While Veeck waited for Greenberg to decide, he announced the radio broadcast schedule for 1948. Jack Graney and new partner Jimmy Dudley would call the games on WJW. A native of Alexandria, Virginia, Dudley had done the play-by-play for the Chicago White Sox and Chicago Cubs before arriving in Cleveland, and for Cleveland Barons hockey on WJW in his first year in Cleveland. WJW would broadcast the entire home season, but a decision had not been made yet on the out-of-town games. The growing Indians radio network now included fifteen stations, eight AM and seven FM, extending throughout northeast Ohio and beyond.

Several Major League teams now had television coverage, but Veeck so far was noncommittal on the subject. The major radio networks were quickly adapting to the new medium, however. NBC offered TV coverage with three cameras that could follow the ball until the conclusion of the play, as well as a monitor for the announcer to note exactly what was being broadcast. CBS used two cameras, one on the ball and the other on the runner. One unintended feature that television gave viewers was the ability to read the players' lips, especially after a bad call by an umpire. Viewers grew to love the closeups.

Two days before the Indians were to leave for Tucson, Jim Hegan ended his holdout, saying he would arrive in Cleveland in time to leave with the rest of the ball club. Hegan reportedly received a $4,000 raise to $12,500. He told the papers, "I just don't want the Cleveland fans to think I'm a sorehead. I've always wanted to play with the Indians, and I think we've got a good chance for the pennant." Aside from the team's final offer, Hegan may have been spurred on by the front office playing up Hank Ruszkowski and rookie Joe Tipton as replacements, as well as Veeck's offering Hegan to the White Sox straight up for pitcher Ed Lopat. Whether they were sincere or just trying to put pressure on him, he ended up agreeing to their terms. Days later in Tucson, Boudreau told Hegan to call all the pitches going forward.

On Friday, February 27, the Indians departed Cleveland for the forty-four-hour train ride to Tucson. They arrived Sunday morning and began workouts the following day. Veeck was already in Arizona, along with Lefty Weisman and his new assistant Wally Bock, as well as Emil and Harold Bossard, who were working on the diamond. Hank

Greenberg soon showed up too. Hank had not decided on Veeck's offer, but planned to practice with the team.

Among the pitching candidates was Cleveland Browns star halfback Edgar "Special Delivery" Jones. As a high schooler, Jones had pitched well enough to draw offers from Major League clubs but chose to play football at the University of Pittsburgh. After spending World War II in the navy, Jones signed with the Browns as part of a talented backfield with Marion Motley and quarterback Otto Graham. Still wanting to give professional baseball a try, but not willing to toil in the minors, he worked out an arrangement with the Indians: he would either make the opening day roster or go back to football.

Camp began with workouts from 10:30 to 3:30, concentrating on bunting, sliding, and properly rounding first base. On balls hit to the outfield, Boudreau wanted his hitters to bend their path in a slight arc to the right before reaching the bag. They could then hit first base with their left foot and take a direct line to second. Many of his players were going straight to the bag and having to adjust their stride after they rounded it. Boudreau believed they were losing a second or two and missing opportunities for doubles. Coach Tris Speaker supported this style, having used it himself during his playing days along with smart baserunners like Ty Cobb and Eddie Collins. Gradually the players adopted the technique, fine-tuning their baserunning for the regular season. Boudreau was pleased with the good physical shape of his ball club. Steve Gromek had overcome a bad knee, while Allie Clark and Hal Peck were healthy after suffering problems with their throwing arms.

On Wednesday, the Indians played their first intrasquad game. With home runs from Larry Doby and Pat Seerey and three hits and three RBIs from Al Rosen, the B's routed the A's 10–1. Bob Lemon pitched three scoreless innings for the winning squad. Doby was working exclusively in the outfield, getting helpful pointers from Greenberg and Speaker. The team already had a veteran center fielder in Thurman Tucker, and Dale Mitchell could play there as well. Doby possessed better skills than all the other outfielders, but needed experience before he could win the job. Veeck wanted to give him a long look to see if he could handle the task of learning a new position.

Among the new pitchers, Gene Bearden was the favorite to win a place. Another intriguing candidate was Mike Garcia, a twenty-four-year-old from California. He had signed with Cleveland after high school, but like most of his contemporaries spent several years in the armed forces. In 1947, Garcia compiled a 17–10 record for Wilkes-Barre and earned a spot on the Eastern League all-star team. His best pitch was his fastball, followed by his curveball, which Mel Harder had taught him.

Cleveland opened the exhibition season with their friendly rivals the New York Giants, then left for California to play eighteen games in Hollywood, Oakland, San Francisco, Los Angeles, and several other stops. Before opening day, the Indians would travel 6,000 miles while visiting nine different states and seventeen cities. With them on the tour was a new signee, second baseman Roberto Avila from Mexico. He had caught the attention of Cleveland scouts when he batted .346 for Puebla of the Mexican League in 1947. Just twenty-three years old, Avila was slated to be sent to Baltimore, but Boudreau wanted to give him some playing time before the International League season began. Later Boudreau would call Avila "one of the best prospects I have seen in a long time."

Spring training is rarely the final word on how a ball club will fare in the regular season. Some players look tremendous, then fizzle out by late April or early May. But the Indians, based on their March performance, appeared to be a team to watch out for, banging out home runs and base hits at a rapid pace. Boudreau, Gordon, Doby, and Robinson were the long-ball guys, while Lemon, Feller, and Gene Bearden pitched well from the outset. At the very least, Cleveland fans could dream a little.

Near the end of the month, Hank Greenberg agreed to a contract with the Indians as second vice president, supporting Harry Grabiner and Veeck. His duties were vague, including coaching and maybe pinch-hitting from time to time. With Veeck making just about all the decisions and Grabiner acting as his consultant and sounding board, where Greenberg fit in was anybody's guess. Newspaper reports claimed he had purchased $100,000 in team stock, which if true would make him the second-largest shareholder in the organization. Hank told reporters he was still thinking about playing but could not say more than that. He was willing to help the club in whatever form he could, even shagging balls in batting practice. Maybe Veeck believed having Greenberg around every day would somehow add another ten to fifteen feet to the batters' fly balls and raise their averages accordingly.

In early April, Veeck made some heads turn when he purchased the contract of Russ Christopher from the Athletics for a reported $25,000. The tall, slim thirty-year-old, who threw a tough sinker submarine style, had the ability to help in the bullpen, and his arm was in fine shape. What was concerning was his serious health problems. As a child in California he had suffered from rheumatic fever, a serious illness that often shortens one's life. While playing high school ball he had been diagnosed with a leaky heart valve. Doctors strongly advised him against playing baseball, but Russ was a competitor and refused to listen. In 1944, while he was playing for the A's, doctors again urged him to quit the game, fearing he could have a heart attack at any moment. At one point Russ was confined to bed with a constant heart rate of 130 beats a minute, well above the normal range. Modern medicine can correct the problem, but in the 1940s there was little that could be done.

Christopher explained to Veeck that he only planned on playing the 1948 season, then retiring to some type of desk job that would put no strain on his heart. He was trying to take advantage of the Major League pension plan, under which players were eligible for a pension with five years of service. The amount they received would go up with every additional year. He was aiming for seven years, which he would reach if he made it through the season.

Christopher, who had a wife and two small children at home, was gambling with his life, and Veeck deserves to be criticized for aggressively pursuing a player whose health was in jeopardy. As late as May of 1948, Christopher told reporters he could only run from foul line to foul line one time before being winded. He should not have been playing baseball.

During the barnstorming tour with the Giants, the Indians dropped a 14–13 slugfest at Oklahoma City. Pat Seerey slammed three home runs, one of them hitting the top of a building a block away from the ballpark. All spring Seerey stayed hot and cold, blasting tremendous home runs then going hitless for several games. With all the outfielders in camp, it appeared "the People's Choice" might not be in an Indians uniform much longer.

Days before the start of the season, in Topeka, Kansas, Eddie Robinson injured his ankle, causing vice president Greenberg to suit up and play against the Giants. Without any real training, he showed the batters how it was done, knocking in three runs in his one game as an Indian. Fortunately, X-rays on Robinson's ankle were negative, allowing Greenberg to return to a suit and tie.

On Saturday, April 17, the Indians and Giants arrived in Cleveland. "Special Delivery" Jones got the chance to start in front of 8,197 football and baseball fans. He gave up four runs in six innings, prompting the team to give him his release. They could have released him earlier but chose to give him his moment in the stadium where he took handoffs and caught passes. It was a class move. Even without Jones, the ball club had an overabundance of pitchers that would need to be pared down by opening day or at the May roster cutdown.

On Sunday, the Indians wrapped up the exhibition schedule with a 13–2 pasting of the Giants. Larry Doby had two hits, scored twice, and pulled off a neat double steal with Thurman Tucker. Boudreau had not yet announced his starting lineup for the opener, but Doby had made a strong bid with an excellent spring. He had made great strides in his hitting while already playing a better-than-average outfield. Early during camp Boudreau had said Doby needed to play every day, either with Cleveland or in the minors. As opening day approached, it looked as if it would be with Cleveland.

With the start of the season came the annual luncheon at the Hotel Statler. Sounding fairly optimistic, at least for him, manager Boudreau said, "The boys have shown a fine spirit and they've worked hard. I can't say that we'll finish any higher than third, but we have a chance of making it tough for the Yankees and Red Sox." Previously Boudreau had said this team was the strongest he had seen since he started managing. Fans picked up on his confidence, buying tickets at a furious rate.

In the days leading up to the season opener, the Indians' front office mailed 35,000 ticket applications and distributed 350,000 schedules. They found 2,500 locations across northeast Ohio that would sell copies of the 1948 Indians sketchbook, containing facts and figures and images of all the players. From early January to mid-April, Veeck visited eighty different organizations that might be ticket buyers. It did not matter if 2,000 or 200 people attended the talks, Veeck would give them a stirring presentation to convince them to attend ballgames. Many of the talks were in the evenings, but when Veeck arrived home the work continued through the wee morning hours. He would sleep a little, then rise at 7:00 a.m. to jump right back on the phones to sell more tickets. The other owners no doubt had to shake their collective heads, having neither the ambition nor perseverance of Bill Veeck.

On opening day, Tuesday, April 20, the opponent for Bob Feller and the Indians was the toothless St. Louis Browns. An excellent crowd was already expected, but the warm temperatures, predicted to reach an unseasonably high seventy-nine degrees, brought out even the casual fans. All the municipal parking lots were crammed full of cars, forcing many to take their chances in the no-parking zones. The city, seeing money for the taking, called out every available tow truck. The crowd slowly pushed their way up the pedestrian ramps to the stadium, while the impatient ones ran below and dangerously navigated their way across the railroad tracks. It was a remarkable scene as over 73,000 people tried to reach the ticket windows and turnstiles all at once. Another Major League record opening day, thanks to Veeck and his exceptional marketing staff.

Once most of the fans had been seated, the pregame activities began with a volley of daytime fireworks. When the smoke cleared, Mayor Burke threw out the first ball to the popular band leader Spike Jones. Jones and his City Slickers wrought havoc on the hits of the day, turning them into comedy routines with whistles, sirens, and irreverent vocals.

The most notable thing done by the Cleveland owner might have been off the field. Near the Gate D entrance, inside the concourse, Veeck had a nursery built that he claimed could hold four hundred kids. Parents could drop off their children aged two to six to be cared for by a nurse and three attendants, watch the game, and pick them up after the final out. Moms and dads left their names, addresses, and seat numbers on a sign-up sheet in case of emergency. The nursery had cribs for the little ones and toys and games for the preschoolers. It would be open for all home games throughout the season.

Even with all the elaborate planning, the Indians and WJW radio got their wires crossed, so to speak. The original start time of 2:00 p.m. was changed to 3:00. The station had plenty of time to rearrange its programming, but WJW executives failed to tell the program director about the change until the day before the game. By then it was too late to move enough paid programming to fit the game in. The station put the game to FM, limiting the audience to the two or three thousand fans with receivers, and went to the game on AM at 4:30, denying most listeners the chance to follow along with Jack Graney and Jimmy Dudley until the late innings.

The Indians' lineup that took the field was the same as last season at pitcher, catcher, and the infield positions, but the outfield was totally new. Allie Clark was in left, Thurman Tucker in center, and Larry Doby in right. Dale Mitchell, a .300 hitter in 1947, was on the bench, and

Boudreau offered no explanation as to why. Doby had earned the job with a terrific spring, but Tucker was an average hitter and Clark had played in only a handful of games with the Yankees last season. One of the knocks against Boudreau as a manager was that he did not handle younger players well. He would indiscriminately pull them in and out of the lineup, confounding fans and sportswriters. Mitchell had played only one full season but had already shown plenty.

In the bottom of the first inning, Tucker walked and stole second, Doby struck out, but Boudreau singled to center, driving in the first run of the game. The Indians added another run in the second on singles by Clark, Keltner, and Hegan to go up 2–0. Feller had the Browns under control, allowing only a hit and a walk through four innings. In the home half of the fourth, Robinson and Clark singled, but Keltner bunted into a double play, Robinson taking third. Jim Hegan powered a fastball on the outside corner into the right field seats. The Indians led 4–0, with three of those runs provided by their catcher. The Browns could do nothing against Feller, who allowed only one more hit and one more walk in the 4–0 victory.

On Friday the Indians were in Detroit to begin a three-game series. Bob Lemon made his season debut against Freddie Hutchinson, one of the better pitchers in the American League. In the top of the sixth inning, Cleveland was out in front 2–1 when Joe Gordon doubled, Robinson fanned, and Allie Clark popped up for out number two. Ken Keltner, who had already homered, smashed another one into the left field stands, scoring Gordon ahead of him for a 4–1 lead. Jim Hegan singled and Bob Lemon cracked a home run to increase the lead to 6–1 and send Hutchinson to the showers. Lemon cruised to an 8–2 win. Larry Doby added three hits, including a shot to the upper deck in right field, his first Major League home run. Boudreau contributed three more hits, while Keltner had four RBIs.

On Sunday, Keltner blasted two more home runs, including a three-run game-tying drive in the fourth inning that caused the Indians players to run out of the dugout and jump all over the veteran third baseman. Keltner was off to the best start of his career, setting an example for Boudreau and Gordon. Al Gettel started the game but was yanked after yielding four runs in two innings. Bob Muncrief and Russ Christopher pitched seven shutout innings in relief for the 7–4 win and a series sweep. Not only were the hitters on fire, but the newly acquired bullpen help showed that Veeck had made some smart decisions.

The Indians finished April 6–0, their best start in many years. Boudreau had a batting average of .519, Robinson .462, and Keltner .375 with five home runs. The one concern was the lack of starting pitching behind Lemon and Feller. Al Gettel and Don Black were the prime candidates, while Gene Bearden waited patiently for his name to be called.

On Saturday, May 8, in Washington, Bearden finally got his first Major League start. The Indians scored a run in the first inning and Bearden was off and running, facing just twenty-two batters through the first seven innings. In the visitors' half of the eighth inning, Joe Gordon tripled to deep center field. Keltner lifted a fly ball to center, far enough for Gordon to tag up and make the score 2–0. Jim Hegan doubled to left field and scored on a Bearden single. Thurman Tucker beat out an infield single, and Larry Doby followed with a tremendous drive to dead center. The baseball was still rising when it hit the top of the thirty-five-foot wall, and it bounced off several loudspeakers before coming back to earth. Though it was ruled a home run, Doby raced around the bases and slid home to be sure. The three-run homer brought even the Senators fans to their feet. After the game, fans and sportswriters remarked that they had only seen one other ball hit the wall with such force, one hit by Babe Ruth in the 1920s.

Bearden tired in the ninth inning, losing the shutout but easily winning the game, 6–1. For the moment he had earned the chance to become the third starter, passing Gettel and Black. If Bearden could win consistently, the Indians would be in the unfamiliar position of challenging preseason favorites Boston and New York for their first pennant in twenty-eight years.

The winning continued at Fenway Park with a Sunday double-header sweep of the Red Sox, followed by a 12–7 win on Monday. Dale Mitchell had entered the lineup a week earlier in left field, ready to work on another .300 season. The reasons for his previous absence were not discussed in any of the papers.

The third game at Boston produced a rare triple play, pulled off by the Indians in the bottom of the eighth inning. With runners on first and second, Billy Goodman scorched a line drive in Lou Boudreau's direction. Boudreau speared the ball and flipped it to Joe Gordon, who stepped on second base, doubling off Wally Moses. Birdie Tebbetts strayed too far off first base, leaving an easy play for Gordon, who threw to Eddie Robinson for out number three. It's safe to say the team was meshing fairly well.

The series sweep boosted the Indians' record to 11–4. Whether hitting, pitching, or fielding, they were playing extraordinary baseball, far from the usual effort the Cleveland fans were accustomed to. When the road trip ended, Boudreau still sported a batting average in the .400s, while Keltner's RBI total stood at twenty, second to Ted Williams. The hometown fans were poised to jam Municipal Stadium to the rafters when the Indians returned.

The month of May brought a milestone to Cleveland baseball, the arrival of televised home games. WEWS Television invested in equipment for broadcasting live from the stadium, with a picture sharp enough for home viewers to recognize the players without squinting. Veeck had been negotiating quietly for seven months before a satisfactory deal was reached. WEWS agreed to broadcast the remaining seventy-four home games, paying the Indians $75,000 for the rights.

Van Patrick, who had done radio games in 1946 with Jack Graney, was hired to handle all the television duties. General Electric consented to be the sole sponsor of the games. A main camera would be placed near the first base line, showing closeups of the pitchers delivering the ball. Shots of the scoreboard would be mixed in, letting viewers have a quick look at scores from around baseball.

Almost immediately the bars and taverns around Cleveland were scrambling to find television sets and install them to draw more customers. They cleaned out the local department stores, then offered cash to anyone willing to turn over a used set. Soon it became commonplace to walk to the nearest establishment, order a cold beer, hop on a stool, and watch the ballgame.

The initial broadcast went on the air Saturday, May 15. Behind back-to-back home runs from Gordon and Keltner, the Indians beat up on the White Sox, 7–1. Bob Feller coasted to his fourth win of the season. Despite the convenience of being able to view the game from their living room or the nearest watering hole, the fans still bought tickets at a record pace.

After less than two years as owner, Bill Veeck was swimming in money and acclaim. He had acquired radio and television rights, produced unimaginable crowds at the stadium, and made the right moves to put the Indians in contention. His world seemed just about perfect—except for his leg. For the third time in less than two years, he grudgingly entered a Cleveland hospital for an operation. The surgeons found it necessary to remove one more inch from the right leg, confining Veeck to his hospital bed indefinitely. Knowing his propensity for sneaking out and staggering his way to the stadium, the doctors should have posted a guard at his door.

The Yankees came to town on Sunday, May 23, for a doubleheader. Though the season was barely a month old, it was an important matchup. The World Series champions were on the hunt for another crown, while the upstart Indians were ready to knock them off their perch. All the box and reserve seats had already been sold before Sunday, causing the front office to believe a crowd of 80,000 fans was possible. Despite rain showers in the morning, people lined up at the box office, gobbling up 15,000 general admission seats before noon. The nursery accepted one hundred children and had to open the storeroom for additional dolls, bicycles, and games.

By game time, 6,000 more tickets had been sold, and the entire stadium was full except for the center field bleachers, which were left empty because the fans' white shirts would reflect the sun back at the hitters. Instead, a standing room area between the bleachers and the rear of the outfield fences was opened to accommodate 3,000. Even with a short rain delay, attendance reached 78,431, a spectacular crowd for a May afternoon.

Among the massive throng were 1,000 children, presumably over the age of six. Weeks before the game, the marketing department had placed ads in the newspapers, offering a special $1.00 package just for kids. The offer included a grandstand ticket, a 1948 sketchbook, the Indians sleeve insignia on a patch, a decal, and a copy of *Indians News*. Mom and Dad could stash the youngest children at the day care, send the older ones to the $1.00 grandstand seats, and enjoy the game by themselves.

In the fourth inning, the final attendee hobbled through the turnstiles, straight from the local hospital. Veeck could not handle lying in his bed and watching the games on television. He got dressed, snuck out through the lobby, and hailed a cab for the stadium. On crutches he made his way to the press box, where reporters were not in the least surprised to see him.

Both managers chose their best pitchers for game one, Feller for Cleveland and Allie Reynolds for the Yankees. After Feller retired the side in the top of the first, the Indians jumped all over their former teammate, touching up Reynolds for four runs. The big blow came off the bat of red-hot Ken Keltner, who whacked a home run with two runners aboard.

The lead held until the fourth inning, when Joe DiMaggio belted a two-run blast off Feller, narrowing the score to 4–2. Reynolds bore down and kept the Indians from any further scoring. Two innings later DiMaggio connected again, this time a three-run homer that gave the Yankees the lead, 5–4. Feller left after seven innings, replaced by Bob Muncrief, who was greeted in the top of the eighth by DiMaggio's third round-tripper of the game, a solo shot. Cleveland scored once in the ninth, but reliever Joe Page held on for the 6–5 win, courtesy of the Yankee Clipper.

In the second game, starter Don Black went six innings, surrendering just one run. Russ Christopher threw three shutout innings to earn his fifth save of the year as the Indians won 5–1. The fans went home happy with the split, knowing their team could compete with the Yankees. Max Axelrod of Cleveland Concessions had to be smiling, having sold approximately 5 tons of hot dogs (80,000 buns) and 50,000 bags of popcorn. Though Veeck and his lawyers had sought to replace him, Axelrod fought to retain his rights to all the concessions at the stadium. While he had them, he was raking in fantastic sales, with several mountains of food and drinks still to go.

On the last day of the month, the Indians split a doubleheader with St. Louis, winning the first 8–3 and dropping the second 6–0. The standings were as follows:

Philadelphia	26–12	.684
Cleveland	23–11	.676
New York	21–15	.583
Detroit	19–20	.487
St. Louis	16–17	.487

The A's were the surprise team, but not expected to remain serious contenders. The race was thought to be between Cleveland and New York. Boston was languishing in seventh place but had lots of time to get back in the race.

Before the Indians boarded their train to set out on a thirteen-game eastern road trip, which would include three games each at Washington, Philadelphia, and Boston, followed by four games at Yankee Stadium, Boudreau related his thoughts on the importance of making a good showing. Though it was early in the year, a losing streak now could kill their momentum and send the season spiraling out of control.

On June 2, Washington took the first game 2–1 as Ray Scarborough outpitched Bob Lemon. The next day the game was rained out, but news came of another trade. Veeck had sent Pat Seerey and Al Gettel to Chicago for twenty-seven-year-old outfielder Bob Kennedy. Seerey's inability to curb his strikeouts led to his demise, while Gettel no longer fit into the Indians' plans. Kennedy, a .262 batter in 1947, was another good defender and fair hitter to add into the mix. With plenty of power hitters for once in Keltner, Gordon, Doby, and Robinson, the team could afford to let go of Seerey and his occasional monstrous home runs.

The final game in Washington was a virtuoso pitcher's battle between Bob Feller and lefty Mickey Haefner. Neither team plated a single run through Feller's eleven innings and Haefner's twelve. Bob Muncrief relieved Feller and blanked the Senators through the fourteenth. In the fifteenth, the Indians exploded for five runs, aided by triples by Joe Gordon and Walt Judnich. Muncrief retired the side in the bottom of the inning to get the victory in the 5–0 win.

After the Indians won in Philadelphia the next day, they played the A's in a Sunday doubleheader. Before a sellout crowd, Bob Lemon won his eighth game of the season, 5–3, and in the nightcap Steve Gromek, replacing an injured Don Black, pitched a complete game for a 11–1 victory. First-year backup catcher Joe Tipton had a perfect day with five hits in five at bats, while Dale Mitchell added four hits and five RBIs. The sweep put the Indians two and a half games in front of the A's.

After pitching ineffectively the last two years while dealing with his problem knee, Gromek was the forgotten man of the pitching staff. He appeared to be healthy now, ready to be used as a spot starter or the fourth man in the rotation. His apparent comeback and the emergence of Gene Bearden meant that manager Boudreau could now lessen the load on Feller and Lemon.

After another rainout the Boston series ended split at one game apiece. The Indians moved on to New York, where both teams were prepared to play as if it were a late September weekend with the pennant on the line. Friday night's game, despite overcast skies and a rain delay of twenty minutes, drew 67,924 wound-up fans. The Indians quieted the crowd by scoring five runs in the first two innings. The Yankees answered off Bob Lemon in the bottom of the third when Tommy Henrich tripled, Johnny Lindell walked, and catcher Yogi Berra slammed a three-run homer to close the gap to 5–3.

In the Indians' next turn at bat, Berra got into a heated argument over balls and strikes with home plate umpire Cal Hubbard. It was a comical sight seeing the 5'8" Berra and the 6'2" Hubbard, a former NFL star, going toe to toe. Hubbard threw Berra out of the game, but Berra refused to leave the field until manager Bucky Harris raced from the dugout and persuaded him to hit the showers. The fans threw bottles, beer cans, and fruit at Hubbard, and one fan jumped out of his box seat near first base and charged umpire Joe Paparella, who had nothing to do with the argument. Mel Harder, coaching at first, wrestled with the fan until the police arrived and took charge. Just another night at Yankee Stadium.

New York took the lead in the fifth on another three-run shot, this time by first baseman George McQuinn. The Indians struck back in the seventh with four more runs on a bases-loaded double by Joe Tipton and a single by Dale Mitchell to go up 9–6. They added one more in the top of the ninth, setting the stage for a last-ditch Yankee rally. With two outs, Joe DiMaggio homered off reliever Ed Klieman to make the score 10–7. A single and a base on balls ended Klieman's night, bringing in Bob Feller to try and close out the game. Another single and a walk to Phil Rizzuto tightened the score to 10–8. With the bases loaded, Feller's one-time teammate Sherm Lollar came up as a pinch hitter. With the crowd on its feet, Feller struck out the young catcher to end the hard-fought game. The Indians had drawn first blood, but there were three games left to play.

Saturday's doubleheader brought another fired-up crowd of 68,586. Joe Gordon, the new Yankee-killer, crushed three home runs against his former club to help the Indians take both games, 7–5 and 9–4. With one more game left on the road trip, they had won eight out of ten, placing them solidly in first place over the Athletics and Yankees. If they could win Sunday's game, it would be icing on the cake.

On Sunday the Yankees were celebrating the twenty-fifth anniversary of Yankee Stadium. There was an old-timers' game between the 1923 World Series champion Yankees and an all-star team of recently retired Yankees, but the marquee attraction was the retirement of Babe Ruth's iconic uniform. The most beloved Yankee in team history, the man with 714 home runs, would step onto the field and say a few words to his fans. After a few moments, the Babe, wearing the famous 3 on his back, walked slowly to the Indians' dugout. The players crowded around him like little boys, eager to shake his hand and say hello. They saw how gaunt and frail the Babe looked, and someone grabbed a bat, which happened to be Bob Feller's, from the bat rack for him to lean on. The cancer had spread through his body, and Ruth had only a few more months to live.

The brief ceremony began with Yankees broadcaster Mel Allen introducing former general manager Ed Barrow, who met the Babe at home plate with a warm hug. Dan Topping, the team president, presented Ruth with a handsome watch with an inscription. The crowd of nearly 50,000 erupted in a stirring ovation as Ruth made his way to the microphones. Leaning heavily on Feller's bat and speaking in a whisper, Ruth said, "Ladies and gentlemen I just want to say one thing. I am proud I hit the first home run here against Boston in 1923. I'm telling you it makes me proud and happy to be here." Will Harridge then told the crowd, "As president of the American League I declare Ruth's uniform officially retired. It never again will be worn by a Yankee player either at the stadium or on the road. It is with deep appreciation for what he has done for baseball that I hereby present his uniform to the Hall of Fame." Wreaths were then laid in deep center field next to the monuments of Lou Gehrig, former owner Colonel Jacob Ruppert, and manager Miller Huggins. Finally the old-timers took the field. Babe went to the Indians' dugout again, where the players asked him to sign the bat. Somehow Eddie Robinson wound up with it, and he kept it in his personal collection for many years. Eventually the bat was purchased back by Feller and displayed in his Van Meter, Iowa, museum. After Bob's death, the bat went to the Indians, and it now resides at Progressive Field in Cleveland.

Due to the pregame activity, the Yankees-Indians game did not begin until 4:00. Berra and Rizzuto each hit two-run homers and Joe DiMaggio belted two triples to lead the Yankees to a 5–3 win, salvaging the last game of the series. But the Indians were still sitting in first place, three games ahead of Philadelphia and five in front of the Bronx Bombers. They had proven they were no pretenders.

Before leaving New York, the Indians stopped in Brooklyn for their exhibition game against the Dodgers. Lou Boudreau hit a two-run home run, but Jackie Robinson did the same, leading Brooklyn to a 6–2 win. More important was the $15,000 raised for the Brooklyn Amateur Baseball Federation. In July, the two teams would meet in Cleveland to complete the series and donate the receipts to the Cleveland Baseball Federation. With Bill Veeck running the show, it was likely the CBF would receive a record amount.

Chapter 13

A TREMENDOUS RACE

On the eve of the June 15 trading deadline, Bill Veeck made one final deal, paying an amount believed to be $100,000 and a prospect to the St. Louis Browns for left-handed pitcher Sam Zoldak. If the stockholders somehow missed the $50,000 paid for Johnny Berardino, this one should have made them fall out of their chairs. Zoldak, a starter-reliever, had compiled a lifetime record of 23–27 with the Browns. To be fair, he played for a club that usually finished near the bottom of the standings. Still, he did not seem the kind of pitcher who was worth that kind of money. Veeck evidently believed Zoldak would be a helpful addition to the Indians, who could provide run support and solid defense behind him, and money was not a concern for the free-spending owner. Since his arrival in Cleveland, Veeck had increased the payroll significantly, paying out high salaries and bonuses at a dizzying rate. His aim was to make the ballplayers happy and in turn get a better quality of play from them. In 1948, his approach seemed to be on target. With his win-now attitude, piles of money to spend, and some good old-fashioned luck, the long pennant drought in Cleveland looked like it might be over.

On Sunday, June 20, the Athletics were in town for a doubleheader. As they had a month ago when the Yankees were at the stadium, fans began lining up at the ticket windows hours before game time. Sales went swiftly all morning, and by 12:30 p.m. all the seats were taken. Standing room tickets then went on sale until management decided it was time to cut them off.

The final attendance was a gargantuan 82,781 fans, breaking the Major League record of 81,841 set by the New York Yankees in 1938. Once again Veeck had one-upped the Yankees, as he had done with the 1946 nylon stockings giveaway. In the second game, he took to the public address system microphone to thank the crowd for topping the attendance mark.

Buoyed by the sold-out stadium crowd, the Indians swept the doubleheader 4–3 and 10–0. In center field for the Indians was Larry Doby, who had recently begun starting there after playing in right for most of the season. Boudreau recognized that Doby was the best athlete on the club and well able to handle the center field position now and for the future. Doby and Mitchell were the two regulars in the outfield, with Allie Clark, Thurman Tucker, and Walt Judnich also getting playing time. While the infield still needed the regulars to stay healthy down the stretch, the outfield was deep and capable.

At the end of the month, the Indians were on the road to play the Tigers. In the first inning, Mitchell reached on an error before Boudreau doubled to drive him in, took third on another error, and scored on Hank Edwards's sacrifice fly. Bob Lemon had all his pitches working, throwing fastballs, curves, and sliders past the Detroit hitters. In the bottom of the fourth, George Kell ripped a line drive down the left field line. Mitchell raced to the corner, leaped, and hauled the ball in near the 340-foot sign. That was the closest to a base hit Detroit came in the first eight innings.

In the bottom of the ninth, pinch hitter Vic Wertz rapped the ball sharply toward the pitcher's mound. Lemon speared the ball with his glove and threw to first for the out. Eddie Mayo fanned for the second out, and George Kell bounced the ball right back to Lemon, who threw him out easily at first. Lemon faced just thirty batters in throwing his first Major League no-hitter. After the ballgame, he was the calmest person in the clubhouse. "I had as good stuff as I've ever had, and I got wonderful support," he said. "You don't see many catches like that one Mitchell made in the fourth." It was Lemon's eleventh win of the season, five of them being shutouts. Sooner or later he would be regarded as the new ace of the staff.

Going into July, the Indians were in first place:

Cleveland	39–23	.629
Philadelphia	40–27	.597
New York	38–26	.594
Boston	32–29	.525

In June, the Red Sox had awakened with a vengeance, winning eighteen of twenty-four games. If they continued at that torrid pace, three teams would surely be in the hunt, with the Athletics being the dark horse. The All-Star break was a few days away, giving the clubs a short rest before the real battle begun.

While fans nationwide voted for the All-Star game starting lineups in record numbers, Bill Veeck was working overtime trying to find another pitcher to complete his staff. The trading deadline had passed, leaving the usual options of a waiver deal or promoting a minor leaguer. Instead, Veeck got the attention of the entire country when on July 7 he proudly announced the signing of Negro Leagues star Leroy "Satchel" Paige.

Numerous sportswriters denounced the move as another Veeck publicity stunt, a ploy to bring even more fans to the stadium. Paige, who was somewhere in his early forties, was too old, they said. "To sign a hurler at Paige's age is to demean the standard of baseball in the big circuits," wrote the *Sporting News* in an editorial. "Further complicating the situation is the suspicion that if Satchel were white, he would not have drawn a second thought from Veeck." They felt that American League president Will Harridge should void the contract.

Veeck quickly fired back at the criticism, insisting his reason for acquiring Paige was the pitcher's ability and nothing else. In the spring of 1947, Veeck had hired promoter Abe Saperstein to scout the best Negro talent available. Saperstein scoured the country and reported back that Paige could help the ballclub. Now, needing one more pitcher to aid in the pennant race, Paige was the man he turned to. Veeck recalled a barnstorming game last fall where the Bob Feller All-Stars were beaten by Paige and his standouts 16–0. Satchel pitched the entire game, striking out sixteen, including Johnny Berardino four times.

Before Veeck offered the contract, he called Boudreau to meet him at the stadium to look over a pitching prospect. Seeing Paige there, Lou realized his boss wanted his opinion on whether to sign him. He asked Paige to throw fifty pitches, almost all of which were strikes. Boudreau would tell the press, "He showed me plenty. It was the first time I had ever seen him and now I can believe some of the tall stories they tell about his pitching."

For his part, Paige took the signing in stride, politely answering questions and playing down the stories attached to him over the years. Paige came from Mobile, Alabama, and gave his birth date as September 1908, making him thirty-nine years old. The *Call and Post* decided to investigate this, phoning a doctor in Mobile who knew Satch and believed him to be either forty-four or forty-five. They also contacted the pitcher's mother, who said he was forty-four. Later research would reveal that he was born on July 7, 1906.

The nickname "Satchel" was given to him at an early age, but the reason for it is still debated today. One suggestion is that in his youth he spent time as a porter, carrying suitcases and satchels.

Paige was 6'3" and was on the slim side, about 180 pounds. He had played professional baseball for at least twenty-one years. Since first appearing in a box score for the Chattanooga Black Lookouts in 1926, he had played for a host of teams in the Negro Leagues, including Birmingham, Baltimore, Pittsburgh, and most recently the Kansas City Monarchs. He had pitched in Latin America and Mexico and barnstormed in the fall against teams led by Feller and Dizzy Dean.

Satch was so popular around all of baseball that the *Cleveland News* assigned sports reporter Hal Lebovitz to follow him around for a couple of weeks. Paige moved at such a rapid pace that Lebovitz would sometimes lose track of him. Articles soon appeared regularly in the *News* about Satchel's background from his early days up to his signing with Cleveland. Soon the stories were printed as a short book titled *Pitchin' Man: "Satchel" Paige's Own Story*. It cost a mere twenty-five cents and included photos and testimony from Veeck and Boudreau.

Numerous tales circulated about him, such as that he was a voracious eater who once downed twelve hot dogs during a game and ate half a turkey and a whole watermelon for dinner. Satch denied this, saying he never ate hot dogs or even hamburgers. He refuted other stories that claimed he liked to sleep in his new cars rather than a hotel room. All he really wanted to do, he said, was prove a Black pitcher could compete in the American League. "I took this job because I think I can help the Indians," he told reporters, "and because I think it will be a big boost for my race."

Fans did not have to wait long to see Paige on the mound. On Friday, July 9, the Indians were trailing the Browns at home 4–1 when Boudreau called him in to pitch the top of the fifth inning. While Satch took a slow walk to the mound, photographers snapped hundreds of pictures for the morning news. The Cleveland fans, realizing the historic moment, stood and cheered loudly for their new pitcher. Deploying his wide assortment of pitches and variety of windups, he managed to hold St. Louis scoreless for two innings. The Browns won the game, 5–3, but all eyes were on the forty-something rookie in his first Major League appearance.

The signing of Satch and Veeck's antics put Cleveland in the national spotlight. For a time the news was positive, reflecting the team's good play and the almost daily attendance records. But the good vibes were interrupted when Bob Feller announced he would not participate in the All-Star game. The decision caused a firestorm among fans and newspaper reporters. Feller was ripped for thumbing his nose at an American institution. Bucky Harris, managing the American League stars, said that if he had the choice he would never again pick Feller for his team. A National League player rep wrote to the owners suggesting that anyone who refused to play should be fined. Another player might not have come under the same scrutiny, but this was Bob Feller.

At the midyear owners' meeting in St. Louis several of the owners criticized Feller to Veeck, saying he had disrespected the tradition of the All-Star game and his fellow players, who felt honored to attend even if they were injured and unable to play. Much too late, Veeck stood up for his pitcher, telling them it was his decision to pull Feller from the lineup. Feller pitched on Sunday the eleventh, the last game before the All-Star game, and Veeck preferred that he not throw any more innings before his next start. "Feller's primary job is to pitch for the Indians and that's what he'll do," Veeck said. "It's not his fault." One pitcher from a team should be enough, and Bob Lemon was already on the All-Star squad.

His explanation did not mollify at least six or seven of the owners, who reminded Veeck that the proceeds of the game went towards the players' pension fund and that Feller's presence might have put more paying customers in the stands. Several owners were quoted afterward saying that Veeck was pulling the same stunts he had in Milwaukee, that he was boosting attendance with circus acts and nightly giveaways so he could eventually attract a buyer who would pay him an exorbitant amount for the team. They expected him to sell the team as early as next year.

That was likely just sour grapes, but Veeck was not making any friends among the ownership group and he seemingly did not care. His attending owners' meetings without a suit and tie and his unprecedented marketing techniques bothered many of the old guard. His claim, which he made several times, that his only concern was to win a pennant and nothing more came off as selfish to the many owners who felt they were deeply involved in the game and all its different aspects. Veeck could have avoided criticism in this case if he had allowed Feller to attend the game but asked that he pitch just an inning or two. But apparently he had tunnel vision when it came to the pennant chase and cared little for league matters. This was not his finest moment.

Minus Feller, the American League still won their eleventh victory in fifteen tries, though Stan Musial of the Cardinals gave the hometown fans a thrill by knocking a two-run homer. The Indians had three-fourths of the starting infield in Gordon, Boudreau, and Keltner.

The next day the Dodgers came to Cleveland for the finale of their two-game exhibition series. The 65,922 fans got to see Larry Doby, Satchel Paige, Jackie Robinson, and Roy Campanella all on the same field. The ageless Paige entered the game in the seventh with the score tied 3–3. He struck out the side on twelve pitches, dazzling the crowd with what the newspapers described as a corkscrew windup. In the eighth he retired three straight Dodgers, capping a superb appearance and making headlines again. Jim Hegan singled in Joe Gordon with the winning run in the eleventh in a 4–3 victory.

The big winner for the night was the Cleveland Baseball Federation, which was presented with a check for $90,000. CBF officials were stunned by the amount, which would go to buy U.S. savings bonds for emergencies and would bankroll equipment and medical costs for many years ahead. The CBF presented a plaque with their thanks to Hank Greenberg, filling in for an absent Bill Veeck. Big things at Municipal Stadium were becoming a nightly occurrence.

The second half of the season kicked off in Philadelphia. After the Indians swept the Thursday doubleheader, Bob Feller started the next evening. The four days' rest he had enjoyed seemed not to have helped him, because he managed to retire just one batter before leaving the game, surrendering five runs on five hits in the 10–5 loss. His performance did nothing to validate Veeck's decision to hold him from the All-Star game. His record stood at 9–11, a major disappointment for himself and the team.

After winning three of four in Washington, the Indians moved on to face the Yankees in a three-game series. They split the opening doubleheader, losing game one 7–3 but taking game two on Jim Hegan's first career grand slam, 12–8. The next day Feller, who had struggled in his last start in Washington, had a 3–2 lead heading into the bottom of the fifth when the Yankees loaded the bases for Joe DiMaggio, who hit a grand slam to put New York ahead 6–3. Cleveland answered with two runs, but the Yankees held on to win 6–5.

The Indians finished their eastern swing against the Red Sox, the winners of nine in a row. On Saturday, July 24, two late runs gave the Red Sox a one-run victory in both games of a doubleheader and knocked Cleveland out of first place for the first time since June 1. The next day Boston made it twelve straight behind Joe Dobson's shutout, 3–0. The important fourteen-game road trip ended with four straight losses and a disappointing record of 6–8.

July finished with a shakeup in the standings. With two full months to play, just two games separated the first- and fourth-place clubs:

Boston	57–38	.600
Philadelphia	58–40	.592
Cleveland	53–38	.582
New York	54–39	.581

On the first day of August, the streaking Red Sox were in town to play a Sunday doubleheader. In game one, Cleveland exploded for nine runs in the first three innings to embarrass Boston 12–2. Bob Lemon pitched effectively and starred with the bat with three hits, including his fifth home run of the year. When Lemon was on the mound, the ball club enjoyed something close to a designated hitter. Opposing pitchers could not afford to ease up on the number nine batter in the lineup. Among the full-time hitters, Larry Doby also had three hits and a home run, and drove in four.

In the second game, Sam Zoldak blanked the Red Sox until Ted Williams's ninth-inning solo home run. Joe Gordon blasted his twentieth home run, but the play of the day came in the second inning. Lou Boudreau was on third base and Eddie Robinson on first. While Boston pitcher Mickey Harris's attention was on Robinson, Boudreau edged away from third. Just as Harris was about to deliver the ball to the plate, the slow-footed Boudreau took off for home, shocking everybody at the stadium. When he was called safe, the crowd erupted. The Indians' 6–1 victory moved them to within a game of first place.

Each game played was getting more nerve-racking, not quite do or die, but extremely important. On Tuesday, August 3, Satchel Paige took the mound against Washington for his historic first Major League start.

He allowed two runs in the first inning, but only one more over the next six before being lifted for a pinch hitter. Ed Klieman finished with two scoreless innings to save the game for Satch, 4–3. The win moved the Indians into a four-way tie for first place, percentage points ahead of New York, Boston, and Philadelphia.

In the clubhouse, the reporters crowded around Paige's locker. Asked if he had run out of gas, he replied, "No I'm not tired. Starting a game is a lot easier than going in to try to save one." Asked if he could take a regular turn in the rotation, a smiling Paige said, "I used to start every second day and then do relief in between. Every four days would be a vacation."

Two days later Gene Bearden shut out the Senators, 3–0. Jim Hegan, having the best season of his career, clobbered two solo home runs while Bearden added another to account for all three runs. With over thirty home games still to play, the Indians had topped their 1947 attendance record with a total of 1,530,224 fans. The good news was overshadowed when a collision at second base with the Senators' Gil Coan forced Lou Boudreau to leave the game, suffering from a sore shoulder, bruised knee, and sprained ankle. His loss meant Johnny Berardino would have to play shortstop for an indefinite time. While a great clubhouse guy, the motion picture actor was a liability at bat. All hoped for a speedy recovery by the All-Star player-manager.

The timing of the injury could not have been worse. With the Yankees coming Friday to begin a key four-game series, the pennant race was in high gear. After that, the Indians had a great opportunity to distance themselves from the other contenders. While the Yankees were playing the Red Sox and Athletics, Cleveland would be playing also-rans Chicago, St. Louis, and Detroit. If the three eastern teams beat up on each other and the Indians took care of business, the pennant would be that much closer.

On the night of August 6, the Indians began the critical series against New York. Bob Feller was back on the mound, facing the usually difficult Ed Lopat. The Yankees scored three runs in the first two innings, but Feller held them scoreless over the next five. The Indians knocked Lopat out of the box after four innings, and in the bottom of the seventh, with Cleveland already leading 6–3, Joe Gordon launched his twenty-first home run of the season, a three-run shot that made the score 9–3.

Staked to a big lead, Feller blew up in the top of the eighth, letting in four runs to narrow the score to 9–7. Ed Klieman and Russ Christopher held on over the final one and two-thirds innings to preserve the victory. Feller had won his eleventh game, but the Yankees' ten hits, seven runs, and five walks left the fans wondering when and if he would turn things around.

On Saturday the Yankees' Vic Raschi shut out the Indians 5–0. The game saw another attendance record broken, not at the gate but at the nursery, which admitted 274 children, shattering the previous high of 168. Hopefully Veeck had hired more nurses and attendants to look after them.

The Sunday afternoon doubleheader brought 73,484 animated fans to the stadium. As was becoming a custom, large groups of fans came from out of state. The municipal airport noted seventeen private planes arriving with guests from Illinois, Michigan, and Indiana, and the New York Central Railroad brought special trains from Niagara Falls and Buffalo carrying ten to twelve cars of crazed baseball fans. At 8 a.m. there were already around 3,000 people lined up at the ticket windows.

The stage was set for two of the best teams in the Major Leagues to battle it out for a leg up in the pennant race. With Sam Zoldak on the mound for Cleveland, the Indians were down 4–1 after five innings and 6–1 going to the home half of the seventh. With two out, the Indians came fighting back against Frank Shea, the Yankees' starter. With Ken Keltner on first, Johnny Berardino homered to close the gap to 6–3. While the fans were still cheering Berardino, Eddie Robinson clouted another homer, slicing the lead to two runs. Jim Hegan singled and pinch hitter Allie Clark walked to put runners on first and second. The crowd raised the noise level several more decibels, enough to wake the sleeping babies in the nursery. Dale Mitchell, the next batter, topped a slow roller in the grass and beat the throw to first. The bases were loaded for Thurman Tucker, but before he stepped to the plate he was called back to the bench for a pinch hitter. Fans craned their necks to see which Indian was walking toward the bat rack. To their astonishment it was Boudreau! With the game on the line and ace reliever Joe Page staring down from the pitcher's mound, Lou walked gingerly to the plate, clearly still aching from the collision a few days before.

The fans listening on the radio got up from their easy chairs and crouched over their sets, straining to hear every word from Jack Graney and Jimmy Dudley. This would be a singular time for Indians baseball. A base hit would not assure the pennant, but the momentum gained could not be understated.

This was by far Boudreau's most pivotal at bat in his ten years as a Major Leaguer. He was a perennial All-Star and having another great season, but little of that mattered when he slowly stepped into the batter's box. With 73,000 hearts pounding, he worked the count to 2–2, then lined a base hit to center field, electrifying the entire stadium. Hegan scored and Allie Clark motored around third to tie the game at 6–6. Boudreau had delivered. Only moments after the bat connected, Ed McAuley was leaning out of the press box, watching Boudreau's laser-shot single. After a few minutes he put down his thoughts for Monday's edition of the *News*. "In all this reporter's years on the sports beat he never heard an ovation to compare with the one which that mammoth crowd gave the crippled manager." His words testified to the absolute magic at the ballyard.

Satchel Paige held the Yankees in check in the top of the eighth. In the home half, Johnny Berardino walked with two outs, giving Eddie Robinson a chance to break the tie. On the first pitch from Joe Page, the big first baseman slammed the ball into the right field seats for his second consecutive home run. The Indians had come all the way back from down 6–1 to leading 8–6. Russ Christopher replaced Satchel with two outs in the ninth and retired Charlie Keller to record his fourteenth save and preserve one of the Indians' greatest victories.

In the break between games, the Ink Spots sang their hits live, including the classic "If I Didn't Care," while the fans tried to calm down and restart their hearts. The concession stands and vendors must have done good business selling soda pop and beer to folks who had screamed themselves hoarse.

Steve Gromek shut the Yankees out for the first five innings. In the bottom of the fifth, Eddie Robinson blasted his third home run of the afternoon, a towering drive that put the Indians up 1–0. The Yankees tied the game in the top of the sixth, but in the bottom of the seventh Joe Gordon singled, Johnny Berardino sacrificed him to second, Robinson was intentionally walked, and Jim Hegan singled to score Gordon from second. Ed Klieman blanked the Yankees through the last two frames, gaining the save and securing the sixth win of the year for a reenergized Gromek.

It probably was a good thing the Indians won both games, because the huge crowd had to push and squeeze its way through the wooden bridge leading from the stadium. As before, some of the pedestrians ducked under the bridges and across the railroad tracks. It took an hour for the happy mob to thin out, but all made it home safely.

The next day the Indians were off on a ten-day western road trip, with stops in Detroit, St. Louis, and Chicago. Boudreau pinch-hit in one of the games against the Tigers, and returned to the lineup against the Browns, playing every inning of two doubleheaders in two days. If he was still hurting, it didn't show in his play, as he went 9 for 18 in those four games.

In the second game of the second doubleheader, Gene Bearden, another of the Indians' good-hitting pitchers, belted a three-run homer in the first inning, part of a nine-run outburst. After three innings the score was 13–0, but the visitors were just warming up. The final score would be 26–3, and the Indians would have twenty-nine hits, including four apiece by Bearden and Hal Peck and three each by four other Cleveland players, and four home runs, by Doby, Judnich, and Hegan in addition to Bearden. The twenty-six runs just missed the team record set in 1923 at League Park, when the Indians crushed Boston 27–3, though in that game Cleveland had no home runs and "only" twenty-four hits.

The next game was in Chicago. Satchel Paige was slated to start. He was always a big draw in the Windy City, having pitched many Negro Leagues games there over the years as well as numerous all-star contests. By game time all seats were taken, with another 15,000 people outside, hoping to find a way into Comiskey Park. Some of the ticketholders came late and tried to ram their way to the turnstiles. Inevitably, fights broke out, resulting in eighteen people being injured and two unhappy folks carted off to jail.

Paige held the White Sox scoreless through the first four innings. Cleveland scored the first run of the game in the top of the fifth when Larry Doby bashed a triple and rode home on Jim Hegan's sacrifice fly. They added four more runs in the eighth and ninth innings to help Paige breeze to his fourth win of the season, 5–0. He allowed five hits while not issuing a single base on balls. Apparently pitching only once every four days really was a vacation for Satch.

The successful road trip ended with seven wins in ten games. The Indians, with a record of 67–42, held on to first place, a game and a half ahead of the A's, who were still refusing to fold. The Red Sox were just a game behind Philadelphia, and the Yankees had fallen to five games behind the leader.

On Monday, August 16, America and the world were saddened by the death of Babe Ruth at age fifty-three. Cleveland fans remembered his July 11, 1914, pitching debut, when a nineteen-year-old kid from nowhere beat the Indians 4–3, and they recalled a much older, larger Ruth blasting his five hundredth career home run into the stratosphere over League Park. Now he was dead of throat cancer, his body lying in state at Yankee Stadium, a place of honor for the one and only Babe. Outside the ballpark a gigantic crowd of men, women, and children waited patiently to pay their respects. The funeral took place at St. Paul's Cathedral in New York City, where mourners bid farewell to the greatest baseball player to wear a Major League uniform. His 714 home runs were eventually surpassed by Henry Aaron, but baseball will probably never see a force of nature like Babe Ruth again.

Back at home, the Indians won both games of a series against the Browns, both by shutout. On Friday night, a giant crowd of 78,382 fans flooded the stadium to see Paige start a second time against the White Sox. Veeck was staging his latest extravaganza, Mayors' Night. The mayors of every city in Ohio were invited. Twenty tents were set up before the game, and the mayors who attended were served food and drink accompanied by strolling musicians and an autograph session with Boudreau and his coaches. Dessert featured a huge four-tier cake with two baseballs on top. Paige was just as sharp as he had been the week before. In the fourth inning, singles by Boudreau, Keltner, and Doby scored the only run he would need as he defeated the White Sox 1–0, allowing only three hits. Paige was marvelous in hurling his second shutout of the season and the Indians' fourth straight win. The staff had rung up thirty-nine scoreless innings in a row, dating back to Sunday at Chicago, and the streak would reach forty-seven before the White Sox scored three late runs off Bob Lemon to beat the Indians 3–2 on Saturday.

After an eight-game winning streak, the Indians lost eight out of thirteen games to end August in third place:

Boston	76–48	.613
New York	75–49	.605
Cleveland	75–50	.600

Only one and a half games separated the three contending teams, while Philadelphia, at four and a half games back, was starting to fall out of contention. In September, the Indians would play eighteen out of twenty-seven games at home, including a long homestand from September 8 through 22. Playing so many home games afforded the Indians a critical advantage in their drive to win the pennant. Further aiding their fortunes was that the Red Sox and Yankees would have to play six games against each other.

September began with a road game against the Athletics. In the first inning, Ken Keltner walloped a bases-loaded triple, then jogged home on Eddie Robinson's single. Bob Feller was his old self, ringing up nine K's in the 8–1 win. The next few days saw Cleveland lose three out of four while New York and Boston went on win streaks, dropping the Indians to an alarming four and a half games behind. It was time either to reel off a bunch of wins or to step back and watch the Red Sox and Yankees battle for the flag.

On Wednesday, September 8, the Tigers were at the stadium, intent on ruining the Indians' pennant hopes. Back in July, Boudreau had told a reporter from the *Cleveland News* he believed the pennant race would be a tight one right down to the end of September, and the team he feared most was the Tigers and their good pitching staff, featuring Hal Newhouser and Freddie Hutchinson.

When Cleveland knocked Hutchinson out of the box in the fifth and led 7–3, it appeared Boudreau could relax a bit. However, Detroit chipped away at the lead, scoring two runs off Bob Lemon and tying the score in the eighth when Satchel Paige walked the bases loaded and Ed Klieman allowed a two-RBI single. The game was still tied in the eleventh when Doby singled, his fourth hit of the night, Gordon walked, and Keltner sacrificed the runners to second and third. Not interested in pitching to Boudreau, the Tigers walked him intentionally. Walt Judnich grounded to second baseman Neil Berry, who fired the ball home in time to retire Doby, but the throw was low and in the dirt and Doby slid in with the winning run. Cleveland survived eight walks by Lemon and four by Paige to win 8–7.

Attendance for the night was 43,707, not a fabulous number by this season's standards but enough to raise the season total to a whopping 2,011,662. The Yankees were the only other Major League ball club ever to reach 2 million. With most of the remaining schedule to be played at home, the Indians were going to bump that figure considerably higher.

Thursday evening was another Bill Veeck evening of entertainment. Ken Keltner, having a career season, was the guest of honor at Ken

Keltner Night. The event was originally the idea of Keltner's Milwaukee friends, but Veeck took the plans and enhanced them like no other. On hand for the celebration were Keltner's mother, wife, and nine-year-old son, Randy. Younger brother Jeff, not up for traveling, stayed in Milwaukee with family.

Veeck presented his third baseman with a check for $1,000 and set up bank accounts in the same amount for his two boys. A new Chevy station wagon was driven to the infield along with a truck, carrying a television, luggage, and furniture estimated to be worth $6,000. The final gift was an adorable collie puppy, which got the unanimous approval of Randy and the family. Keltner thanked the crowd for ten great years in Cleveland. Fans cheered loudly, remembering his fantastic plays at third base, particularly the one on July 17, 1941, that stopped Joe DiMaggio's fifty-six-game hitting streak, and his solid hitting over the years. Keltner had had many highlights in his career, but there were still a few more big ones to come.

On the mound that evening was Bob Feller, squaring off against Hal Newhouser, the pitcher Boudreau feared most. The game went as advertised, with the Indians clinging to a 2–1 lead going into the ninth inning. Once again Satchel Paige faltered in relief, surrendering the tying run. The "$100,000 man," Sam Zoldak, took over for Satchel and held the Tigers scoreless through the thirteenth inning. In the home half, Keltner drew a walk and Thurman Tucker singled, bringing Eddie Robinson to the plate. He hit a blooper off the handle, but far enough to drop safely in the outfield and score Keltner with the game winner, 3–2.

On Friday the Indians led from the start and won easily, 10–1, to pull within three and a half games of Boston. The St. Louis Browns were in town next for a Saturday doubleheader. In the first game, Steve Gromek gave up no hits until the fifth inning and only four in the game as the Indians won 4–1. Whenever the Indians needed an extra starter, Gromek ably filled the slot, usually turning in a stellar performance. In the second game, Bob Lemon won his twentieth of the year, 9–1, while Keltner batted in three to boost his total to 101. The Indians were catching fire again.

With Lemon, Bearden, and Feller pitching well in September, Don Black got few chances to start, but he remained positive, always ready and waiting for a chance to contribute. On Monday, September 13, Boudreau named him to start that night against St. Louis. Earlier in the day, Black talked with reporters about his state of mind and new outlook. "I'm living a new life," he said. "I'm 100 per cent improved. I'm grateful to a lot of folks, in and out of Alcoholics Anonymous, who helped keep me from sliding all the way down." His decision to quit drinking and his willingness to go public about it doubtless encouraged others to seek help.

Eager to show Boudreau and the fans he could still get the job done, Black put away the Browns in the first two innings. At bat in the home half of the second, he fouled off a pitch, then dropped the bat and grabbed his head with both hands, obviously in great pain. He staggered for a moment, then dropped to his knees. Lefty Weisman flew out of the dugout and helped support him. It would have been best to call for a stretcher, but Black stubbornly rose to his feet and walked with help toward the dugout. Just before reaching the steps he collapsed again, vomited, and lost consciousness. Inside the clubhouse, Dr. Castle was waiting anxiously to examine him. He inserted a syringe into Black's spine. Within seconds the syringe filled with blood, verifying Dr. Castle's suspicion of a cerebral hemorrhage. An ambulance rushed Black to St. Vincent Charity Hospital, where doctors confirmed the diagnosis. Their foremost concern was the possibility of further blood being released from the brain, which could be fatal. Black's wife, Joyce, and two young daughters, who had watched him rebuild his life and were hoping with him he could go on to a long career in baseball, were devastated.

Shaken, the Indians lost the game to St. Louis, ending their win streak at seven. They had little time to worry about their teammate, as the Yankees were coming to the stadium to play a single game. Bob Lemon started against Ed Lopat, and three runs in the bottom of the sixth put the Indians up 4–2. But in the top of the seventh, pinch hitter Charlie Keller hit a two-run homer off Lemon, sparking a four-run rally that put the Yankees up 6–4. With one out in the bottom of the ninth, the Indians loaded the bases. Pinch hitter Joe Tipton lofted a sacrifice fly to close the gap to one run, but Dale Mitchell grounded out to second, and the Indians fell one run short, 6–5. The loss dropped the Indians to four games behind Boston with just fifteen games left to play. Nobody was throwing in the towel, but making up the ground would take a huge effort. The standings on September 15 looked like this:

Boston	87–50	.635
New York	85–52	.620
Cleveland	84–55	.604

Some hopeful news came when doctors announced Don Black had shown slight improvement, though he remained unconscious. The *Plain Dealer* reported that they had received five hundred calls to the switchboard inquiring if there were any updates on the pitcher's condition. Though Black had not contributed much to the Indians' exceptional season, the fans were behind him. A day later Black opened his eyes briefly and asked for orange juice. He recognized his wife before drifting back to sleep. The doctors were cautiously optimistic about a recovery, though it would be a long and difficult one.

Before the Indians faced the Senators on September 16, the commissioner's office announced that the first two games of the World Series would be played in the National League park beginning on October 6. Tickets would be $8 for a box seat, $6 for reserved, and a buck for general admission. The Mutual Broadcasting System, at a price of $249,000, was awarded the radio and television rights to send the game to five hundred radio stations in the United States and Canada. In addition, the radio broadcasts would be carried over the North Atlantic to the soldiers and sailors in Europe. The television broadcasts and the number of stations included were not yet released. For the tenth year in a row, Gillette Razors would be the sponsor for the broadcasts. Of the $249,000 paid by Mutual, $150,000 was earmarked for the players' pension fund, while the other $149,000 would go to the Major League offices.

Whether the Indians were thinking about the World Series or not, they began the Washington game with a loud bang. Dale Mitchell led off with a single, Thurman Tucker walked, Boudreau popped out, and Joe Gordon was hit by a pitch to load the bases. Keltner walked, scoring Mitchell, and Larry Doby hammered a pitch four hundred feet over the right center field fence for a grand slam and a 5–0 lead. Gene Bearden pitched steadily to pick up his fifteenth win, 6–3. The victory, combined with a Boston loss to St. Louis, pulled Cleveland to within two and a half games.

The next afternoon the Indians took on the Senators once more. Rising to the occasion, Bob Feller struck out eleven batters in a neat 4–1 victory. It was his fourth straight win in crunch time. His resurgence came at just the right time, with Bob Lemon struggling and no designated fourth starter on the staff.

Bill Veeck announced that the game on Wednesday, September 22, would be a benefit for Don Black and his family. The Indians would keep the ticket receipts from the first 25,000 customers and pay the visitors' share to Boston and all remaining money to the Blacks. No free passes would be given out, meaning all writers and radio people would have to pay to get in. The Red Sox front office offered to donate their share, but Veeck declined, believing the stadium would be filled and a huge amount left over for the Black family.

On Saturday the Indians, behind three-run homers by Boudreau and Hegan and four hits from Dale Mitchell, finished the series sweep against Washington. Sam Zoldak, doing his best to justify his $100,000 price tag, held the Senators to a single run in a 10–1 victory. The hapless visitors went down to defeat for an unfathomable eighteenth straight time. The Indians had won ten of their last twelve games.

Though the American League pennant was still very much in the air, accolades began pouring in for the Indians. The *Sporting News* named Lou Boudreau Player of the Year in the American League and Bob Lemon Pitcher of the Year. The selection of Lemon was truly remarkable, considering he had arrived in the Major Leagues just a few years earlier as a third baseman–outfielder. Switching from position player to pitcher, and vice versa, in the minor leagues is not unheard of, but to make the conversion successfully while maintaining a spot in the Majors is rare.

With every remaining game on the schedule a matter of do or die, the Indians pressed on. The day after the Washington series, a Sunday doubleheader against Philadelphia brought 75,382 fans to the stadium. The season total of 2,300,893 smashed the Yankees' Major League record. A two-run homer in the bottom of the ninth by Larry Doby won the first game, 5–3, and the second game was all Steve Gromek and Lou Boudreau. The former scattered three hits while the latter homered twice for a 2–0 win. Meanwhile the Red Sox lost twice to the Tigers, closing the gap to half a game. With ten games left in the season, only seven percentage points separated Boston, Cleveland, and New York. On Tuesday the twenty-second, the Indians would host Boston in what was billed as the biggest game of the year. A win would give the Indians a leg up in the race. Of their eight remaining games, six would be with Detroit and two with Chicago. The Red Sox and Yankees would meet another five times, most likely dropping one of them out of contention.

On Monday, Joe Gordon hit his twenty-ninth home run and had three RBIs as Gene Bearden won his sixteenth game of the year, 6–3. Tuesday was a day off for the team and its fans to take a few deep breaths and check their blood pressure before the Red Sox arrived. Probably thousands of Cleveland radios were tuned in for updates on the Red Sox–Tigers game. Boston, behind Mel Parnell, won 10–2, increasing their slim lead to a full game. It was Parnell's fourteenth victory.

On Wednesday night Bob Feller started the Don Black benefit game, while sixteen-game winner Joe Dobson pitched for Boston. Black was making steady improvement, though not enough to stay awake and listen to the game. Joyce Black wanted to be at the stadium, but all her neighbors were going to the game, leaving her without any babysitters. She and her daughters had to listen to the play-by-play on the radio. An enormous crowd of 76,772 fought their way down the pedestrian bridges, eager to lose their voices for the Indians and support Don Black. Scalpers on Euclid Avenue were reported to be asking and getting a remarkable $15 per ticket. Wally Bock, the Indians' assistant trainer, tried to purchase nineteen tickets for members of the Cleveland Browns and was told at the box office all seats were gone. If this was not the World Series, it felt a lot like it.

Feller retired the side in the top of the first inning, and in the home half Thurman Tucker drew a walk off Dobson, stole second, and came home on Joe Gordon's single. Ken Keltner socked his twenty-eighth home run, scoring Gordon ahead of him and staking Feller to an early 3–0 margin. With the crowd making enough noise to shake the stadium's foundation, Feller kept the Red Sox hitless for the first five innings. In the bottom of the seventh, Cleveland added two more runs on RBI singles by Doby and Walt Judnich. The fans were dancing and singing as they watched Feller pitch one of his finest games of the season, surrendering only three hits in winning his seventeenth, 5–2.

Only two and a half weeks ago the Indians had trailed the Red Sox by four and a half games. Incredibly, they had made up all the ground and were now tied with Boston for first place. Asked about the cheers directed at him throughout the ballgame, Feller wisely remarked, "A hero one day, and a heel the next in this game. But it was good to win."

After the Indians took their part of the gate and paid the Red Sox their portion, just over $40,000 was left for Mrs. Black. Her husband would not immediately learn about the Clevelanders' terrific generosity, but the money would give him the security he needed while he continued his recovery. In addition, there might be a World Series share still to come.

Chapter 14

A BATTLE TO THE END

Locked in a tie for first place, the Indians made a leap of faith and announced that World Series tickets would go on sale. Ticket orders would be accepted beginning on Tuesday, September 28. Each fan could apply for up to four box or reserve tickets for each home game, with general admission tickets sold at the box office on game day. At the appropriate time, the front office would notify all the successful applicants when to go to the stadium and pay for their tickets. The demand for seats was expected to be colossal since Cleveland had not won a pennant in twenty-eight long years.

On September 24, as the fans filled out their applications, the Indians were in Detroit facing the Tigers and Freddie Hutchinson. In the top of the sixth inning, Ken Keltner launched a solo home run for a 2–1 Cleveland lead. The Tigers tied the game in their half of the sixth, and struck again in the seventh when Vic Wertz doubled in two more runs off Bob Lemon to make the score 4–2. Joe Gordon's solo home run in the eighth finished the scoring as the Tigers won 4–3. The Yankees beat the Red Sox 9–6, creating an unusual, especially this late in the season, three-way tie for first place. American League president Will Harridge announced that if all three teams tied for the pennant, two of them would play on October 4, with the third awarded a bye, and on October 5 the two teams left would play for the title. Rarely had the American League seen such excitement.

On Saturday, September 25, Gene Bearden pitched against the Tigers' Virgil Trucks. The Indians led 2–0 after four innings, then erupted for five more in the top of the fifth, keyed by singles from Keltner, Robinson, and Bearden. They added two more runs over the last four innings, helping Bearden coast to his seventeenth win, 9–3. Boston defeated New York to stay tied with Cleveland, while the Yankees fell a game behind in third place.

The rubber match on Sunday featured Bob Feller against Hal Newhouser, seeking his twentieth win and more than eager to knock the Indians out of first place. A near-sellout crowd of 58,919, many of them fans who had driven up from Cleveland, packed Briggs Stadium. In the top of the third, Joe Gordon homered with Boudreau on base, putting the Indians out front 2–0. Feller was in magnificent form throughout, striking out nine batters and walking none as the Indians won 4–1. Fans glued to the scoreboard saw New York defeat Boston 6–2. Cleveland was back in sole possession of the harrowing race's lead for the first time since August 26.

As Monday dawned, the schedule showed Cleveland with five games left to play, two with Chicago and three with Detroit. With all of them at home, the oddsmakers made the Indians the favorites to win the pennant. Exceptional pitching, led by Feller, Lemon, and Bearden, with a large assist from Gromek and Zoldak, and solid hitting, especially by Gordon, Doby, Boudreau, Keltner, and Mitchell, had carried them through the September surge that took them to the top. Now the stars would need to keep up their torrid pace all the way to the finish line.

Although the Indians' office had its hands full with thousands of ticket requests, Veeck found time for one more nighttime extravaganza. A few weeks ago he had received a letter from a fan named Joe Early asking why the club did not have a night to honor an average Joe. Intrigued by the idea, Veeck decided to honor Early himself as the average Joe. Tuesday, September 28, would be Joe Early Night, and it would be something special even by Veeck's standards.

On Tuesday morning the postal service informed the Cleveland front office that it had 65,000 World Series ticket applications ready to be forwarded to the stadium. Fans had until 11:00 p.m. to have their applications postmarked and delivered on time. Based on the mail already received, the number of tickets requested was 780,000, more than three times the total number of seats available for all three home games. Realizing he had woefully underestimated the demand for tickets, Veeck told the three Cleveland newspapers he would be changing the ticket-distribution plan. From now on, for each application received only two tickets to one game would be processed. That way roughly 120,000 applications could be accommodated, which allowed a lot more individual fans to see a game rather than under the original plan. To placate the fans mailing applications from out of state, 30 percent of the tickets would be set aside for them. The fans would have no choice but to accept the one-game allotment or deal with the scalpers.

The downtown Cleveland post office designated a window for all fans dropping off applications. Throughout the entire day and until the 11:00 p.m. deadline, the line never slowed down as hopeful men and women waited to drop off their precious requests. Many post offices around northeast Ohio extended their deadlines to 11:30 p.m. to accommodate as many fans as possible.

The City of Cleveland chose this of all moments to express their displeasure with the current lease agreement, which would pay the city $60 per one thousand people at each World Series game held at the stadium. If three World Series games were played in Cleveland and each game drew approximately 80,000 spectators, the city would receive $4,800 per game and $14,400 for all three. The concession agreement guaranteed them $5,000 per game or $15,000 for all three. The total revenue would thus be $29,400, a paltry sum in view of the potential revenue to be distributed to the players and the league. The city would still get the parking revenue but would need to hire an army of police officers for traffic and crowd control. It was no wonder city officials were bitter. Veeck had evaded them so far on renegotiating the one-sided agreement, and was in no hurry to change things now.

Joe Early Night was held in front of 60,405 fans. The late September weather cooperated, with temperatures topping seventy degrees. The first 20,000 ladies who attended received a free orchid to pin on their coats. The orchids had been shipped to Cleveland from the Biltmore Flower Plantation in Hawaii on a temperature-controlled DC-3, along with a flower company representative and a grass-skirted flower girl, all of which cost $30,000. Imagine what the shareholders must have thought. To start the fun, Veeck stepped in front of the microphone and called Joe and his wife out onto the field. Moments later an old Model T Ford stuttered across the outfield toward home plate, followed by a cow, several pigs, rabbits, chickens, roosters, and a horse. When they were all assembled, a group of beautiful women popped out of the rusty antique car. That would be unacceptable today, but in 1948 dazzling women were considered part of the pageantry and subject to whistles and cat-calls from the men. As he had done when he owned the Milwaukee Brewers, Veeck read off ticket numbers and the winners came out of the grandstand to collect their animals, whether they wanted them or not. One lucky winner took home a collection of four wooden ladders. There was no rhyme or reason to the gifts. They were just another example of Veeck and his off-the-wall entertainment.

Attention then turned to Joe Early, a war veteran and security guard at the local Chevrolet plant. Joe received a spanking new 1949 Ford convertible with a year's supply of gas, a radio-phonograph set, a washing machine, work clothes, and a stack of books. The crowd cheered for Joe, an average guy trying to make a living. He was not honored for hitting home runs over the fence or pitching shutouts against the Yankees but for being a good hardworking citizen and neighbor. In Veeck's two-plus years as owner of the Cleveland Indians, this was the most charitable of his wacky promotions.

After some necessary cleanup, the Indians and White Sox were ready to play ball. Dale Mitchell led off the bottom of the first with a home run, and his teammates added two more runs to make the score 3–0. Intent on putting the game away quickly, they pushed the lead to 5–0 after four innings and 11–0 in the bottom of the fifth. That was the final score as the Chicago hitters could manage only four hits against Gene Bearden's floating knuckleballs. It was his eighteenth victory. The good news got better when the Red Sox and Yankees both went down to defeat, stretching the Indians' advantage to two games over both teams. With four games left, the pennant was there for the taking.

The next morning, twenty workers in the stadium office began sifting through the enormous number of ticket applications. Some came with letters pleading for tickets as if they were the difference between life and death. One letter read, "Send me a ticket or send me flowers for if I don't get the tickets I know I'll just die." Another asked for Bill Veeck's seat "because he paces back and forth and rarely sits down." Whatever system the workers used to distribute tickets would still leave thousands of fans with no alternative other than television, radio, or devious ticket scalpers.

The Wednesday night finale against Chicago featured Bob Feller on the mound, looking for his seventh win in a row. After five innings the

Indians trailed the White Sox 2–0. Lou Boudreau, leading off the bottom of the sixth, drew a base on balls and jogged home on Joe Gordon's thirty-second home run. Ken Keltner followed with another homer, his thirtieth, and the Indians led 3–2. An inning later the Indians added two more runs on back-to-back doubles by Gordon and Keltner. Dale Mitchell had two singles to reach the 200-hit mark, becoming the first Cleveland hitter to reach that number since Earl Averill and Hal Trosky in 1936. Feller won his nineteenth of the year, 5–2, and had another start coming to try to achieve another twenty-win season.

The Indians rested on Thursday, waiting for the pesky Tigers to arrive for the final three games of the year. Pennant fever was rampant all around the city, including the local libraries. The Cleveland Public Library loaned out practically all its baseball books to boys and girls caught up in the anticipation of a World Series at the stadium, and the downtown branch created a special room equipped with a radio where students could socialize and listen to the games.

The downtown Cleveland hotels were booked to capacity, obliging the Cleveland Convention and Visitors Bureau to set up hospitality desks in the lobbies. The bureau assembled lists of local homeowners willing to rent rooms to out-of-town guests. Folks who had witnessed the near-hysteria of the 1920 Cleveland world championship anticipated a repeat of those crazy days, with three or four times the commotion.

Winning two or three of the games against the Tigers would mean the pennant, while one win would guarantee at least a tie. Both New York and Boston had won on Cleveland's day off, and if one of them swept the two games between them, then a Detroit sweep would mean the Indians' season was over. But the fans tried not to think about that horrifying possibility. Friday's game would match up veteran Virgil Trucks, a .500 pitcher that year, against Cleveland's best, Bob Lemon. Freddie Hutchinson was a scratch for Saturday's game, in bed with a fever, and whoever took his place would be up against nineteen-game winner Gene Bearden. Though someone being ill was nothing to celebrate, the Indians must have been glad not to face Detroit's number two starter. Hal Newhouser was alive and well and scheduled to pitch on Sunday, which the Indians hoped would be a meaningless game.

On Friday afternoon, the Indians struck quickly in the bottom of the first when Mitchell and Doby singled, Boudreau sacrificed, and Gordon grounded out to score Mitchell. The Tigers took a 2–1 lead in the top of the sixth, but the Indians countered in their half when outfielder Walt Judnich coaxed a walk with the bases loaded. With just one out and three runners still on base, the fans expected a big inning, but Trucks bore down and retired the next two hitters to leave the score at 2–2. One inning later Mitchell singled again and scored on Boudreau's double, giving Cleveland the lead, 3–2, with just six Tiger outs to go.

Lemon held the Tigers in the eighth, Trucks followed suit, and now the Tigers were down to their last three outs. Eddie Mayo opened the ninth with a slow roller down the third-base line. Lemon fielded the ball, slipped, and uncorked a wild throw into right field, allowing Mayo to race to second. Lemon struck out pinch hitter Johnny Bero, but then, at this crucial moment in the game and the season, his control failed him. After he walked the next two batters to load the bases, Boudreau came out to the mound and waved Russ Christopher in to pitch to Johnny Lipon.

Christopher had been outstanding all year at getting ground ball outs. Boudreau was hoping he could do it once again so the Indians could turn a double play or at least throw home for the force play. Maybe it was end-of-season fatigue, but Russ could not throw a strike, walking Lipon to bring in the tying run. The next hitter was Neil Berry, who swung at a low pitch and hit a routine grounder to Keltner. The throw went to Hegan, who stepped on the plate for one out then threw to first for the double play. As luck would have it on this day, regular first baseman Eddie Robinson had been removed for a pinch hitter and Walt Judnich had moved from right field to play first. The throw was in time but Judnich dropped it, allowing the Tigers an extra at bat. Jimmy Outlaw then slashed a single to center, scoring two more runs. Sam Zoldak came in to get the final out of the inning, but the damage was done. Art Houtteman retired the side in the bottom of the ninth to save the win for Trucks, 5–3.

The standings on October 1:

Cleveland	95–57
Boston	94–58
New York	94–58

The Indians could win the title with two straight wins. If they won only one of the games, they could still win if Boston and New York split their games, or tie if one of those teams won out. If the Red Sox and

Yankees split their remaining two games with each other, the Indians would need only one to clinch. Two Cleveland losses would mean either a playoff game or an unthinkable second-place finish.

Waiting to see how the final two games shook out were the National League champion Boston Braves. The Braves had won the pennant handily behind the standout pitching of Johnny Sain and Warren Spahn, backed by reliable starters Bill Voiselle and Vern Bickford. Their hitting was not on par with any of their potential opponents, but Bob Elliott at third base, last year's MVP, provided good power, with 24 home runs and 100 RBIs, and Al Dark, Eddie Stanky, and Tommy Holmes were all .300 hitters.

The Braves had another power hitter in the outfield, but in a September 29 game against the Brooklyn Dodgers he had tried to score from second base on a single to right field. The throw was right on target, forcing the runner, Jeff Heath, to try to slide hard under Roy Campanella's tag. His spikes caught the side of home plate, causing a painful fracture of his left ankle. Heath was taken to the nearest hospital, where doctors set the leg and applied a cast up to the knee. The former Indian would miss the World Series and a chance to set his sights on the medium-distance fences at Municipal Stadium. The accident probably also ruined any chances for the Cleveland sportswriters to pen numerous columns about the return of the prodigal son. At the time Heath was batting a healthy .319 with 20 home runs and 78 RBIs. Now he could only watch the World Series from the press box.

The vital Detroit-Cleveland series continued Saturday with Gene Bearden facing Lou Kretlow, recently called up from Williamsport of the Eastern League to take Freddie Hutchinson's place. Kretlow had appeared in four games for the Tigers, winning two of them. Many of the fans and writers at the stadium thought of an eerie similarity to a game played on September 28, 1940, when the Indians were two games behind the Tigers and needed to sweep the three-game series to bring home the pennant. Bob Feller was up against Floyd Giebell, who had been with the Tigers for only two weeks. The fans smelled blood when Giebell took the mound, but he shocked the world by pitching a shutout and clinching the pennant for Detroit. Now, almost eight years to the day, another unheralded rookie pitcher would be facing the Indians in a must-win game.

For three innings neither team was able to mount a threat. Fans began to fear they were seeing Floyd Giebell all over again. Their concerns were eased when Larry Doby slammed a double off the right field fence and went to third when outfielder Pat Mullin juggled the ball. Boudreau grounded out to Kretlow, but then Joe Gordon doubled to left, scoring Doby, and Ken Keltner's grounder to third was booted by Jimmy Outlaw, allowing Gordon to come in with the second run of the inning. Judnich walked and Robinson hit the third double of the frame, scoring Keltner. Dizzy Trout came on to pitch and immediately gave up a two-run single to Jim Hegan. Given five runs to work with, Bearden shut the Tigers down to win his nineteenth game, 8–0. In the clubhouse, Bearden was too busy happily chasing his eight-week-old cocker spaniel puppy around the room to talk to reporters.

In Boston, the Red Sox beat the Yankees 5–1, eliminating last year's champs. One game back and with one to play, Boston could only hope and pray for the Tigers to win on Sunday. If they did and the Red Sox won again, the two teams would meet on Monday, October 4, in a play-off game, the first in American League history.

Sunday afternoon Bob Feller, with a terrific September behind him, matched pitches with the Tigers' best, Hal Newhouser. In a day with perfect weather for football, Cleveland baseball fans jammed the stadium with a final regular season crowd of 74,181. The attendance boosted the season figure to an all-time Major League record of 2,620,627, almost 250,000 more than the Yankees, who Veeck loved to beat at anything. The first two innings went quietly, but in the top of the third Feller walked Johnny Lipon, Neil Berry singled, and Vic Wertz belted a double to left field, scoring Lipon with the first run of the game. Pat Mullin drew Feller's second walk of the inning, loading the bases for Dick Wakefield. With so much at stake, the moment had arrived for Feller to clamp down and stop the rally. But to Indians fans' dismay the Tigers outfielder got a piece of the next pitch, lifting a shallow pop fly down the left field line. Ken Keltner raced out after it, but the ball dropped out of his reach in fair territory. Berry and Wertz flew around the bases, extending Detroit's lead to 3–0, and Wakefield ended up at second base and Mullin at third. Boudreau decided that was enough for Feller and called for Sam Zoldak. Lou waved the outfielders in so that on a short fly Mullin would have to hold at third, but Eddie Mayo ruined the strategy by lofting a fly ball over Allie Clark's head in right. Mullin trotted home to extend the lead to 4–0. Ed Klieman came on to retire the side on a double play, but the Tigers had given Newhouser all the runs he would need. The twenty-game winner breezed to a 7–1 victory while Boston was clobbering the

Yankees 10–5. With a playoff game to be held in Boston, the champagne would have to stay on ice.

Despite the all-night train ride and the hostile environment they would face in Boston, the Indians players were ready to leave home and do battle. Boudreau told reporters he was undecided on who to pitch on Monday. He had used his best three starters in the Detroit series. Feller was out after pitching the day before, Bearden would have had only one day's rest, and Lemon would have had two. Should he roll the dice and try Zoldak, winner of four in September, or possibly Satchel Paige or Steve Gromek? The choice likely came down to Lemon or Bearden, but in the end it was Bearden, the hottest pitcher on the staff. Throwing the knuckleball, which put less stress on the arm, he was capable of pitching on short rest. Boudreau had made his decision before the team left for Boston, but to keep the writers from bothering his pitcher, he did not reveal it publicly until just before the game.

Red Sox manager Joe McCarthy had the luxury of picking from several different starters. The best choice seemed to be Mel Parnell, who sported a record of 15–8 and a fine ERA of 3.14. Parnell was rested, having last pitched on September 30. Ellis Kinder, with a 10–7 record, was another option; he had last pitched on September 29. McCarthy surprised everybody in the baseball world, including Parnell and Kinder, by selecting thirty-six-year-old righty Denny Galehouse. McCarthy may have been thinking of Galehouse's eight and a third strong innings in relief against the Indians back in July. Overall, though, Galehouse had a record of only 8–7 with an ERA of 3.82 in only 14 starts.

The Indians departed Cleveland Sunday night by train, and the next morning two chartered airplanes followed, all the seats taken by fans. Even though Monday was a workday, many businesses and shops would have their radios blaring, while schools were permitting teachers and students to tune in to the start of the game at 1:30.

Despite Galehouse being right-handed, and thus presumably tougher on right-handed hitters, Boudreau still chose to load his lineup with righties, including Allie Clark at first and Bob Kennedy in right. He was hoping they could reach the thirty-seven-foot-high wall in left field. The wall, which would come to be known as the "Green Monster," stood an inviting 310 feet at the foul line. Playing Clark at first raised a lot of eyebrows, given that it was his first game at that position in either the Majors or the minors. Calling on him to make his debut at first base in a playoff game was an unorthodox move. If Clark dropped a throw or booted a ground ball, Boudreau would be second-guessed for the rest of his time in Cleveland.

Galehouse retired the first two men in the first inning, but then Boudreau launched a solo home run over the left field wall. Boston tied the game in the bottom of the inning when Johnny Pesky doubled and scored on a single by Vern Stephens. Neither team scored in the next two innings, but in the top of the fourth the Indians began their dismantling of Denny Galehouse. Boudreau and Gordon singled, bringing Ken Keltner to the plate. He worked the count to two balls, two strikes, then blasted the next offering high over the left field wall and into the screen. The three-run homer was Keltner's thirty-first of the season, and without a doubt the biggest of his career. The Indians led 4–1, and Galehouse's day was over. Larry Doby greeted Ellis Kinder with a double to left center. Bob Kennedy sacrificed him to third, and Jim Hegan grounded out to short while Doby raced home with the fourth run of the inning.

With two outs in the fifth Boudreau hit another towering drive over the left field wall for his second home run of the game. Fenway Park grew silent as Lou slowly circled the bases and crossed home plate with Cleveland's sixth run. The home run marked another chapter in one of the most sensational years an Indians ballplayer ever had. If Bill Veeck had any lingering thoughts about getting another manager or shortstop, they must have been erased by now.

In the bottom of the sixth, the Red Sox tried their best to get back in the game. With one out, Ted Williams hit a pop fly over second base that Joe Gordon dropped for an error. Vern Stephens struck out, then Bobby Doerr straightened out one of Bearden's knuckleballs and drove it over the fence to cut the lead to 6–3. But that was all the offense the Red Sox could muster. The Indians added two more runs to win the historic playoff game, and the pennant, 8–3.

When Birdie Tebbetts grounded to Keltner for the last out, the Indians players mobbed Bearden, jumping all over him, pulling off his cap, and tousling his hair. Bill Veeck climbed over the railing behind the Indians dugout and hobbled as fast as he could to congratulate the winning pitcher. In just forty-eight hours Bearden had won two crucial games. In remarkable fashion, his win on Saturday saved the season, and his win on Monday won the pennant. He would have a chance for an encore in the World Series.

The game ended at 3:54 p.m., setting off the largest celebration in Cleveland since VJ Day in 1945. Factory whistles blared and church bells rang, signaling the people of Cleveland to get to public square downtown and make merry. The crowd started a snake dance through the city streets, gathering new members at every corner. People inside the office buildings opened their windows and threw confetti, ticker tape, newspapers, and even toilet paper down on the crowds below. From Euclid Avenue and 9th Street a steady bombardment of fireworks added to the deafening noise. Folks stuck in traffic in their cars simply blew their horns and sat in their seats, content to wait out the celebration. The newspapers estimated that close to 150,000 deliriously happy fans gathered to let off twenty-eight years' worth of steam. They would pack the streets for several hours before giving way to a fifty-man city street crew to clean up the tons of paper strewn about. There were no complaints from anyone, including the people leaving work and just trying to make their way home.

Meanwhile, in Boston, the Cleveland players showered and dressed and headed to the Kenmore Hotel for a victory party given by Veeck. In the Silver and Embassy Rooms, just off the main lobby, Veeck had managed to schedule an evening of music and dancing with a lavish spread, including Cape Cod lobster and roast beef. All team rules were put aside, meaning no limit on the champagne, beer, and liquor. The players did not hold back, eating and drinking without any concern for the next day. Suddenly, for no apparent reason, a fight broke out, then another and another. A Boston newspaper reported at least four fights, naming Joe Tipton, Eddie Robinson, Joe Gordon, and Ken Keltner as the main combatants. Hank Greenberg and Bill Veeck attempted to stop the fighting, and after newspapermen and other guests had been escorted out of the dining rooms Greenberg shut the doors until order could be restored. When all was quiet, several players were sent to their rooms for the night and the party doors reopened. The same Boston newspaper reported Tipton had a cut above the eye and Gordon and Keltner had welts on their noses. The fighting was attributed to an extreme amount of alcohol and boys being boys. The Cleveland newspapers tried to play down the conflict, saying it took nothing to separate the fighters and all was well in a few moments. Either way, the incident and the out-of-control behavior did not reflect well on the ball club on the eve of the World Series.

Chapter 15

VICTORY AT LAST

Since the World Series would begin in Boston against the Braves, the Indians remained at the Kenmore Hotel. Both teams worked out on Tuesday at Braves Field, an old, rusty ballpark dating back to 1915. Despite its age, the park seated 40,000 fans, an adequate number to host a World Series. The fences were 337 feet down the left field line, 370 feet to center, and 319 down the right field line, no problem for Gordon, Keltner, Doby, and the rest of the boys.

The players, even those with hangovers, were surrounded by newspaper writers from around the country. The Cleveland papers sent a large delegation, including veterans Gordon Cobbledick, Ed McAuley, Ed Bang, and Franklin Lewis. Some younger reporters also made the trip, including Harry Jones and Chuck Heaton, as well as feature writers and Jim Doyle, who would send his limericks and witticisms back to the *Plain Dealer*. Mutual Broadcasting set up their television cameras around the field as well as radio equipment for the national coverage. Handling the World Series radio play-by-play were Mel Allen from New York and Jim Britt from Boston. Jack Graney and Jimmy Dudley would not be broadcasting the games.

Regional television networks had recently been created for broadcasting games to different cities. The Eastern Network sent signals around New England and the East Coast states but had no connections with areas outside their broadcasting range. Similarly, WEWS Television in Cleveland, which had the broadcast rights for the three home games, set up live coverage to a small network of midwestern cities, including Chicago, Detroit, St. Louis, and Milwaukee, as well as Buffalo to the east. Cleveland fans would be unable to see any games from Boston, and vice versa. To compensate, WEWS placed a baseball diagram on screen together with a moving scoreboard. Van Patrick, with help from Tris Speaker, would get results off a telegraph wire and inform the viewers what was happening. When the games were in Cleveland, Patrick would work with longtime radio play-by-play man Walter "Red" Barber, currently doing the Dodger broadcasts.

Castle Films had the rights to shoot the entire series and sell the footage to baseball fans everywhere. The film would be available in eight and sixteen millimeter, offering highlights for $2.75, with sixteen millimeter feature length for $8.75 and $17.50, the latter with sound.

The expanded Tuesday sports pages in Cleveland featured three-quarter-page advertising from most of the downtown department stores. The Indian front office took out a large ad thanking the fans for their season-long support: "This is your pennant fans! It will fly over Cleveland Stadium because you put it there with enthusiasm—with faith—with support that surely stands unequalled in all baseball history. Thanks a million—more than two and a half million—Bill Veeck, President." The ad ended with a reminder that souvenir programs would be available at the stadium for only fifty cents. Veeck knew his audience and the mad rush there would be to purchase the programs.

Early Tuesday morning thousands of fans lined up at the stadium ticket windows by gates A and C. These were the fortunate ones notified by mail that their ticket requests were being honored and the tickets would be available until Wednesday evening. Hordes of out-of-town ticket buyers joined the locals for the day, standing in line for hours to claim their seats. Dropping fall temperatures and heavy gusts of wind from Lake Erie made the long wait even more difficult. Buyers had to pay by money order or certified check, no cash accepted.

The first game of the World Series was slated for Wednesday, October 6, at 1:00 p.m. Despite his Sunday troubles with Detroit, Bob Feller received the starting assignment to face twenty-four-game winner Johnny Sain. Feller's long, brilliant career and his status as one of baseball's all-time greats led Boudreau to choose him over the more rested Bob Lemon. Feller would be itching for the chance to pitch in a World Series and ready to give his best effort.

Johnny Sain was twenty-eight years old and had just completed his third full season with Boston. Like Feller, he had lost years to the military, but since returning home he had posted three consecutive twenty-win seasons. It would be a compelling matchup and likely a low-scoring game. The lineups were as follows:

Mitchell lf	Tommy Holmes cf
Doby cf	Al Dark ss
Boudreau ss	Earl Torgeson 1b
Gordon 2b	Bob Elliott 3b
Keltner 3b	Marv Rickert lf
Judnich rf	Bill Salkeld c
Robinson 1b	Mike McCormick cf
Hegan c	Eddie Stanky 2b
Feller p	Johnny Sain p

Marv Rickert was a last-minute call-up from Milwaukee to replace the injured Jeff Heath. Eddie Stanky was working his way back from a broken leg and was nowhere near 100 percent. The Indians enjoyed a clear hitting advantage, but based just on this season the pitchers were fairly equal, with a slight edge to Sain.

The pregame ceremonies featured former secretary of state James Byrne throwing out the first ball with Commissioner Chandler standing by his side. The Boston front office invited members of the 1914 "Miracle Braves" to the game, the only World Series winner in team history. The team's thirty-four-year drought was even longer than the Indians'.

Johnny Sain threw his warmup tosses on the mound as Dale Mitchell stood by, waiting to lead off the game. National League umpire George Barr took his place behind catcher Bill Salkeld and called "Play ball!" and the 1948 World Series was on. Sain threw nothing but curveballs to Mitchell, who flied out to center field. Larry Doby flied out to center as well, then Boudreau flailed at a breaking ball and lifted another fly ball down the left field line that Marv Rickert tracked down. Feller did his part, easily retiring the first three Braves he faced. The game developed into a memorable pitcher's battle, Sain baffling the Indians with a variety of curves that broke in and out around the plate and Feller showing his famous fastball, mixed in with sliders and breaking balls. Joe Gordon singled in the fourth and stole second but was left stranded after Ken Keltner fanned and Walt Judnich flied out to right. Marv Rickert led off the bottom of the first with a single, the Braves' first base hit, and was sacrificed to second, but Feller pitched out of any trouble.

That was how it went until the bottom of the eighth inning, when Bill Salkeld led off with a walk, then took a seat on the bench for pinch runner Phil Masi. Mike McCormick laid down a perfect sacrifice bunt, advancing Masi to second. Boudreau thought for a second, then motioned to Jim Hegan to intentionally walk Eddie Stanky. The move set up a force play at any base, but writers would later second-guess the decision, based on how well Feller was pitching. Johnny Sain hit a fly ball to right field for out number two. With Tommy Holmes at the plate, Feller suddenly whirled around and fired toward second, where Boudreau was racing toward the bag. Boudreau grabbed the throw and whirled to tag Masi, who was diving headlong back to the base. National League umpire Bill Stewart flashed the safe sign, starting a controversy that lasted for years.

The Indians had honed their pickoff play to perfection. They practiced it faithfully throughout the year and had used it in several games. American League umpires were aware of it and always kept a careful watch when an opponent reached second base. Apparently Stewart knew nothing about the play and was not in position to make the right call. Boudreau argued heatedly, but after several futile minutes play resumed. Photos and film of the play seemed to show Boudreau's glove on Masi's shoulder before his hand reached the bag.

With Masi given another life, Tommy Holmes singled sharply past Ken Keltner. Masi rounded third and streaked home with the first run of the game. Al Dark grounded out, but the Indians were down to their last at bat. With two out in the ninth, Keltner grounded to Bob Elliott, who threw wildly past first base. Keltner raced to second base, where he represented the tying run, but Sain bore down and struck out Walt Judnich. Boston had drawn first blood.

Sain was tremendous, surrendering four hits, all of them singles, fanning six, and not walking a batter. Feller delivered one of his finest games, throwing only eighty-three pitches while allowing just two hits and one tainted run. There were still plenty of games to play, but losing the first one this way left the Indians with a bitter taste.

Thursday's game featured Warren Spahn against Bob Lemon. In the bottom of the first inning, umpire Bill Stewart struck again. Al Dark grounded to Joe Gordon, who juggled the ball but threw to first apparently in time to get the runner. But Stewart, umpiring first base, signaled him safe, drawing the wrath of every Indian on the field and in the dugout. To add to the frustration, the Braves poked two singles off Lemon to bring Dark home for the first run. Incidentally, Earl Torgeson, who hit one of the singles, took a leadoff from second base and was caught dead when Lemon spun and fired to second. With all the umpires now alerted, there was no mistake about the call this time.

The 1–0 score stood up until the top of the fourth, when Cleveland staged their first rally of the series. Boudreau lashed a double just inside the right field line. Joe Gordon stroked a base hit to left, scoring Lou, and took second base on the throw home. One batter later, Larry Doby lined a single, scoring Gordon and putting the Indians out front 2–1. In the following inning, Mitchell singled, Clark sacrificed, and Boudreau drove a base hit to center to increase the lead to 3–1. The Indians scored once more in the ninth to make the final score 4–1 and even the series at one game apiece. Bob Lemon pitched masterfully in his first World Series game, scattering eight hits but giving up only the one unearned run.

After the game both teams hopped on a train for Cleveland to resume the series on Friday. Trains from all over converged on Cleveland, bringing baseball fans from Boston, from Richmond, Virginia, from Pittsburgh, and from Chicago. On the subject of trains, the Baltimore and Ohio Railroad installed a television set on a train, tuned in to the second game of the World Series. It was the first time rail travelers had been able to watch live television. Newspapermen reported that the picture was surprisingly clear and many passengers stopped by to take a look.

Late Thursday evening people began lining up at Municipal Stadium in hopes of securing a bleacher seat or a standing room ticket the following morning. Many came prepared with portable radios, sandwiches, and blankets to sleep on. Unfortunately, rain in the early morning hours forced fans to put the blankets over their heads and sit on the hard concrete. Undeterred, they continued their vigil. If anybody failed to get a seat, there were always the scalpers. The Indians ticket sales staff opened two restrooms for people to use and to dry off in.

The city of Cleveland was well set up to handle the influx of approximately 75,000 people. While the hotels were full, the Cleveland Convention and Visitors Bureau lined up 1,500 homes that could accommodate up to 5,000 visitors. Mayor Burke ordered all the downtown streets to be spruced up to make a good impression on the visitors and the eight hundred sportswriters from the United States, Canada, and Mexico. He assigned 250 police officers to patrol the streets from morning until night.

The Masonic Auditorium on 36th and Euclid offered television coverage of the game for those who could not find tickets. They installed a huge 7' by 9' screen, guaranteeing a good view regardless of where one was seated. Don Black, still recovering in his hospital room, received a television courtesy of General Electric. He was able to walk around his room and sit in a chair, leaving doctors more confident of a reasonable recovery.

Late Thursday night and all day Friday, the downtown hotels started checking in various celebrities from Hollywood and the sports world. Staying at the Hotel Carter were movie and radio stars Bob Hope, Bing Crosby, and Jack Benny, actress Mary Martin, and actor Peter Lawford, as well as popular comedians Bud Abbott and Lou Costello. Costello was from New Jersey and a fan of Larry Doby. Gangster actor George Raft stayed at the Hollenden Hotel, along with noted sportswriters Grantland Rice, Jimmy Powers, and Arch Ward. In the evenings, the Hollenden Ballroom presented baseball greats like Rogers Hornsby, Frankie Frisch, Bill Terry, and a host of others. The reception area rented one hundred typewriters and brought in one hundred Western Union telegraph operators for the convenience of the many baseball writers.

Among the former Indians arriving from out of town were 1930s favorites Earl Averill and Odell "Bad News" Hale. They joined local old-time stars Bill Wamby, Elmer Smith, Tris Speaker, Joe Vosmik, and George Uhle. For several hours the group reminisced about their teams from the 1920s and '30s. Wamby and Smith, two of the heroes of the 1920 World Series, were given seats directly behind home plate.

The Friday weather forecast called for periods of rain throughout the day, which downgraded the expected turnout to 60,000 to 70,000. In most places that would be an enormous number, but the Indians, despite the iffy weather, had been banking on standing room only. Before fans arrived, they had studied open spaces in the stadium, ready to place extra people at several locations behind the seating areas after all the spaces behind the outfield fences were filled to capacity. To the front office's disappointment, it looked like that would be unnecessary.

The uncertain weather wreaked havoc on the downtown scalpers, who had been hoping for a banner day. Since the game was not a sellout, they were forced to unload tickets for as little as fifty cents apiece. Fortunately for them, there were two home games still to play and a better than even chance to recoup their losses—as long as they could avoid the army of detectives patrolling the streets.

Due to late Thursday congestion at several eastern train stations, the Indians did not arrive in Cleveland until 10:30 a.m., two and a half hours before game time. The train carrying Commissioner Chandler did not roll into Cleveland until 11:00 a.m. From the station he went directly to his hotel and made calls to the other league officials. Satisfied his associates were already situated, Chandler, without changing clothes or shaving, hailed a cab for the stadium. Such was life in the days of back-and-forth train travel during World Series week.

At 1:00 p.m. the Indians, in front of 70,306 fans, trotted onto the field, wearing their home whites with the blue caps and distinctive red bills. The Braves, in their road grays with blue sweatshirts and blue caps, looked somewhat similar to the Indians. Gene Bearden was warmed up and ready to start game three against the Braves' Vern Bickford.

Neither team scored until the bottom of the third inning, when Bearden, playing the role of Superman, clouted a double off the right field fence. Bickford walked Dale Mitchell, bringing Larry Doby to the plate. The outfielder hit a ground ball right at Eddie Stanky, who flipped to Al Dark for out number one. Aware of Doby's great speed, Dark hurried his throw to first base, and the ball sailed into the Indians' dugout. Bearden jogged home on the error for Cleveland's first run.

An inning later, Ken Keltner walked and went to second on Eddie Robinson's single. Jim Hegan brought the fans out of their seats by driving a base hit to right field that scored Keltner. Bearden then scorched a line drive single to load the bases. With Mitchell and Doby due to hit, Braves manager Billy Southworth called in Billy Voiselle to relieve Bickford. Voiselle was up to the challenge, retiring both hitters to end the rally.

Bearden continued his late-season heroics, shutting the Braves down on five hits and no walks while striking out four. The 2–0 victory gave the Indians a 2–1 advantage in the series. At least for September and into October, a case could be made that Bearden was the best pitcher in either league. Veeck had made a lot of great moves since the 1946 season, but his acquisition of Bearden was looking like a stroke of genius.

At the end of the ballgame, a well-dressed gentleman and his wife, daughter, and son-in-law left their box seats in right field and walked to the exits. Alva Bradley had quietly watched the action, noting the large crowd and the huge success of the team. Back in 1927, when Bradley and his investors bought the ball club, he had emphasized promoting the city of Cleveland with a competitive ball club and a modern new stadium on the lakefront. He accomplished both these goals, but the man in charge now was Bill Veeck, not Bradley. Now the former owner was just another well-to-do fan, virtually unnoticed as he walked through the stadium concourse.

On Saturday morning, Cleveland fans pored eagerly over their newspapers, which were crammed with reports of yesterday's game. It seemed as though even the reporters who did not cover baseball had stories to file. The *Cleveland News* ran a column bylined by Bob Hope, originating from a strange location named Boudreauville. The nation's premier comedian threw out enough one-liners and zingers to make the reader spit up his coffee. Hope had been taking full advantage of his part ownership of the Indians, appearing in newspaper ads and taking his turn as a guest sports reporter. His many years of acquaintance with Clevelanders helped him along as well. If anyone was living the dream, it was Hope.

Wanting to give Feller another day of rest, Boudreau chose to start Steve Gromek over Satchel Paige, Sam Zoldak, and Bob Muncrief. As a spot starter, Gromek had a worthy record of 9–3, but he had last started on September 19, nearly three weeks ago. Whether he could shake the rust off and pitch effectively was a big question mark. While the Indians were still at Boston, Gromek had phoned his father in Michigan, telling him there was no need to sit by the radio every minute waiting to hear his son's name called. Before the game started, the elder Gromek, who was babysitting for his one-year-old grandson, turned the radio off to let the boy take his nap. He had no idea what he was about to miss.

On the Braves' side, Billy Southworth decided to start Johnny Sain on two days' rest rather than match him against Feller again on Sunday. He knew the Braves needed to win now, and after seeing how well Feller pitched in the first game, he wanted to use his number one guy in a game he had a better chance to win.

The Saturday weather forecast was perfect: clear skies and temperatures near seventy degrees. With no chance of rain, thousands of people stampeded the box office, lining up for tickets while they lasted. The final attendance was a massive 81,897, a new World Series record. At precisely 1:00 p.m., while fans waved pennants reading "American League Champs 1948," bought from the vendors for $1.25, Steve Gromek walked to the pitcher's mound. He would tell reporters after the game that he had been too anxious to get much sleep the night before. Still feeling some nerves, he managed to get leadoff hitter Tommy Holmes to fly out to right field. Al Dark fouled out to Hegan, but Earl Torgeson stroked a two-out double. Gromek, already over the jitters, retired Bob Elliott on another foul pop-up to Hegan.

Dale Mitchell opened the home half of the first with a single and moved to second on Doby's sharp grounder to first. Boudreau followed with a line drive down the first base line and into the right field corner, scoring Mitchell. Bad ankles and all, he tried to stretch the hit into a triple but was thrown out on a strong relay throw. The out call was made by Indians nemesis Bill Stewart, who was umpiring third base. After several choice words from Boudreau, and the loud boos of the partisan Cleveland fans, play resumed with Joe Gordon grounding out to end the inning.

The score was still 1–0 in the bottom of the third inning when Doby slammed a Sain fastball 410 feet over the right center field fence and into the standing room crowd, where it was snagged by a ten-year-old boy, John Lynch. The young fan had woken up early Saturday morning and arrived at the box office at 8:00 a.m. After getting his ticket, he fought his way to a good spot behind the fence. Men around him offered cash for the home run ball, and after some negotiations he gave it up for the generous sum of $6. After the game he walked proudly to the May Company Department store, where he bought china dishes for his mom and a shirt for his dad. It was a day to remember for the Lynch family.

Staked to a 2–0 lead, Gromek used his lively fastball and knuckle curve to hold back the Braves' hitters. Back home in Michigan, Steve's sister and mother were shopping at a department store when they noticed a television broadcasting the ballgame. His sister gasped, realizing her brother was pitching. The two raced home and woke up Gromek's father, and likely the baby as well, and the radio was quickly turned back on.

In the top of the seventh, Marv Rickert homered to right field to cut the margin in half. Mike McCormick followed with a single, which got the Indians' bullpen up and throwing. However, this day belonged to Gromek, and he retired the side without any further damage. Down to two more chances, the Braves had still not solved the man from Michigan.

After the Braves left a man stranded at second in the eighth, Gromek fanned Rickert and McCormick to start the ninth. Nearly bursting at the seams, the Indians fans rose to their feet with enough noise to be heard in the suburbs. Bill Salkeld came in to pinch-hit for Phil Masi and lifted a routine fly ball to right field for the third and final out. Gromek had stepped up to the challenge, pitching one of the best games of his career to lead the Indians to a 3–1 margin. On cloud nine, Cleveland fans left the stadium feeling confident about wrapping up the series on Sunday. Bob Feller would be rested and ready to go, in likely his last chance to pitch in the series. If there was ever a game he was motivated to win, game five was it.

In the Indians' clubhouse a more than pleased Steve Gromek answered all the reporters' questions. He admitted to being nervous, but said he calmed down quickly. He praised Larry Doby for his key home run and the rest of his teammates for their support. Asked about the homer, a jubilant Doby said, "I don't mind saying, that it was just right for me, though he [Sain] never did plan it that way. A change-up curve ball shoulder high. Nothing or nobody could feel so good as I feel now."

Photographers asked the two ballplayers to pose for a few pictures. Without hesitation, Gromek put his arms around Doby and gave him a tremendous hug. The photographs captured the moment perfectly: two happy men enjoying perhaps their finest moment as ballplayers. Doby would later write about his deep feeling of relief that he was finally accepted as one of the guys without any thought of race. The image, with its undeniable message of friendship between a White man and a Black man celebrating together, would be seen across the United States. Doby would have some trying experiences in the future, but the march toward acceptance took a significant step inside the Cleveland locker room that day. Steve Gromek deserved a ton of credit for hugging his teammate, not at all concerned about what anybody thought.

Early Sunday morning the stadium box office opened its windows to an endless mass of ticket buyers. Since it was the last game to be played in Cleveland, the front office apparently decided to let everybody in without concern for space. When the line finally melted away, the official attendance stood at a mind-numbing 86,288.

Anticipation of a World Series–clinching win ran wild throughout the stadium and the city. The Cleveland reporters believed Feller would wrap things up in a breeze. Even the Cleveland players got caught up in the hype, as few thought to pack a bag for a possible trip back to Boston. In all the buildup, somebody forgot to tell the Braves to lie down and quit.

Tommy Holmes led off the first with a single. Al Dark tapped a slow roller down the third-base line and beat Keltner's throw to first for a scratch hit. Earl Torgeson flied out, but Bob Elliott reached for a high fastball and powered it over the right center field fence, silencing the crowd and giving Boston a surprising 3–0 lead.

Dale Mitchell began the Indians' half of the first with a home run off Nelson Potter. The blow to deep right center buoyed the fans, who were sure Potter would not last the inning. But he scraped through, and the score remained at 3–1 until the top of the third, when Elliott caught up to a hanging curveball and blasted his second consecutive homer. By now it was apparent that Feller did not have his overpowering fastball or sharp-breaking curve. Nobody in the ballpark expected the Braves to be leading 4–1 before three innings were done. The last thing on Boudreau's mind, however, was to get a reliever warmed up in the bullpen. He was confident Feller would turn things around.

In the bottom of the fourth, the Indians came to life with a vengeance. Gordon opened with a single, moved to second on Keltner's walk, and scored on Judnich's bloop single just over Alvin Dark's head into left field. Eddie Robinson popped out, but Jim Hegan bashed a long home run to put the Indians ahead 5–4. This was what the crowd had expected, that the Indians' hitters would send Potter to the clubhouse and keep it up against the Boston relief pitchers. Warren Spahn, the losing pitcher in game two, came on and retired Feller and struck out Doby to end the inning.

Feller put the Braves down in order in the fifth, but with one down in the top of the sixth Bill Salkeld tied the game with a homer to right. Sportswriters wondered aloud if Feller needed to be taken out before the game got out of hand. To that point he had allowed five runs, including three home runs, in five and a third innings. Boudreau had a rested bullpen at his disposal, but chose to live or die with his trusted hurler.

The next inning Holmes singled again, Dark sacrificed him to second, and Torgeson drove him in with a line drive single to center. With the score 6–5 in favor of Boston and Bob Elliott coming to the plate, Boudreau reluctantly pulled Feller and brought in Ed Klieman. Klieman had pitched well in relief all year, appearing in forty-four games with an ERA of 2.60 and four saves. With the great starting pitching the Indians had enjoyed down the stretch, he had the benefit of a full week of rest.

Facing Elliott, who had already hit two home runs in the game, Klieman tried to be too fine with his pitches and ended up walking him. With runners on first and second, Marv Rickert singled to center, scoring Torgeson. Trying to get Elliott at third, Doby overthrew third and the ball bounced into the Braves' dugout, allowing Elliott to score and Rickert to advance to third. Boston's lead was now 8–5. Rattled, Klieman walked Bill Salkeld. Once again Boudreau made a pitching change, bringing in Russ Christopher. He did no better, giving up back-to-back singles for two more runs and a 10–5 deficit.

The next pitcher Boudreau called on was Satchel Paige, who became the first Black pitcher to make a World Series appearance. He retired Spahn on a fly ball to center field, but McCormick tagged up at third and scored the sixth run of the inning. Holmes, batting for the second time, grounded out to end the inning, but the six-run rally had quieted the crowd and taken the wind out of the Indians' sails. Spahn was lights out the rest of the way, and the Braves' 11–5 victory forced a sixth game in Boston. After the game a dejected Feller told the sportswriters, "I haven't any excuses. I couldn't seem to loosen up and I didn't have any control. All I can say is that I just didn't have it."

As the game ended, several of the Indians' wives raced home to pack suitcases for their husbands' 5:00 p.m. train to Boston, then hurried to the train station and wove their way through the 10,000 well-wishers to hand off the bags. Feller and Boudreau, not wanting to face the Cleveland fans, used a neglected freight elevator to reach the train undetected. They were worried a few individuals might take their frustrations out on them and start a riot.

The reporters stuffed their notes into their pockets and rushed off with their typewriters to catch the New York Central train. Usually a trip from city to city meant a lot of eating and sleeping and hobnobbing with the ballplayers. But they would have to spend this trip writing and filing their stories. The next day those stories were not overly critical of Boudreau's choice to stick with Feller, but they did suggest that his loyalty probably cost the Indians the game.

On Monday afternoon Bob Lemon was on the mound attempting to clinch the series against Billy Voiselle. The game was a sellout, with over 40,000 Boston fans fervently praying for a victory and a seventh game in which Johnny Sain could pitch. Though it was not revealed until after the game, Lemon was pitching with a sore arm from several days ago. The night before the game, he had gone to bed with several heating pads on his arm to try and ease the pain. In the morning, trainer Weisman worked on the arm for several hours until just before game time.

In the third inning, the Indians scored first when Mitchell and Boudreau each doubled for a 1–0 lead. In the bottom of the fourth, the Braves evened the score on an infield single by Elliott, a walk, and a base hit by Mike McCormick. There was no scoring in the fifth, but in the top of the sixth Joe Gordon broke the tie with a home run high over the left field wall. Thurman Tucker, getting his first start of the series, singled, Robinson singled him to third, and Hegan grounded into a fielder's choice at second to drive him in.

Warren Spahn relieved Voiselle in the top of the eighth and was greeted by consecutive singles by Keltner, Tucker, and Robinson to make the lead 4–1. With Bob Lemon in great form, the Braves were two innings away from defeat, but they refused to go away and hide. Holmes led off the bottom of the eighth inning, slapping a base hit through the infield. Dark flied out, but the crowd roared when Torgeson, having a fine World Series, doubled to right to put runners on second and third. Lemon stayed in the game to pitch to Elliott, but when he walked him Boudreau called for the Indians' most reliable pitcher, Gene Bearden. With Weisman's help and his own determination, Lemon had managed to gut out seven and a third innings.

With the bases loaded, pinch hitter Clint Conatser surprisingly nailed one of Bearden's offerings, sending a drive to deep center field. Thurman Tucker raced back near the wall and made a superb grab. Holmes scored, but Torgeson could only advance to third while Elliott retreated to first. Phil Masi then lined a clutch double off the left field wall, bringing in Torgeson and making the score 4–3 with the tying and winning runs at second and third. The Braves' hitters looked as if they had figured out Bearden's knuckleballs. Mike McCormick was next. The Boston fans were on their feet, pleading for their guys to extend the inning. Bearden took his time before he delivered. McCormick tapped a roller back to the pitcher's mound, which Bearden fielded and tossed easily to first to end the inning. The Indians still led, 4–3, but the Braves had one more shot to tie or win the game.

Spahn fanned the side in the top of the ninth. In the bottom of the inning, Eddie Stanky led off with a walk and Connie Ryan came in to run for him. Pinch hitter Sibby Sisti then attempted to sacrifice but bunted the ball in the air. Hegan leaped out from behind the plate, grabbed the ball on the fly, then whistled a throw to first to double off Ryan. Instead of having the tying run on second with one out, the Braves were down to their last at bat, in the person of Tommy Holmes. He lofted a high fly to left fielder Bob Kennedy, in for Dale Mitchell. Kennedy glided backwards, reached up, and squeezed the ball in his glove to end the game. The Cleveland Indians were World Series champs! The winning players rushed to the mound and carried Bearden off the field on their shoulders. The twenty-eight years without a World Series win had ended at Braves Field, starting a celebration that would last well into the trip back home.

In the clubhouse, Boudreau managed to quiet down the players for a brief talk. With his coaches standing by grinning ear to ear, Lou told his team, "I and the coaches knew you had the stuff to win the American League pennant and World Series. But we knew too that you had to get a few breaks to reach the top, you got them. So, the tops you are."

The players, glad beyond words, showered and dressed, eager to board their train and return home the following morning. While they were on their way, the city got to work, organizing a colossal parade from the downtown train station to Euclid Avenue and several miles up to University Circle. Fifteen convertibles were hired to chauffer the team past a predicted 150,000 fans lining the city streets to see them. Schools would stay open, but students could attend the parade provided they had a note from their parents, or a convenient forger.

Arriving in Cleveland early were Ken Keltner, Gene Bearden, and Satchel Paige. Rather than endure another train ride, they chose to take a plane from Boston. The story circulated that Satch ate three full meals aboard the plane, declining a fourth because he was tired of eating. Upon arrival at Cleveland Airport, the three players were surprised to see a crowd there to greet them. They signed autographs for all those who wanted them, then scattered for their homes.

At about 8:30 a.m., the train carrying the rest of the squad pulled slowly into the station. The players jumped into the line of classy convertibles, which made their way to Euclid Avenue and the start of the parade. Several motorcycle police led the caravan, followed by a local band perched in a large moving truck. The first car held Veeck, Boudreau,

Mrs. Boudreau, and Mayor Burke. As the procession inched its way east, roses, confetti, ticker tape, and balloons showered the ballplayers and their wives. At some places men and women ran up to the cars pleading for autographs or simply a handshake. The players smiled and took it all in as the enormous throng of people stood and cheered wildly for each and every one of them. Some would experience a pennant and World Series victory again and others would not, but this was a moment they could all take with them for the rest of their lives.

After the parade, the players dispersed. Some would remain in town for a Thursday banquet at the Hotel Carter, while others headed out for their off-season homes. Gene Bearden planned to fly to Hollywood for a screen test, hoping to become the next Johnny Berardino. Bob Feller nixed any barnstorming plans in favor of several months of hunting, fishing, and golf in Dallas, Texas. Joe Gordon left for Eugene, Oregon, to hunt and fish while putting in time at his hardware store. Ken Keltner opened a bicycle shop in Milwaukee, while Dale Mitchell considered returning to the University of Oklahoma to work on his degree.

The players would not go home empty-handed. Largely due to the three games of record-breaking attendance in Cleveland, each one's winning share came to $6,772, the highest amount paid out since 1935, when the Detroit players received $6,544.76. Many World Series attendance and revenue records were shattered, thanks to a baseball-crazed city on the shores of Lake Erie.

For the season, Indians players were among the leaders in multiple categories. Boudreau finished second in the batting race, posting a career high of .355, while Dale Mitchell, at .336, was third. Mitchell was second in hits with 204, just ahead of Boudreau's 199. Gordon and Keltner were second and third in home runs, Joe with 32 and Ken with 31. On the pitching side, Lemon led all American League hurlers with 10 shutouts and 293 and 2/3 innings pitched. Lemon and Bearden finished with 20 wins each, one behind Hal Newhouser. Bearden finished second in the Major League Rookie of the Year voting behind the Braves' Al Dark. Russ Christopher led all relief pitchers with an impressive 17 saves, though saves were not a recognized statistic then. Feller won another strikeout title, fanning 164, while Lemon was second with 147. Other Indians players finished in the top ten in numerous statistics.

And what of Bill Veeck? To the dismay of the old-school owners, he had proven himself the most successful baseball executive in the Major

Leagues. His talents as a first-rate showman and entrepreneur and an astute judge of talent set him far apart from the rest of the pack. Though the baseball season was over, Veeck would soon be on the prowl again, readying himself and his ball club for another pennant run in 1949. Winning two in a row would be no easy task, but for the man with the curly red hair and ready smile it was just another obstacle to try and overcome.

EPILOGUE

B ill Veeck was never a man to rest on his laurels. In two and a half years he had broken every Cleveland baseball attendance record and brought home a rare World Series win. His ball club was the reigning champ, but he had no desire to stand still and see what might happen with last year's roster. In mid-December, he pulled off a major trade, sending Eddie Robinson and Ed Klieman to Washington for former batting champ Mickey Vernon and veteran pitcher Early Wynn. Veeck believed Vernon at age thirty was a better all-around player than Robinson, and he had coveted Wynn for several years, despite a 1948 record of 8–19 and an ERA well over 5.00. He would be a candidate for the starting rotation behind Feller, Lemon, and Bearden.

The Cleveland friends of Larry Doby held a December appreciation night for the star outfielder. With Veeck in attendance, Doby received a lavish gift, a 1949 Buick convertible. The evening included dinner, dancing, and music from the great jazz singer Ella Fitzgerald, backed by the Lester Young Orchestra. Doby received thanks for his superb efforts in helping the Indians win the World Series. He would be counted on to help carry the load in the upcoming season.

The defending champions began the 1949 schedule losing at St. Louis 5–1. Bob Feller left the game after two innings with a sore shoulder, an injury that first came up in spring training. He would be out of the lineup for two weeks, an early indicator of storm clouds gathering. The Indians came back to win the next two games against the Browns, and then the home opener in ten innings behind the effective pitching of Gene Bearden and the clutch hitting of first baseman Mickey Vernon, whose single in the bottom of the tenth gave Cleveland the win, 4–3.

The season started well. Bearden won his first three games in a row, Bob Lemon and Steve Gromek were pitching as they did in 1948, and Mike Garcia won his first two Major League decisions. The offense was potent, with Mitchell, Gordon, and Keltner hitting well. Through the first part of May, the Indians looked like a team ready and able to defend their crown. But then things began to implode. Lemon was out with an injured side, while American League batters began to tee off on Bearden's knuckleball. The defeats started to pile up. On May 17, a loss to the Yankees sank the Indians' record below .500, and by May 26 they were five games under at 12–17. The Indians determinedly battled back, but precious ground had been lost to Boston and New York. Late in the season they climbed as high as second place, but could not catch the Yanks, finishing a distant third.

In comparing 1948 to 1949, it is easy to analyze what went wrong. A year before, the champs had the benefit of career seasons from Joe Gordon, Ken Keltner, and Lou Boudreau, who combined for 81 homers and 349 RBIs, compared to 32 home runs and 174 RBIs in 1949. Boudreau's batting average dropped from .355 to .284, and Keltner's from .297 to .232. Joe Gordon did the best of the three, batting .251 with 20 of the home runs and 84 of the RBIs. With the big three falling back, Dale Mitchell and Larry Doby were left to shoulder much of the burden. Both had All-Star seasons, with Mitchell reaching 200 hits for the second straight year and Doby clouting 24 home runs. The decline of the older players meant some retooling would be needed for 1950.

The pitching dropped off too, with Feller, Lemon, and Bearden going from 59 wins in 1948 to 45 in 1949. Lemon had 22, up from 20, but Feller won only 15, a career low for a full season, and Bearden just 8. Mike Garcia picked up much of the slack with a record of 14–5 and a league-leading ERA of 2.36. Early Wynn had a winning record but an ERA of 4.15. Satchel Paige pitched well but could not repeat his crowd-pleasing heroics of 1948, while most of the bullpen struggled throughout the year. The club did win eighty-nine games, not a bad mark at all, but a disappointment to fans hoping for another pennant. For the second year in a row attendance passed the 2 million mark, a tremendous accomplishment but overshadowed by the third-place finish.

Bill Veeck was certainly not pleased with his team's performance. His magic touch had faded somewhat, and his attention was distracted by the divorce he and his wife were going through, which took away assets that he would normally have spent on baseball. He agreed to set up a trust fund for his children, locking up a significant amount of money for a man who never saved for a rainy day. The only ready cash available to him was his shares in the Cleveland Indians.

Rumors began during the season that the Indians were for sale, and Veeck did little to dispel them. In October, he announced plans to marry a second time after the divorce was final, and on November 17, eager to start a new life, he sold the Indians to Cleveland businessman Ellis Ryan and his group of investors. The sale of his shares went toward the trust fund for the Veeck children.

In a whirlwind three and a half seasons, Veeck had taken control of a losing ball club and transformed them into world champions. His one-of-a-kind promotions and groundbreaking marketing campaigns brought invigorated fans to the stadium in eye-popping numbers. He had made a few mistakes in the process, including publicly criticizing Boudreau as a manager and acquiring too many veteran ballplayers instead of grooming a younger team for the future. But overall he deserved an A for turning around a city with complacent fans and bringing a sense of excitement like no other. Bill Veeck left his mark on Cleveland.

The new regime retained Hank Greenberg as the general manager. He set to work rebuilding the infield, placing Luke Easter at first base, Roberto Avila at second, Ray Boone at shortstop, and Al Rosen, for a departed Ken Keltner, at third. Mitchell, Doby, and Bob Kennedy continued as the primary outfielders, Jim Hegan remained at catcher, and the pitching staff featured Lemon, Garcia, Feller, and a vastly improved Wynn. The core of this team would win another pennant in 1954, though they would fall to Willie Mays and the Giants in the World Series.

Among the ballplayers traded away in the Veeck era, Allie Reynolds went on to have tremendous success with the Yankees. An elite pitcher in the late 1940s through the mid-1950s, he won seven World Series games for New York while being named to the All-Star team five times. In 1951, Reynolds pitched two no-hitters, the first a 1–0 gem against Feller at Cleveland Municipal Stadium. For his career he won 182 games, lost 107, and compiled an ERA of 3.30. The 1946 trade of Joe Gordon for

Reynolds significantly helped both teams, though the Indians benefitted only in the short term. If Bill Veeck could have found a way to keep Reynolds while still acquiring Gordon, the Indians might have brought home several more pennants.

Eddie Robinson became a four-time All-Star with several American League teams. From 1950 to 1953 he averaged 23 home runs and 96 RBIs yearly. He appeared in another World Series, this time with the New York Yankees. After his playing days Robinson served as general manager with the Atlanta Braves and Texas Rangers. At age one hundred, he was the oldest living ex–Major Leaguer until he passed away in October 2021. The Indians may have been shortsighted in trading him, though Early Wynn proved to be a special pitcher for many years.

Pat Seerey continued his hit-or-miss batting with the White Sox, but on July 18, 1948, in Philadelphia, he walloped four home runs in a single contest to join a mighty exclusive club, including Hall of Famers Ed Delahanty, Lou Gehrig, Chuck Klein, and later Willie Mays and Mike Schmidt. The last home run broke an eleventh-inning tie, giving the White Sox a 12–11 win. The next season, overweight and out of shape, Seerey was sent to the minors. He played several more years, but never returned to the big time. "The People's Choice" had a relatively short career, but in his time he gave baseball fans more than a few thrills.

After the 1948 World Series, Russ Christopher wisely retired from baseball. Two years later he underwent a risky heart surgery, which doctors believed to be a success. Feeling fairly healthy for the first time in years, Russ attempted a comeback with minor league San Diego, but was unable to stick with the team. On December 5, 1954, he died suddenly of heart failure at the young age of thirty-seven. To play baseball as long as he did showed tremendous courage, with some audacity mixed in. In 1944, when doctors advised him to quit the game, he replied frankly that if he had to die there was no place better than on a baseball field.

Don Black recovered from his near-fatal cerebral hemorrhage, even trying a brief comeback with the Indians. He found himself too weak to keep up with his teammates, but reportedly Bill Veeck, as a courtesy, paid his 1949 salary. Black made his permanent home in northeast Ohio, where he sold insurance and automobiles. In 1958, injuries from a serious car crash forced him to retire as a relatively young man. On April 21, 1959, Black was at home, peacefully watching the Indians game on television, when he slumped in his chair. An ambulance rushed him to an Akron hospital, where he was pronounced dead. He left behind his wife and two teenaged daughters.

Jim Hegan was another who had his life shortened by illness, though he was able to accomplish much more in baseball. He stayed with the Indians through the 1950s, buying a home in Cleveland while opening up a combined gift shop and jewelry store with buddy Otto Graham, the great Browns quarterback. After his playing days were over, Hegan became the New York Yankees bullpen coach in 1960. There he had the privilege of seeing his son Mike break in with the Yanks. The younger Hegan would eventually join his father as an All-Star and World Series champion, with the 1972 Oakland Athletics.

Jim Hegan coached in New York for many years, serving as a confidant to manager and close friend Ralph Houk. In 1974, Houk moved on to pilot the Detroit Tigers and convinced Hegan to join him there for the next four years. In June of 1984, Jim, now a part-time scout with the Yankees, was doing an interview at his Massachusetts home when he suffered a heart attack. An ambulance hurried him to the hospital, where he was dead upon arrival. He was just sixty-three years old.

In his career, Hegan caught some of the best pitchers in baseball, including Hall of Famers Bob Feller, Bob Lemon, Satchel Paige, and Early Wynn. A five-time All-Star and member of the Cleveland Indians Hall of Fame, Hegan was one of baseball's finest defensive catchers.

As for the provocative Cleveland Indian Jeff Heath, he returned to the Boston Braves in midseason of 1949. He still had problems with the slow-healing leg but managed to belt 9 home runs in thirty-nine games. Unable to play the outfield as in the old days, he was released at the end of the season. After a brief stay with the Seattle Rainiers of the PCL, he retired for good. Later he became a color commentator for the Rainiers, known for downing mass quantities of hot dogs while broadcasting games. Heath never quite got over his quick temper, getting into several brawls before he died of a heart attack at the age of sixty. His legacy is preserved by being voted as one of the Cleveland Indians' one hundred greatest players. There were times when he exasperated fans and even a manager or two, but more often than not he was truly a gifted ballplayer.

Six of the players on the 1948 ball club are in baseball's Hall of Fame. Bob Feller entered in 1962, followed by Lou Boudreau, Satchel Paige, Bob Lemon, Larry Doby, and Joe Gordon. Bill Veeck, the architect of the fabulous season, was elected in 1991. Front office vice president

Hank Greenberg and coach Bill McKechnie are also Hall of Famers, though Greenberg was elected for his hitting prowess for the Tigers and McKechnie for his managing skill in the National League.

Third baseman Ken Keltner enjoyed an excellent career, but saved his absolute best for the 1948 season. Outfielder Dale Mitchell was an elite hitter for several years, especially in the championship season. Steve Gromek went on to have a long career, first with the Indians, then with the Tigers. The balance of the 1948 roster, including Sam Zoldak, Ed Klieman, Walt Judnich, Bob Kennedy, Thurman Tucker, and Hal Peck, complemented the everyday players, and all had their moments in reaching the pinnacle of the baseball world. The 1948 world champs were beyond doubt a marvelous team, all working together unselfishly to reach the ultimate goal. Though there may have been World Series champs with heavier bats and stronger arms, this team was brilliant in winning it all.

ACKNOWLEDGMENTS

O f all the books I have endeavored to write, this was certainly the most challenging. I began as usual with mapping out the chapters and listing the subjects to research. I had barely began the process when the ghastly pandemic took shape. For most of the next few months, I spent my time checking statistics and birth and death dates for the ballplayers.

Sometime in the following spring, the Cleveland Public Library partially opened and the cooperative research staff agreed to accept an emailed list from me to locate the necessary articles in the three Cleveland newspapers. A short time later the Hall of Fame library in Cooperstown forwarded me the player files needed and I was off and running.

I am deeply grateful to the folks at the Cleveland Indians offices for their assistance in connecting me with several of the families of the 1948 Indians. My thanks to vice president of Public Affairs Bob DiBiasio, vice president of Communications and Community Impact Curtis Danburg, and coordinator and team historian Jeremy Feador. Their help was fundamental in developing a number of biographical sketches.

Many thanks to Bruce Milla and Gordon Kramp for lending a hand with photos and copies of rare 1940s baseball programs. A big thank-you to the Edmon Low Library at Oklahoma State University and the Oklahoma Historical Society for information on pitcher Allie Reynolds. The Hamtramck Historical Museum in Michigan provided valuable background on pitcher Steve Gromek.

A special thanks to my publisher, Ohio University Press, for sticking with me and turning my jumbled-up manuscripts into books that I am proud of.

My sincere love and gratitude go to my wife, Vicki, for her extraordinary patience and support, and to Blair, the dog, for holding down the barking, and to Morris and Stormy, the two cool cats, for sitting on my notes and materials and keeping them organized. And last, but certainly not least, to Addison, my adorable first great-niece who came along during the final portion of my writing. She has ten to twelve years before this book becomes mandatory reading.

VICTORY ON TWO FRONTS

SOURCES

Books

Allen, Lee. *The American League Story*. New York: Hill and Wang, 1962.

Boudreau, Lou, with Russell Schneider. *Lou Boudreau: Covering All the Bases*. Champaign, IL: Sagamore, 1993.

Dickson, Paul. *Bill Veeck: Baseball's Greatest Maverick*. New York: Walker, 2012.

Freedman, Lew. *A Summer to Remember*. New York: Sports, 2014.

Montville, Leigh. *Ted Williams*. New York: Doubleday, 2004.

Moore, Joseph Thomas. *Larry Doby: The Struggle of the American League's First Black Player*. New York: Dover, 1988.

Paige, Satchel, as told to Hal Lebovitz. *Pitchin' Man: "Satchel" Paige's Own Story*. Cleveland: Cleveland News, 1948.

Robinson, Eddie. *Lucky Me: My Sixty-Five Years in Baseball*. Lincoln: University of Nebraska Press, 2011.

Schneider, Russell. *The Boys of the Summer of '48*. Champaign, IL: Sports, 1998.

Sickles, John. *Bob Feller: Ace of the Greatest Generation*. Washington, DC: Brasseys, 2004.

Spink, J. G. Taylor. *Judge Landis and Twenty-Five Years of Baseball*. New York: Thomas Y. Crowell, 1947.

Tye, Larry. *Satchel: The Life and Times of an American Legend*. New York: Random House, 2009.

Veeck, Bill, with Ed Linn. *Veeck—as in Wreck: The Autobiography of Bill Veeck.* Chicago: University of Chicago Press, 2012.

Wancho, Joe. *Pitching to the Pennant: The 1954 Cleveland Indians.* Lincoln: University of Nebraska Press, 2014.

Periodicals

Baseball Digest (1942–49)
Baseball Magazine (1942, 1948)
Cleveland Call and Post (1942, 1947–48)
Cleveland News (1942–49)
Cleveland Plain Dealer (1942–49)
Cleveland Press (1942–49)
Sporting News (1942–49)

Libraries and Archives

Cleveland Heights–University Heights Library
Cleveland Indians
Cleveland Public Library
Cuyahoga County Public Library
Hamtramck Historical Museum, Hamtramck, Michigan
National Baseball Hall of Fame Library, Cooperstown, NY (player files)
Oklahoma Historical Society
Oklahoma State University Library (Allie Reynolds Collection)
Society for American Baseball Research

Personal Communications

Family of Larry Doby
Family of Steve Gromek
Family of Jim Hegan

Internet Sites

http://www.baseball-almanac.com

INDEX